BERLIN BODIES

BERLIN BODIES

ANATOMIZING THE STREETS OF THE CITY

STEPHEN BARBER

REAKTION BOOKS

Published by Reaktion Books Ltd
Unit 32, Waterside
44–48 Wharf Road
London N1 7UX, UK
www.reaktionbooks.co.uk

First published 2017
Copyright © Stephen Barber 2017

Gedruckt mit Unterstützung der Gerda Henkel Stiftung, Düsseldorf
Printed with the support of the Gerda Henkel Foundation, Düsseldorf

Printed and bound in Great Britain
by TJ International, Padstow, Cornwall

A catalogue record for this book is available from the British Library

ISBN 978 1 78023 720 6

CONTENTS

1
BERLIN BODIES

THE CITY DEAD . GHOSTS . SPECTRES . REMNANTS .
INHABITANTS . SPECTACLES . ANNEXES . CODAS .
STRATA . SCARS . MARKERS . EXPANSIONS . AMASSINGS .
CONCENTRATIONS . RESIDUES . DETRITA . SKINS .
TRACES . THE HUNTED DOWN . THE MALFUNCTIONED .
DANCERS . FOOTFALLS . MEMORIES . ABSENCES .
INERADICABLES . TRANSFIGURATIONS .
EMITTERS OF NOISE . ENACTORS OF SILENCE .
CONJURATIONS . DATA . PROLIFERATIONS .
DIGITIZED PRESENCES . IMAGE-RENDERED ENTITIES .
TRANSACTORS . ACTORS . PERFORMERS . BERLIN BODIES

THE CITY DEAD

Caught in the present moment, Berlin bodies now hold, project and perform the accumulated city dead. The entirety of Berlin's dead – permeated to the bones by the city which also often destroyed or subjugated them – are intimately layered into its contemporary anatomies, so that those present bodies compulsively disgorge and gesture out the city dead, in a unique manifestation of the conjunction between corporeal space and city space, between corporeal time and city time, which exists in no other amassing of bodies, in no other city.

The dead are more living than the living, in Berlin. The living are not really deeply there yet, until they are dead. The conjunction of the human body and the city invariably forms a zone of dense interconnections, of subterranean conduits and ligamental musculatures, moving in near-simultaneous oscillation in one direction and then its reverse, and projected through performances, images, textual traces and histories. Often, the body cannot be disentangled from the city, or the city from the body, except at the moment of death. The body may always direct and conduct any city, in the way that, in the Soviet Union in 1922–3, in an extreme instance, the sound artist Arseny Avraamov, displayed on a raised platform, used flaming torches held overhead in both hands to conduct the factory sirens and accumulated weaponry of Baku and Moscow for his *Symphony of Sirens*; generals or dictators in warfare may also order the comprehensive razings of cities, as Hitler did for Paris in 1944.[1] The city itself, in an infinity of historical instances, can also choreograph and conduct the human body, individually and in its amassings, in complicity or against its will, and impel it, as in the contemporary moment, via digital devices and screens, to move through urban arteries and dimensions. But in Berlin, above all cities, the dead form the vital anatomical conductors and manipulators of urban transformations and bodies' manoeuvres.

When urban cinematographers first entered the body-packed open spaces and avenues of Berlin, from 1896, and positioned their devices within those sites, along Unter den Linden, at the Hallesches Tor and in the Alexanderplatz, they recorded faces and figures instantaneously cognizant, as they looked at the film-camera lens, of their own deaths. Film animates the city dead, in the very moment of their bodies' seizing via celluloid, through sequences of images. Faces never ignore the film-camera in such sequences. Instead, they eye it directly or askance, in puzzlement and amuse-ment, and thereby counter or intensify that device's capacity. With gestures of recognition, and with nuances of delight and joy, those figures and faces perform their own status as the imminently city dead, soon to be projected on screens, or archived away in image vaults. In such visualizations, history embodies the city dead.

Bodies may be dispatched in massive consignments from the city for their erasure, as in the sending of much of Berlin's young male population of the First World War years to their slaughter, and in the transportation of stigmatized populations corralled, three decades later, in freight-train carriages, from the platforms of the Grunewald railway station, and other Berlin stations, to destinations at Nazi work camps and death camps. Every such transported body is precipitated elsewhere, towards whatever site its expulsion towards death took it, and simultaneously remains still there for all time in the city. But such bodies were also often fixed in stasis, for their mass rendering into the city dead, as in the immense aerial incinerations of 1943–4, and the killings of those who either would not or could not flee from the Soviet army's invasion of April 1945, and thereby became engulfed by it. Berlin bodies may also become the city dead through an act (or arrested act) of moment-ary traversal, as in the figures attempting to cross the walled 'death strips' or equally lethal waterways between East and West Berlin, in the decades of the city's division. Berlin bodies' riotous crossings of the city in protest may also transmutate them into the city dead, at the hands of police or security agents, in the arena of demonstrations, from the 1950s to the present moment. The generation of the city dead is not always a spectacu-lar process; it may also occur with maximal mundanity, but still leave unprecedented residues.

The city itself can appear to be living, but may really be dead, or be carrying its deaths within itself, as in the East Berlin half-city that existed, with its gestures, languages and images, and its urban rituals, from the end of the 1940s to the end of the 1980s, and then abruptly became a dead-body city, both in the remembering of its bodies, and also in that lost city's ineradicable projection via the contemporary city. The more that the pasts of a dead-body city are actively forgotten, the more they carry the potential imminently to infiltrate and resurge through the phantasmatic fabric of the contemporary city's apparitions.

Berlin remains inhabited by its infinite dead, and by the multiple media of their deaths. Envisioning the history of that city invariably forms an evocation of corporealities – momentarily enclosed within edifices and subterranes, or exposed on plazas, and always in place for an instant that is already changed, blurred or gone – in which the city dead remain the initial and finally enduring presences, the primary and terminal components, the first and last to speak, the first to appear and the last to leave, through the cracked-open mouth of the city. This book forms an exploratory history of Berlin bodies that incorporates the city dead as well as – and embedded within – the city's contemporary sensations and visions: fragments around urban anatomies, torn from the streets of Berlin. It proposes that the cultural history of a city, exemplified above all by Berlin, is always primarily one of human bodies and their projections, visions and archivings – in incessant transit between memory and oblivion – and only secondarily one of architecture, media and power.

GHOSTS

Berlin ghosts pass simultaneously through the momentarily frozen body and the captivated eye of its contemporary occupants, to come back to the city which they lost, in death. Berlin ghosts form a contrary population to that of the city dead, who are monumentally amassed in historical subterranes and edifices, coagulated onto the celluloid surfaces of moving-image sequences, and multiply archived in the form of text. Berlin ghosts, by contrast, remain always in individual flux, traversing the urban spaces – wastelands, crossing points, interzones – at which the bodies of the city's contemporary inhabitants can momentarily serve as their medium, for split-second apparitions that have vanished before they are ever visualized.

Berlin ghosts emerge pre-eminently from within the missing elements of the city: those points at which it has been irreparably incised, gouged and dematerialized. Such excoriated points form irresistible nodes of assembly for contemporary Berlin bodies. And whenever such voids are corporeally sealed, for example with tactile digits, Berlin ghosts can traverse that channel between the erased city and its contemporary form. On the Monbijou pedestrian bridge at the western tip of Berlin's Museum Island, traversants often pause within the semicircular area off to one side, which once held a statue of Kaiser Friedrich III but now holds nothing, and either turn back to look at the facade of the Bode Museum or else place their hands on the bridge's

parapet, to gaze straight down at the Spree or to follow the river's course in the direction of the Friedrichstrasse railway station, towards the next bridges and the buildings surrounding them. Their fingers touch the elements of the blackened stone parapet that are missing, such as the indentations created by stray bullets that lodged in that parapet in April 1945 during the fierce final stage of the Soviet army's assault on Berlin, or by white-hot fragments of shrapnel. They also touch the larger voids where an entire section of the inner parapet wall has been blown away by a projectile, leaving an absence that all five fingertips can trace simultaneously, along with the palm of the hand, in a tactile excavation that transmits the body into the city's absent surface and receives, in return, the sensation of the mismatched, misaligned completion of the city by the body. At that instant of intimate disjuncture, in which the body is directly layered into the city's surface, flesh pressed to stone, to form an aberrant compound, Berlin ghosts may project themselves through those exposed fingertips, via the medium of that contrary body-screen, which serves momentarily to guide Berlin ghosts back into the city. Berlin ghosts also pass through the gazing eye that looks outwards at the cityscape or focuses in on the site of absence in which the fingertips are placed, since such a revivification can only take place as an instantaneous amalgam of vision and flesh, annulled an instant later, when the eye blinks to cast out its ghosts, and when the electrified fingertips are abruptly detached from the parapet wall, which is then returned to the contemporary instant, emblazoned with spray-canned graffiti naming the Dinamo Bukarest football team, with heart-iconed declarations of love, and other inscriptions that overwrite, in their immediacy, that parapet's incised absences.

Berlin ghosts once wholeheartedly inhabited the city, and participated in great struggles, obsessive projects and social movements to expand or amend that city – the impossible struggles and acts that pre-eminently generated Berlin's innumerable absences and incisions – or to prevent its overturning into an intolerable space of subjugation. If Berlin had been rendered irrelevant to such ghosts by death, they would not take the trouble to locate a corporeal medium by which to re-enter that city's space. A Berlin ghost's momentary reoccupation of the city is always a serious undertaking, but it can only be accomplished by a devious, trickster manoeuvre – the opportunistic inhabitation of the eyes and body of that city's contemporary inhabitants – which also makes that urban haunting appear fraudulent or ludicrous, invested with the fear-edged ridicule that the living direct towards the ghostly.

So many Berlin ghosts died violent and unjust deaths – clubbed from behind with a rifle butt, as in the 1919 death of the Socialist revolutionary Rosa Luxemburg, or shot down in the course of everyday bicycle journeys through the city, as in the 1968 mortal wounding of the student-movement leader Rudi Dutschke (the actual moment of his death deferred for a decade or so) – that their appropriation of contemporary city bodies may also be experienced as an extreme anatomical and ocular jarring. A Berlin ghost's corporeal passage – into and then back out of the city – is never a quiet one, even when its duration is near zero and its sensory consequences are already beginning to deliquesce even as they emerge; that ghost transit's absence archives the city via the intermediary of the body, creating urban marks of the not-there.

Berlin ghosts also encompass the afterlife detritus of multiple surpassed Berlins, often architecturally devised and corporeally generated with immense ambition, and still perceptible as barely-there Fata Morganas, in peripheral vision, many years after their erasures or transmutations. This is especially so on journeys through the city whose physical and ocular momentum accentuates those thin-air ghost residues, as with those residues of East Berlin's cityscapes, in such manifestations as the Alexanderplatz variant created in the 1960s and the demolished Palace of the Republic, together with many other repudiated or obsolete urban components. Such ghost-city elements were often directly oriented towards death at their inception, as was the German Democratic Republic's monumental Memorial to the Socialists, in the eastern district of Lichtenberg, which incorporated the grave sites of Rosa Luxemburg and Karl Liebknecht, along with adjacent gathering spaces (now permanently voided) for inhabitation by masses of chanting, activist bodies whose invocatory work of performance was explicitly that of the intended corporeal resuscitation, whether they desired it or not, of eminent ghosts. Berlin ghosts, in obstinacy, will not be called; they will abruptly infiltrate the bodies of the city's contemporary occupants at unforeseen moments, when they are least expected, then vanish.

SPECTRES

Berlin spectres form bodies of power that their death only magnifies, so that they appear just a translucent membrane of skin away from the immediate arena of the contemporary city. Berlin spectres will not be dispelled or consigned to subterranean space. The profound damage they inflicted on the city itself accords them the inalienable right to corporeally haunt that city, not as infiltrating ghosts or the teeming city dead, who elude sustained vision, but as spectres whose urban tenacity stems from their pre-death obsessional re-envisioning of the city. Among those spectres are Albert Speer and Hitler, with their colossal project for the Triumphal Arch, People's Hall and North–South Axis avenue that had already led to the enforced clearing of wide areas of central Berlin before that plan was suspended for more pressing destructive priorities in 1939; and the GDR's leaders Walter Ulbricht and Wilhelm Pieck, with their realized project for the dynamiting of central Berlin's part-ruined imperial palace (Stadtschloss) and the subsequent transformation through all-out levelling of the Alexanderplatz, the monumentality of that vision signalled vertically through the construction, across the second half of the 1960s, of Ulbricht's Television Tower (Fernsehturm). The obsession with transforming Berlin is a uniquely corporeal one that perceives the human figure as determining urban parameters and forms; architecture is only one potential medium to transmit and stage such visions, alongside ocular hallucination, spatial modelling, performance and film. Berlin spectres are the survivors of such visions, ostensibly dead – even consigned to oblivion – but still vitally embodied in the contemporary city.

At the same time, Berlin spectres constitute the most melancholy and stultified of all the multiply death-traversed components of Berlin bodies. Even when those spectres razed and overhauled the city, or subjected it to other variants of upheaval, and now appear only a hair's breadth (that of death) away from being ready to extend that work or restart it from zero, they can do nothing, as though the minuscule obstacle of being dead possessed an even greater power than that of their once-omniscient capacity to reformulate the city unstoppably. Spectres are always frozen a fraction of an instant away from resurging into the contemporary moment of Berlin, invariably stilled a fragment of a void away from re-entering its space: breathlessly poised sprinters who can never start, marathon runners who may spectrally circle the city but cannot re-enter it.

To test, for the satisfaction of Hitler, the logistical feasibility and rationality of his Berlin obsessions, in

1941 Speer built a unique concrete structure which he called the 'Heavy-load-bearing Body' (Schwerbelastungs-körper), between the Kreuzberg district's Viktoriapark and the city's southbound railway cutting. That vast cylindrical 'body', simultaneously propelled upwards and extending downwards into Berlin's subterranes, weighed many thousands of tons. Its gradual sinking into the city's sand soil over several years would indicate the potential risk for Hitler's triumphal arch, planned for future construction in that same area, eventually to subside or even be overturned by the geological flux of Berlin's underworld. The 'Heavy-load-bearing Body', although conceived as an experimental entity solely to generate test results, was not intended for erasure during the programme of construction required for Hitler's transmutation of Berlin into the world-dominating city of Germania, but would instead be incorporated into it, engulfed invisibly within the city's new ground level, which would be raised far above its current level during the construction programme. In the event, that 'body' sank only marginally during several years of tests. Once Speer and Hitler had been consigned to spectrality (Speer not even dead, but imprisoned until 1966 in Spandau prison on post-war West Berlin's periphery, then finally released to begin obstinately reformulating the city once more, in his media appearances and writings), it could not be safely destroyed, and remained nailed deep into the city's surface, as an aberrant and semi-abandoned corporeal presence poised directly alongside the railway cutting, so that Berlin's contemporary urban exploring young bodies now often infiltrate it at night, scale its surrounding fence and enter its overgrown terrain, ascend to its summit, and descend into its subsurface levels. That experimental concrete body – holding the Berlin-focused obsessions of two of the city's pre-eminent spectres – envelops the bodies of those momentary nocturnal occupants, so that they inhabit spectral visions.

Even before the ambitions of the GDR state had fully taken form, in the post-war years during which Berlin's ruins were being heatedly contested between its city dead, its ghosts and its spectres, Ulbricht and Pieck were determined that the reconfiguration of the city would itself form a corporeal spectacle. In May 1950, seven months after the founding of the GDR state, and shortly before they ordered the dynamiting of the city's central palace, Ulbricht and Pieck arranged for a vast gathering of the young bodies of Soviet-zone Berlin (along with those from other zones across Europe), the Deutschlandtreffen der Jugend, during which they oversaw, from a succession of podiums, intricately choreographed demonstrations of amassed corporeality in a newly built sports stadium – a stadium named after Ulbricht: the Walter-Ulbricht-Stadion – together with great banner-wielding processions moving along the rain-lashed, still decimated Unter den Linden avenue, towards the site, directly alongside the palace's ruins, where Ulbricht and Pieck, performing the glacial smiles of the already dead, directed and incited them with imperious hand gestures, as though that immense influx

of young bodies surging, in coordination and propelled by vocal chants and banners' textual exclamations through the wastelanded city, could serve to resuscitate it. In colour film documents of the processions of several hundred thousand figures, shot from high elevations and taking in the entirety of Berlin's central district below stormy skies, those great pulses of wide-eyed, raw-faced young bodies on the city's avenues form an instrument of spectral power, launched via the bodies and visions of Ulbricht and Pieck, and are amassed too as untold spectres of the future city.

Berlin's spectres can also comprise maximally autonomous, disengaged presences whose preoccupations still contrarily permeate and derange the city from their isolation, even against their will. In the last winter of his life, that of 1923–4, a time of acute financial crisis in Germany, Franz Kafka rented a room in a large boarding-house villa on Grunewaldstrasse, in Berlin's Steglitz district, together with his final lover, the activist Dora Diamant, whom he had met during the previous summer in the Baltic sea-coast resort of Graal-Müritz, exclaiming his admiration for her blood-ied hands on their first encounter as she prepared meals from just-slaughtered chickens at a holiday camp for the impoverished Jewish children of Berlin; Kafka worked in that period on editing his final collection of stories, *A Hunger Artist*. That couple, existing in anonymous isolation from the city they momentarily inhabited together, would take the local urban train northwards from Steglitz station, past the future sites of Hitler's Germania obsessions, to find specialist vegetarian restaurants in the Friedrichstrasse district at which the spectral Kafka, already emaciated from the effects of tuberculosis and corporeally disappearing before Berlin's eyes (his saved funds also fast dwindling, to his horror, in the city's economic meltdown), could find sustenance for his body, before finally conceding defeat and leaving his spectre behind in Berlin, for his return journey south to Prague and finally to his death from starvation at the Sanatorium Hoffmann in Klosterneuberg, outside Vienna. Berlin spectres may, in autonomy, incise, destabilize and dissolve all manifestations and evidence of power, as well as form its death-immersed directors and advocates.

REMNANTS

Contemporary Berlin bodies form phantom presences within the city, corporeally occupying the city's central avenues but simultaneously projected into an outlandish zone, intimately in touch with the city dead, the ghosts and the spectres who overpopulate Berlin to excess. An overwhelming sensation in looking out over any crowded street-crossing or plaza in central Berlin, such as the Potsdamer Platz, is that the traversing and harried figures, heading in all directions, are the moribund remnants of all previous Berlin populations now posthumously consigned into phantasmatic space, and concentrated into that immediate instant. Those bodies also form the remnants of the city itself that, in its multiple transformations and razings, has undergone such severe pressurization that time itself may explode into an aberrant medium which negates linear duration – as visualized notably in Ludwig Meidner's apocalyptic cityscapes from 1912–13 depicting, among others, convulsed figures fleeing spectacular detonations in the Halensee district and the Friedenau district in which they were painted – thereby propelling the city forwards as well as backwards, so that Berlin bodies comprise the remnants of acute urban malfunction, scattered in haywire trajectories and pulses across its terrain.

Speer's 'Heavy-load-bearing Body' architectural experiment possesses its own spectral histories and dimensions, but it is also a contemporary and prescient remnant that is iconic of Berlin's contrary sensory movements. The elated narcotic rush to accentuate and elevate corporeal sensations, integral for example to the relentlessness of the city's nightclub culture, is countered by the gradual downward pressure of exhausted comedowns that load Berlin bodies, requiring self-calibration in degrees of instability, loss and physical hairline cracks, just as Speer's engineers meticulously calibrated the inexorable sinking of that vast concrete cylinder into the city's sandy soil. An urban anatomical equation of a Berlin body calculates, as a remnant sum, whatever the city has extracted and eroded out from it, against whatever that body has itself assimilated in urban matter and vision from its

movements through the city.

The form of a Berlin remnant intimates that it constitutes an entity which is at its last moment, and is transmitting its final traces. It may no longer be able to hold itself together in a coherent form, having been part-consumed or excoriated until almost nothing is left, and so it articulates its urban experience in the form of fragments or last gasps and final breaths. It has not yet reached the definitively terminal stage of the city dead, and will never possess any maleficent spectral power, but nor can it ever fully return to the intact world of the living; if it still possesses a tangible body, it may be vampirically living off the last of itself, and if it enduringly owns and processes memories, they will be uniquely haunting ones, to the point of compulsive obsession and repetition. At the same time, a Berlin body as remnant forms a distillation of urban encounters with corporeality: its final configuration, just before death, results from multiple abrasures inflicted over time, as well as tender and ecstatic contacts.

Often, on the urban trains and subways of Berlin, remnant bodies make their apparitions to perform a final vocal appeal, exclaimed or muttered through clenched teeth, to the present occupants of the city. In anticipation of monetary donations, they will incant last-ditch narratives in which sequences of calamities (alcoholism and drug addiction, but also less definable urban malfunctions) have rendered them into city remnants. In that sense, they embody the city itself in its most corrosive and oblivious manifestations and effects, and that process of embodiment itself constitutes a justification of their final appeal. The nature of that appeal is that it cannot be narrated only once, but must be repeated incessantly, through every carriage of each subway or urban train, from Zoologischer Garten station to Ostbahnhof and back again, until the remnant body slips silently over into the domain of the city dead. Even when the narrated catastrophes and mishaps have actually taken place in another city, or another country, their culmination in Berlin allots remnant bodies their space in the city, since Berlin's population (notably in its great expansion across the decades from the 1870s, and in the chaos of mass human movements and expulsions from 1945, but also in the contemporary moment) was often vitally one of exiles, refugees, the displaced, the uprooted: those who ran aground everywhere, elsewhere, and finally came to Berlin.

A remnant may, as well as making exclamatory urban apparitions, also return. With a little mid-word scrambling, a remnant is also a 'revenant'. The repro-cessed city dead, ghosts and spectres who utilize the corporeal screens of the city's contemporary occupants in order to reappear in the city or to be remediated by it, for a split second or longer, stake the entire future of their urban haunting upon Berlin's anatomical dimen-sions. The returned dead still need to transit the city, to see what has become of it since they were last alive there. Since they previously had an existence in the city, revenants can also potentially be recognized by the living, but they may have undergone a transmutation, in death, that accords their reappearance in the city an aura of horror and bodily disintegration.

In Wim Wenders's 1995 film *A Trick of the Light* (*Die Gebrüder Skladanowsky*), two long-dead family members of the Skladanowsky brothers – Berlin's innovators of filmic projection and the first film-makers to create celluloid moving images of the city – return to Berlin as corporeally intact revenants (the brothers themselves do not reappear, remaining in the world of the dead, since film is always seminally of that world). Those two figures, a child and an acrobat, traverse the city in the interior of a horse-drawn, funereal carriage, from the Pankow district southwards to the Alexanderplatz area – filmed for the first time by the Skladanowsky brothers in the summer of 1896 – and look out at its recognizable remnants, such as the Marienkirche, along with that area's newer components. But their carriage is finally engulfed into void space, within the endless construction work then under way around the Potsdamer Platz, as though that site were the abysmal orifice leading into the subterranean repository of all Berlin's city dead, ghosts, spectres and revenants. A corporeal remnant of Berlin presupposes its own imminent extinguishment and disappearance, into history, into an image or archive, or into the city itself.

INHABITANTS

For Berlin bodies to inhabit the city – to mesh themselves corporeally into Berlin's edifices, surfaces and screens, in such a way that an aura of sustained duration is created – entails a deep-rooted perception of displacement. Berlin possesses relatively few multi-generational occupants in the context of Western European megalopolises. The city only began to expand around its growing population from the 1870s. Many of its inhabitants arrived unwillingly, in states of emergency, such as the population influxes from 1945 on, especially into Berlin's Soviet-controlled eastern zone, from formerly German cities – Stettin, Breslau, Königsberg – whose populations had been summarily expelled in their transformation into cities of Poland or the USSR. In later decades, notably the 1960s and '70s, other new inhabitants arrived in West Berlin to elude military conscription or what they perceived as social stultification and sexual constraint in the Federal Republic – in order to melt from sight and thereby dis-appear within West Berlin, or else to riot and blatantly generate political and sexual experimentation and spectacle there – as well as via forms of enforced flight, such as that of the Austrian artist Günter Brus, who in 1968 fled a prison sentence and media harassment in connection with his performance artworks, condemned as illicit and criminal in Vienna, and wryly conceived an Austrian 'government in exile' sited around the canal-side restaurant Exil in West Berlin's Kreuzberg district.[2]

To inhabit a city entails exposure to every last history of expulsion and deportation belonging to that city. Once a city accumulates a sufficiently strong history of deportation, as Berlin did in the 1930s and '40s alone, that expulsive dynamic also belongs integrally to the future of its urban inhabitation. The city itself then generates arbitrary refusals of inhabitation, as for example in the administrative and secret-police decrees of the 1980s by which East Berlin's punks (and other urban miscreants) were prohibited from inhabiting all or parts of that half-city. The exiled, the refugees and the uprooted who, on arriving in contemporary Berlin, now attempt an act of inhabitation always face that act's potential annulling. Many contemporary Berlin inhabitants can only maintain a tenuous hold on the face of the city, as with a mountaineer's ice-pick incision into a precipice rockface which, if that attempted incision is repelled or misfires, risks plunging the mid-air body into the monocultural abyss of the remainder of Europe, or beyond. Processes of gentrification, as with those undertaken in eastern Berlin districts such as Prenzlauer Berg and Friedrichshain from the mid-1990s, which appear (as they begin to consolidate themselves over several decades) designed to establish secure material means to inhabit the city, concurrently form incitations and acts of exposure to the expulsive dynamics of Berlin.

To inhabit a city means to live in it, to establish the existence of a body that can conduct rhythms and habits there, however erratic they may be, in order to constitute a tangible corporeal performance of inhabitation. But Berlin is already pre-emptively populated by its city dead, ghosts, spectres and revenants; the living have to squeeze their way in, alongside that excessive population, who rightfully exert their priority as inhabitants, with the result that the corporeal rhythms of the living become seismically charged and infused with an acute sense of their own imminent cancellation. In that sense, it may appear that the living only live in Berlin so that the dead can deploy them as corporeal and ocular screens for their own manifestations and momentary reinhabitations of the city. The dead inhabit the living who inhabit Berlin, so that the living form interstitial presences who would become obsolete if only the city dead were able finally to suture the great fracture in time and space – that of death – that disqualifies them from their renewed presence in the city. As a result, the living inhabitants of Berlin are often compelled to devote great swathes of their time to excavating, interrogating and embodying the traces within Berlin of its ghosts. The act of Berlin's inhabitation constitutes an archiving and mediumistic voicing of death, in which each contemporary instant's urban inhabitants – through their gestures of desire and ecstasy, as well as in the performance of their obsessional habits – prefigure their own forthcoming deaths and spectral disappearances. In Berlin, effacings from the city today may prove as abrupt and unforeseen as they have been throughout its history's multiple strata of corporeal vanishings.

Art images and photographic images of Berlin bodies are often imprinted with momentary corporeal inhabitations of urban space, in which the blurring of the figured appearance of those living bodies across that of their spectral accompanists is apparent. More so than in any other city, the urban environment surrounding such bodies in Berlin is prone to being no longer extant or recognizable, so that the body figured in the image appears stranded in space, staring out in bewilderment at its spectator. Film images of Berlin bodies extend those split-second, displaced city-death moments of art and photography into the form of sequences in which something irreparable has happened to a body, so that the act of inhabitation abruptly lapses. In the first minutes of Fritz Lang's 1931 film *M*, for example, the child Elsie is abducted from Berlin's streets and murdered on her way home from school as the film's initiating action, so that the subsequent minutes – as her mother waits with increasing desperation for the sound of Elsie's steps ascending the staircase of their tenement building – constitute the duration in which the body's subtraction from life in the city, and the accumulating perception of that subtraction, become marked. In many images of Berlin bodies, across all media, that act of inhabitation, together with its time and space, is under duress from all sides: contested, and subject to its invalidation or erasure.

To inhabit a city also implies that the urban body and eye may become so attuned to their environment, in their gestures and in their manoeuvres through it, that the city eventually falls from sight, through habituation. It fades out as through a process of irradiation, but its attuned inhabitants still occupy it, as though blind or sensorially numb. But Berlin, for all its vanishings, appears exempt from that acquired habituation; it will impinge itself inexorably upon the eye and body, and impel unprecedented ways for that body and eye to unpeel the act of Berlin's inhabitation and reveal its uniquely raw contingencies.

SPECTACLES

Berlin bodies irresistibly enact spectacles in the city, and even the act of intentional withdrawal and the negation of visibility, for the body in urban space, itself forms an inverse spectacle that demonstrates the profound tension – acute in Berlin above all other cities – between corporeality and the urban screen. The city embodies a spectacle driven and simultaneously impeded by the living figures and spectres that inhabit it. In innumerable textual accounts, film documents and photographs of Berlin across the six decades from the 1870s to the 1920s, the city emanates the sheer intensive corporeal effort that was required to generate and maintain the transmission to itself – and to its inhabitants and momentary traversants – of its own spectacle: for example, the labour involved in constructing and upkeeping its buildings and transport infrastructure, the effort and expenditure demanded to provision the city with its immense resources of food, drink, clothing and items of consumption, and the reservoirs of exhilaration and desire needed to propel the city's velocity-impelled spectacle. To launch and sustain that corporeal entity of Berlin in relentless sensory pleasure, over those six decades, formed a spectacular act of parallel intensity to that involved in the subsequent destructions of the city, in which even ruins had to be painstakingly decimated; a corresponding, unrelenting corporeal exertion is also at stake in the levelling and annulling – via banalizing monocultural spectacles – of the contemporary city's textures and layers.

In 1950 the dynamiting of the extensive ruins of the Berlin city-centre palace – constructed from the fifteenth century onwards, with its form coalescing in the mid-eighteenth century – was recorded in monochrome 35mm film as a twelve-minute silent document, *Sprengung des Berliner Schlosses* (*Detonation of the Berlin Palace*).[3] The future of those ruins had been in disputed suspension for the five years since the palace had been struck and badly damaged by wartime incendiary bombs during the first months of 1945, with polarized debate over whether the palace should now be comprehensively razed, or reconstructed from its courtyards' intact foundations. Those ruins had appeared months earlier as a backdrop to the spec-tacular Deutschlandtreffen der Jugend parade of many thousands of young bodies traversing Berlin under the moribund eyes of Ulbricht and Pieck. The razing

process eventually ordered by Ulbricht itself formed a colossal undertaking, six months or so in duration and demanding the participation of numerous large-scale demolition crews. But the film document of that process of destruction – shot haphazardly by cinematographers whose clapperboard-holding figures appear between the camera lens and the ruins at the beginnings of several sequences, as phantasmatic corporeal apparitions poised an instant before those ruins explosively erupt – transforms that anti-architectural spectacle into one focused primarily on incidental physical movements and spectatorial acts, such as the intricate transits around the site of the demolition crews and the sudden amassings of curious audiences before they disperse to shield themselves from the detonations. Originally intended to be edited into a newsreel and shown to cinema spectators in the Soviet zone of East Berlin, the film was instead consigned unedited and unseen to an archival existence, eventually forming part of the film-document collection of the German Bundesarchiv. That suppression may have resulted from the heated debate on the ruins' survival, or from the realization, by the document's instigators, that Berlin's film spectators of 1950 were already exhausted with viewing acts or images of the city's erasures. Instead of concentrating the time of destruction, through editing, in order to generate a spectacle of the ostensibly self-combusting city (as can be seen for example in familiar films of the spectacular detonations for entranced crowds of obsolete buildings, such as crumbling skyscrapers or Las Vegas casino hotels), that film document of the detonation of the Berlin palace forms an accumulation of detached fragments of corporeality, interposed by void intervals, in which intent gangs of bodies conduct and observe a mysterious scorched-earth ritual of ruins' razings.

Plazas, open spaces, wastelands and the voided sites of demolition enduringly form pre-eminent locations for the contemporary appearances of Berlin bodies and their acts' rendering as spectacle, above all through the mutation of corporeality into the images and filmic sequences that record those bodies. The body in urban space is always displaced into *something else*, into another entity, once it has traversed the medium of moving images. The intended grandiosity of the body's spectacles can be nullified and reduced to a minuscule incident, and its most tangential, slight gesture may be magnified into an all-engulfing spectacle. Berlin bodies cannot endure indefinitely in exposed space, such as that of the city's axis points and plazas; while their image-recorded acts may endure as spectacles, those already evanescing bodies themselves are simultaneously in the process of being archived away into their own vanishing.

Spectacles, for Berlin bodies, are often involuntary exposures to the dynamics of time and death, in which the desire to project a spectacle outwards, with optimum external visibility, is countered by an interior collapse, into anti-spectacle, which would be correspondingly spectacular, if that deflation's implosive sensory and body-interior dimensions could also clearly be seen and perceived, in the way that a building's eye-seizing detonation may be caught in both its outwards and inwards trajectories if cameras are positioned to record the destruction of both its exterior and interior spaces. Corporeal spectacles – projected externally in the media of performance and display, but also through the insistent scouring and interior infiltration of Berlin bodies by urban elements – invariably prefigure and incite the imminent outlandish mutation, via spectrally infiltrating presences, of those bodies into death. The negation of visibility enacted by bodies that attempt habitually to refuse spectacle – by silently and invisibly hiding themselves within the city's occluded zones – forms a vital element conspiring (even against such bodies' intentions) in death-propelled spectacular corporeal acts that 'disappear' the body in urban space.

Death and time may delimit the parameters for Berlin bodies' spectacles, by which such spectacles risk being doubled by their own spectacular implosive erasure. But Berlin bodies' nightlife spectacles contrarily demand an exemption from such parameters. Rather than the negation of visibility, nightlife spectacles envision the maximal corporeal projection of invisibility, under cover of darkness, so that the body resurges from its city deaths. When the city loses all light-fixed limits, its ostensible parameters become the adrenaline-dissolved domain of its nocturnal inhabitants, who consume and swallow the space of Berlin as a pivotally corporeal spectacle that leaves behind only haunted, blurred afterimages, from 1920s photographs and films of the ecstatic enactors of Berlin's spectacular nightclub-based culture, through to digital devices capturing (often illicitly, as in nightclubs such as Berghain in which visual documentation is outlawed) sequences showing the contemporary enactors of that culture. Berlin's nocturnal spectacles constitute corporeal detonations in which exhausted, voided bodies may collapse or else endure, but will remain always glaringly visible against the surfaces of the city.

ANNEXES

Berlin bodies' tangible hold upon the core of the city they inhabit or traverse is one that is always imminently about to be prised away, and those bodies are subject to annulling expulsion. As a result, Berlin bodies often form disposable annexes to the all-engulfing spectacles and convulsions of the city which they may attempt to acquisition and re-envision. The infinite capacity of Berlin's urban spectacles to oscillate between the historical moment and the contemporary moment – to *hold* time – enables that city to have annexed all bodies that occupy it, long before they acquire any degree of visibility within it. Berlin bodies may appear as the aberrant, mutating and always extraneous presences that issue from the city's space as its subsidiary, ghosted and voided annexes. The body's subsidiary role in urban space is one that can be contested through,

among other means, a corporeal desire to refute
that annexation, by the body's self-propulsion as
an affront against urban space, in combinations of
wild, cacophonic nocturnal performance and focused
political protest such as those that cross over Walpurgisnacht on 30 April and the city's May Day riots of the
following day, each year. The body is invariably already
annexed by Berlin into a minor role, but that ostensible
servitude of corporeality to urban space also enables
the unruly body to elude all dutifully committed fixity
that the city seeks to impose upon it; Berlin bodies
comprise volatile subsidiaries that cannot ever be fully
incorporated into the city's power agendas.

A Berlin body also forms an annex whose resistant
corporeality may survive – notably through its imprinting
into film sequences or art images – the vanishing of the
urban surfaces from which it appears to issue. The city
itself may be ghosted, while the body endures. In East
Berlin, in the early 1970s, the state authorities of the GDR
formulated a plan to document the daily life of particular streets of the city, via the medium of film, in order
then to intentionally set aside the resulting documents,
in an archive of non-projected films, before finally
showing them to audiences only thirty years later, to
demonstrate those districts' anticipated revitalization.
In 1973 the film-maker Veronika Otten shot footage that
exhaustively documented the inhabitants of an inner-
city street mainly composed of nineteenth-century
tenement buildings, the Ackerstrasse, notably following
their transits along the dilapidated street and through

its striated, semi-collapsed back courtyards. The mostly elderly inhabitants, poised against pitted facades and long-neglected neon or painted signage, vocally evoke to the camera the history of the street and their deep attachment to it, across warfare, political seisms and infrastructural disintegration. The resulting film document, *Berlin Milieu – Ackerstrasse*, was duly archived away, unseen, in anticipation of its eventual projection in 2003 to an audience of future inhabitants of that same district of Berlin, who would then experience awe at the area's intervening transformation through the GDR's urban renovation programme. But by 2003, neither the entity of East Berlin nor that of the GDR state still existed, and the anticipated future audience for the film's projection had also disappeared. Plans for the future Ackerstrasse – of new, prefabricated apartment buildings enclosed by the renovated facades of the otherwise demolished original buildings – had also become obsolete. Any contemporary audience for that film would now form an unimagined one, as though conjured from the mysteries of future visions. But the bodies of the 1973 occupants of the Ackerstrasse remain enduringly intact in that film document, as the obstinate annexes to cancelled urban reconfigurations. A corporeal annex can outlive the dissolution or negation of the city which generates it; that annex endures even when its originating city is gone.

In cartographic projections of East Berlin, from the 1960s to the 1980s, a blank zone often represented the adjoining presence of West Berlin, named with contempt on such maps in one word as 'Westberlin', and devoid of a grid of streets, buildings or any other markers, as though deprived of its tenuous status as a half-city and rendered instead into the outlandish, derided form of an East Berlin annex, too exposed to derision and too resonant of contamination even to take on a subsidiary role, and whose occupants equally endured that blanking out and draining of their corporeal substance. An annex, in the intersections of urban space and its bodies, can be so undesired that it barely achieves representation. But, by 1990, the scathingly named annex of 'Westberlin' had voraciously swallowed and consumed the caustic eye of its mapper, so that East Berlin in turn became blanked space.

During the same era in which East Berlin's run-down Ackerstrasse was being filmed for the projection – three decades into the future – of its occupants and buildings to new or still unborn audiences, the Dutch transsexual performer Romy Haag opened her legendary nightclub, Chez Romy Haag, on a corner of the Fuggerstrasse in one of the more opulent areas of West Berlin's Schöneberg district. By the mid-1970s, that nightclub's aura of sexual and gender experimentation and of sensory excess and confrontational performance – forming an exclusive annex beyond, and in contradiction to, the terrain of the then-stranded, melancholy island city of West Berlin – began to attract the attention of musicians in transit via West Berlin, either for concerts or to record at its studios (the Hansa studios, above all), and also to form the foundation for the development over the following years of an unprecedented nightclub culture, drawing on Weimar-era club culture and experimental performance art as well as the new insurgence of punk rock culture, whose venues stretched across the adjacent Schöneberg and Kreuzberg districts. David Bowie's years in West Berlin, from 1976 to 1979, were instigated pivotally through his obsession with Romy Haag and with her nightclub, and the black and white photographs taken of them in elated intimacy in nightclub spaces show seminal bodies, issuing from an aberrant annex fissure in West Berlin, that finally encompassed not only that half-city, but urban nightclub cultures worldwide, through to the contemporary moment.

During walks into the Prenzlauer Berg district of eastern Berlin in the icy winter of 1990, I often crossed the railway bridge that had formed the site of the originating aperture, during hours of chaos, a year or so earlier, for one-way border traversals, on 9 November 1989. On frozen nights, that deserted bridge (the Bösebrücke, named after an opponent of the Nazis who was executed in 1944) still retained the aura of a strange annex in space and time, poised at a fracture between the two irreconcilable but now-amalgamated Berlin half-cities – one of them now 'annexed' by the other, but, in the vanishing of its urban status, still there – and also between the suspended, tensed bodies that then inhabited them. At that time, the Bornholmer Strasse S-bahn station, located below the bridge – directly in the interval zone between East Berlin and West Berlin during the decades of division, and consequently then a closed-down 'ghost station' – had not yet reopened, and the trains ran through without stopping. One early morning, still under iced darkness, I discovered that the station had been illuminated and reopened, as though nothing had ever happened, and that sense of an annex pierced into the space and time of the city had abruptly gone. I descended the *Blitzeis*-encrusted, decades-unused stairway to the platform, from which trains would arrive, heading north towards Pankow and Buch, or south towards Unter den Linden and Potsdamer Platz.

CODAS

In the propulsions of Berlin bodies through the streets of the Kreuzberg district towards the city's most elevated point – the Viktoriapark – for Walpurgisnacht mayhem and then, the following day, May Day, along the Oranien-strasse and other streets in furious self-reconfiguration as riot bodies, corporeal codas to the city are created in which those bodies interventionally act back upon Berlin's space, to erase its strictures, to annul linear urban parameters and to lividly bruise sensation into the city's surfaces. Berlin bodies as urban codas form the antithesis to subsidiarized corporeal annexes, which the city archives away as malleable material, so pliable to corporate power's priorities and injunctions that it dissolves on touch. The default body in urban space may constitute a subjugated, annexed presence, but that identical body can also transform itself into a coda that turns back upon the city and abruptly reverses its order. Once driven to mutation through desire or fury or aberration, it reconfigures itself as that insurgent urban coda, either at concentrated anniversary moments (such as May Day) or else via an imaginably infinite time of liberated action that Berlin's bodies of the last five decades often dreamed of or else projected towards the contemporary moment.

Urban space itself can generate wayward channels within itself that the corporeal history of the city then reformulates as codas, once Berlin's bodies infiltrate such channels for the performance of an act within them. On the frozen platform of the Bornholmer Strasse S-bahn station on the morning of 22 December 1990, I watched those first, graffiti-inscribed trains follow the course of the obsolete death strip on their journeys northwards and southwards. A further nineteen, and then 24 years forward in time, in the still-freezing Novembers of 2009 and 2014, back up the platform stairs at bridge level, among chaotic and unruly amassings of spectators, I saw the traversals on foot, east to west, of the bodies of eminent figures viewed as being determining in the historical, political or cultural acts that had precipitated the opening of the Berlin Wall, twenty and then 25 years earlier (now aged bodies, such as those of Mikhail Gorbachev, Lech Wałęsa and Wolf Biermann) that had evolved into still-living 'historical bodies' now able to re-imprint that physically carried history upon the city through their on-foot traversals of that bridge,

in the forms of corporeal history codas. Soon, the bridge had been emptied out again; those historical, on-foot movements across determining urban channels formed momentary ones. An hour on, those bodies had already been whisked away in slick black limousines like those that had transported Walter Ulbricht and Erich Honecker, a few decades earlier, at speed along adjacent streets, north to south, from their residences in the outlying districts of Pankow and Wandlitz towards the GDR's central sites of power. Even during those two anniversaries' momentary celebrations, the performances of the bridge's historical traversal had been vocally contested, in cries of anger against urban corruption or hypocrisy, by activist figures in the crowd who, in destabilizing those fixed segmentations of time (twenty or 25 years on from the night of 9 November 1989), themselves formed disruptive corporeal codas, opposing the attempt to consolidate the linear endurance across time of new figures and regimes of power.

The capacity for Berlin bodies as codas to intervene back against the city may extend – in tearings, fragmentations and reversals of time, oscillating between long-gone, mythologized urban time and the contemporary moment – far beyond the twenty- or 25-year anniversaries embodied in the traversals by eminent historical figures of the Bösebrücke. Forty years after opening her nightclub at an obscure street corner in the melancholy West Berlin island city, and thereby precipitating an upheaval in the nightlife culture of that city and far beyond it, the orange-haired figure of Romy Haag appeared in the exposed corporate zone of Potsdamer Platz, on a surveillance-camera-controlled expanse between the tower headquarters of German and transglobal conglomerates, to protest against anti-gay legislation in Russia and other countries worldwide. In front of a small temporary display, miniaturized against the edifices of those surrounding towers, of a map representing global sites of persecution, Romy Haag protested to passers-by that, across the decades since the 1970s, Berlin had become an immeasurably more constricted, intrusive city for its exploratory, experimenting bodies, and not a more open one; she argued that corporeal surveillance now issued above all from digital technologies of intrusion. Against the enveloping corporate space of Potsdamer Platz – a new form of corporate wasteland conjured from zero, through reunified Berlin's 1990s wave of city-governmental financial corruption, from the wasteland death strip and abandoned bombed-out adjacent spaces that had previously occupied the site – that small-scale mapping of sexual persecution and Romy Haag's protesting figure appeared to possess only a tenuous hold. Within a few days, that map had vanished into the fragile status of a memory coda, solely for the eyes of those who had witnessed it. A few months later, and a few hundred metres along the Stresemannstrasse from the site of Romy Haag's protest in the Potsdamer Platz, within the spectator-saturated exhibition rooms of the Martin-Gropius-Bau art museum, a vast installation of digitized

projections of the figure of David Bowie, together with

the now revered historical detritus of his life in the city, formed another memory coda, to his own 1970s years in West Berlin.[4]

In the two decades after the Ackerstrasse and its inhabitants' bodies were filmed by Veronika Otten for a document that would then be hidden away and projected only in the distant future, the infrastructure of that street deteriorated still further, as though subject to a pre-ordained regime of urban disintegration. The elderly inhabitants eventually died away and very few new inhabitants appeared, other than the desperate or those seeking subterranean lives away from the attentions of the secret police, since the final populations of the GDR-era far preferred the new prefabricated estates on the eastern peripheries of the city. But from the mid-1990s, after the GDR's erasure, the Ackerstrasse gradually began to be renovated as part of the comprehensive resuscitation of the Mitte district of central Berlin. Forty years on, at the moment when the secreted film of the 1973 Ackerstrasse was finally unearthed and projected to cinema audiences (a decade or so later than originally planned), that scarred, eroded street had been transformed almost beyond recognition, the renovation and rehabilitation of its facades now complete, as though that once-disintegrated street's reversal back in time to a pristine status had been accomplished, as a perverse coda, in subservient compliance to the GDR city-planners' imperatives.

As the last breath and the last act of the manifold, ever-proliferating archives of the city of Berlin, which hold and incorporate all traces and residues of Berlin bodies, everything known and knowable about that city will arbitrarily mutate into an unknown and unknowable status, and all bodies and their images will be rendered into reversed entities, negative to positive, or positive to negative, at the final instant, in the final coda to the city.

STRATA

The streets of Berlin form anatomical amalgams of bodies and mutating urban elements in which body and city are invariably meshed in intimacy, never identical, often in antithetical tension, but profoundly interlayered, body-stratum posed against city-stratum, overturning one another in incessant oscillation, so that the coda may gloriously supplant the main 'body' of the text in elated urban exclamation but is then subject to immediate obsolescence and oblivion, as with the spectacular physical crossings of the Bösebrücke by pivotal historical figures, then forgotten on the bleak, voided bridge an hour later, or with the riot-debris layered over the streets of Kreuzberg at dawn following split-second insurgencies of the previous day and night. In the intense engagement that Berlin provokes from its inhabitants, and even in those only momentarily traversing or glimpsing the city, the body is stratified into Berlin's infinite layering, but those urban layers are themselves fissured by networks of

disintegration and vanishing that will always engulf the eye implicated in them.

At times, Berlin's strata appear so torn open to reinvention – in its streets' active anatomization by the bodies occupying them, notably at the end of the 1920s, or the beginning of the 1990s – that new eyes and originating visions or gestures are required to incise those strata and to disregard the city's fraudulent and surveillance-defined parameters. Six years on from Veronika Otten's filmic documentation of the Ackerstrasse that followed the elderly, castaway bodies along the then dilapidated street and through its peeled-away back courtyards, another filmic excavation of an adjacent East Berlin street was undertaken. Günter Jordan's *Berlin Auguststrasse* was shot in the hot summer of 1979 in a street just to the south of the Ackerstrasse (the two long streets almost intersect), but focused this time on the lives and bodies of the children of that street. Unlike Otten's hidden-away film, Jordan's was intended to be viewed immediately by its spectators. Since almost no traffic is seen on the Auguststrasse, and the pressing political imperatives of GDR youth culture appear to be a matter of utter indifference for that street's children, they are able to reinvent and reimagine it as their own terrain, as city-strata-creators and expansionists, delineating and stretching the neglected street itself and the surrounding ruinscapes directly through the momentum of their bodies' incursions and excursions, which extend southwards from the Auguststrasse to the stone stairways etched into the northern bank of the river Spree, from which those children's eyes coolly assess East Berlin's state edifices and museums on the far side.

Set together, Otten's 1973 *Berlin Milieu – Ackerstrasse* and Jordan's 1979 *Berlin Auguststrasse* topographically configure via film an East Berlin cityscape in which an ossified stratum of elderly bodies is layered above a mobile, volatile stratum of young bodies: contrary extremes of decrepitude and regeneration, of stultification and exploration, traversing zones of urban and corporeal space. That entire configuration of disparate strata is exposed to being wiped from the face of the city, and supplanted by another. In 1979 the only variances to the Auguststrasse's expanse of decrepit tenement houses were one or two run-down factories and dance halls, notably Clärchens Ballhaus, which had been a tenacious fixture in the street even before the 1920s era of Alfred Döblin's novel *Berlin Alexanderplatz* (in which the hero Franz Biberkopf visits it to dance, undeterred by the recent loss of one of his arms), despite losing the entire front half of its building in wartime bombing. But by 1990, eleven years after Jordan's film of the Auguststrasse children's restratification of that street, it had been overhauled into a new node of nightclub culture for the reunified city – those venues conjured in abandoned or obsolete spaces whose ownership had abruptly been rendered uncertain, such as the subterranes of an electricity generating station and the basement of a defunct margarine factory. The unused street-level rooms of Auguststrasse tenements were simultaneously mutating into art gallery spaces.

The wildly dancing bodies exposed to cacophony and sexual experimentation in those excavated strata for nightlife beneath the city's surface resonated with Romy Haag's instigation of a new, revivifying nightclub culture under the petrified streets of the West Berlin island city, sixteen years earlier.

Berlin bodies form inseparably conjoined components of street strata through the unique prominence which the city accords to urban corporeality, as in the forms of the body's elated exposures, its experimentations, its disintegrations, its forgettings and its razings, once it is intimately layered into the city. The cultural history of the human body in Berlin, notably in its image-focused dimensions, is integrally one in which that body tests and probes its own capacity to infiltrate, inhabit and reconfigure the strata of the city. Berlin corporeality itself is defined by the sensory responses, acquisitions, scarrings and negations that are the results of those probings of urban strata. Once a Berlin body has reached an inextricable degree of entanglement in its profound stratification of the city, via determined obsessionality or tenacious activism, it comes to form an urban stratum itself, and can only project itself through its role as that city-layered entity.

Berlin's unstable sub-ground level – whose shifting sand layers formed a great source of anxiety for Speer in his hallucinated formulation of the new Germania megalopolis and its rationality's testing with his 'Heavy-load-bearing Body' – constitutes a skeletal stratification, many centuries deep but densest in its twentieth-century components, of the accumulated residues of all such layered entanglements with the city, accompanied by other bone remains, many of them of unknown provenance: the residues of battles and massacres, of bombing raids (along with earth-embedded incendiary devices still awaiting their moment to detonate), and of decimating epidemics and plagues. Just as the city holds, beneath itself, the detrita of its previous architectures – their levels often compacted by time into one another – it holds, too, its amassed, uncontainable strata of the dead that double the living on its surfaces.

SCARS

An urban scarring of the body in Berlin is often an accidental, incidental matter: an integral experience of physical traversals via passageways and channels whose edges are serrated, rough, unsuturable, un-cleansable. Such minuscule punctures or gashes, sustained on foot, at ground level and through subterranean transits, gradually accumulate over time into constellations of urban scars. They form mappings of the city whose markings are concentrated at its most jaggedly exposed sites, thereby paralleling Romy Haag's Potsdamer Platz map of those puncture-points of Europe (and further afield) at which sexual prohibitions are exacted against the body. For Berlin bodies, constellations of scars equate to corporeal urban duration. City scarrings may also form networks of superficial abrasures and bruisings that have momentarily skimmed or glanced the skin, leaving residual traces on its surface that could only be perceived if that skin were stripped off and then projected with high-intensity illumination, like a celluloid strip, as a reverse image, and would otherwise remain invisible and imperceptible. Scarrings may enter the body's ears via the domain of noise and cacophony, and the eyes via the propulsions of digital screens and data; they can also leave no discernible trace at all, whenever Berlin bodies are touched by ghosts, spectres and revenants for whom all scarring must be hauntingly phantasmatic in order for those presences to occupy living bodies again for an instant.

In 1979's summer, when the filmed children of the Auguststrasse were engaged in their oblivious corporeal restratification of East Berlin's cityscape, I took my first walks along that street and through the surrounding streets, after emerging from the riverside 'Palace of Tears' (Tränenpalast) at the Friedrichstrasse border station, and constantly thought, as I walked: This is a city of scars . . . The facades of the East Berlin central district appeared so glaringly pitted and incised by configurations of bomb shrapnel and bullet-hole impacts, together with all of the accumulated everyday excoriations and striations inflicted upon buildings that had never been tended to (at least, not since the 1930s). Absences constituted scars too, in the pervasive bomb sites and abandoned interzones that up-ended

the status of the soot-blackened, still standing or newly built components of the wasteland city into that of its aberrant, anomalous element. On walks later that summer through the more peripheral areas of West Berlin, such as the far eastern end of Kreuzberg, that sensation of traversing a city of scars returned, as though each new street that appeared manifested variants of a colossal urban scarring that the tracing eye constantly reanimated. Over 35 years on, almost all of those relentless striations had been sealed over, vanished or been rendered virtual, but remained enduringly intact in those erasures, ready all the more virulently to exist or re-exist for their negation.

Still deeper scars exist, for Berlin bodies. To mark his ninetieth birthday, the jazz guitarist Coco Schumann gave a talk on his experiences of performing in the Nazi-era swing-music scene following his exposure, at a very young age, to American jazz during the Berlin Olympic Games of 1936, playing in nightclubs and larger venues such as the Delphi Filmpalast cinema – often covert performances, since both his playing of outlawed swing music and his half-Jewish status made him vulnerable to arrest – until his deportation from Berlin in 1943, to the concentration camp of Theresienstadt, then that of Auschwitz, where he faced Josef Mengele and performed (as he had at Theresienstadt) in the concentration camp band, and finally to Dachau. When he finally returned to Berlin, he perceived the city as utterly destroyed, every building without exception damaged – though music was still being played in the decimated ruins, as at Auschwitz. He left Berlin to emigrate to Australia, but was pulled back after several years, returning to the city with his guitar to pass though a further six decades or more of its nightclub life. In 1960s promotional photographs, his figure was often juxtaposed against West Berlin landmarks, such as the Europa-Center, to reinforce his intimate association with the city. As he speaks, Coco Schumann's concertinaed face tangibly emanates the scarrings of that time of deportation, over seventy years in the past, while his semi-gasped words also form scars; his body, in its survival and capacity still to project memory, constitutes another seminal Berlin coda that acts back upon the city's fragile, obliterating history, and embeds itself too into the contemporary city. At ninety, he must search deeply for his memories, pitched at the moment before they will vanish, but the act of locating them, against abraded time, makes them insurge.

When scars emerge from the tongue of Coco Schumann and inhabit the space of Berlin, they signal that words form scars, just as images form scars. Propelled against the sensitized surfaces of the city, they possess the capacity to wound it still further, as scars exerted from Berlin bodies into the strata of the city, accomplishing the inverse movement to the stratifications of scars inflicted from the city's serrated edges into the skin of the bodies traversing it. Those words also incant scarred locations, such as that of the former Jewish boys' school in the Grosse Hamburger Strasse (the street interconnecting the Ackerstrasse and

Auguststrasse) transformed by 1943 into an internment centre for those imminently to be deported, at which he awaited that expulsion, together with other bodies, to be lethally jettisoned from Berlin from the platforms of the Grunewald or Anhalter railway stations. The immeasurable, contrary texture of its scarification in itself constitutes an urban cultural history of Berlin that becomes infinitely tangible through its ocular and corporeal transits, across time always ready to freefall – as the experience of listening to Coco Schumann's recitation of his scarred-Berlin decades demonstrates, as well as through the city's imagery, such as that of film, and through its spoken and read text.

Scars may often appear to have annealed and calcified, as though through a process of petrifaction that finally reconfigures their burning sensory fissurations and cataclysms into formless, frozen signals – those of Berlin bodies or locations that once were wrenched or torn apart, but in an act now entirely voided from time. An annealed scar forms the antithesis to a 'healed' scar; it has undergone premature treatment to curtail its still seething resonances. Such annealed scars may then become officially sanctioned corporate spectacles that are publicly displayed and placarded, as the sites for monuments (including those ostensibly commemorating Berlin's deportation of its own Jewish inhabitants), for maximal visibility throughout the city. They exist in opposition to Berlin's contemporary open-woundings, including those inflicted digitally and those that stem from desperations momentarily deferred with drugs and alcohol, that will never scar, in their incessant transmutations, remaining in raw flux and unclosed on the surfaces of the body and the city.

MARKERS

Berlin forms an exploratory laboratory for experiments with the contours, resilience, brutality and visions of the human body – its capacities for excess, extreme sensation, imaginary conjurings, conjoinings, pain, terror, nostalgia, lust – and unendingly subjects its bodies to such experiments in the contemporary moment, as it has throughout its history of the past century and a half, since its expansion into a megalopolis in the 1870s. Whenever Berlin's bodies in transit abruptly stop dead in the streets for an instant, disorientated, bewildered or gazing, they constitute markers inscribed upon the city's ongoing temporal dynamics, thereby bringing Berlin's relentless experimentation to a momentary halt, to a paused breath. Such static figures in the streets of Berlin possess a distinctive monumental status of their own in those instants, marking the resistant outlines of Berlin corporealities, while also negating the city's proliferating institutional monuments of declaredly infinite duration.

As Berlin's figures stand in frozen silence for an instant in its streets, their ongoing dissolution renders them always subject to imminent collapse. All ostensibly fixed markers of Berlin bodies are subject to such collapses, including those that serve to propel the corporeality of Berlin's cultural history backwards through time. In Coco Schumann's gasped vocal and memorial revivification of his experiences in the night-club swing-music scene that was pursued in defiance, including sexual defiance, of Nazi urban edicts, between 1936 and 1943, Berlin's nightclub culture suddenly opens out beyond its familiar history, extending back in time far beyond Romy Haag's own instigation of a defiant nightclub culture in 1974, back towards Berlin's vast nightclub scene of the late 1920s, with its intricate permutations of sexual as well as musical preferences, for which no living voices still subsist; then even further back, to the 1890s and the Skladanowsky brothers' first ever demonstration of celluloid film projection in the lavish nightclub ballroom of the Wintergarten venue. In reverse urban genealogies, such as that of the city's nightclub culture, Berlin bodies deeply imprint each successive moment and its surviving spaces, such as that of the wood-panelled Nazi-era cabaret hall in the Steglitz district's Grunewaldstrasse, or the cavernous, still-resonant mirror room (Spiegelsaal) of Clärchens Ballhaus in the Auguststrasse, an integral part of Berlin's nightlife of the 1920s and '30s before being emptied of bodies, abandoned and used for storage throughout the GDR decades – including the 1979 children's summer of the film *Berlin Auguststrasse* – and beyond. Other spaces, such as that of the Wintergarten ballroom, located within the Central Hotel alongside the Friedrich-strasse station, were obliterated by wartime bombing, their ruins then erased to create wastelands. In all such spaces Berlin bodies mark their momentarily performed presences as intensively as they embed their enduring absences, as in the dance-frenzy incised markings of heel-nicks in the wooden floorings of dancehalls, in violent fistings of never-replaced wall plaster, and in heated falls of sweat onto porous nightclub surfaces. Even when a venue appears to have utterly vanished or undergone unrecognizable transformation, as with the Wintergarten and innumerable other pivotal spaces across more than a century of Berlin nightlife, its bodies spectrally conjure and mark it into the contemporary city.

In Berlin bodies' propulsive experiences of awry reverse momentum, as in that of the city's nightclub culture, they hold the status simultaneously of fixed inhabitants and of involuntary time travellers through the city, those bodies subject at any moment to a through-the-floorboards, vertically launched or sideways transition in time and vision, towards potentially hostile but revelatory pasts and futures (as with the urban journeys experienced by the imprisoned time-traveller figure in Chris Marker's 1962 film *La Jetée*, which begin and end in his death). Berlin forms an always uncertain zonal terrain which demands networks of markers for orientation, but markers themselves, in their incipient collapses and in their capacity for spatial and corporeal experimentation, precipitate a concurrent, overriding visual regime of disorientation.

In the years before the collapse of the GDR, markers accumulated on the West Berlin side of the Wall and of the Spree river boundary to signal the corporeal absences of those who had attempted to traverse that border and been shot down by border guards or else drowned. Those markers often took the form of upright wooden crosses hand-inscribed with the traversant's name and date of attempted crossing, or of flat slabs embedded in stone into the street itself, like those commemorating 1960s escapees crossing the part of East Berlin's frontier which, for a time, coincided with a line of derelict tenements, in the Bernauer Strasse, with that escape necessitating a potentially lethal plummet from upper-storey windows to the street below, which belonged to West Berlin's territory, so that the body's moment of liberation risked coinciding exactly with that of its death impact. Although many of the vertical cross markers disappeared after the GDR's collapse, as though the bodies they named had now been consigned to absence through that state's fall (which led to trials and imprisonments of its border guards), the horizontal stone-slab markers endured, to be supplemented from 1993 through the 'Stumbling Stones' (*Stolpersteine*) project of the artist Gunter Demnig, marking the Nazi-era sitings of buildings – often now vanished – from which Jewish and other occupants had been deported to concentration camps and labour camps, and naming those expelled bodies, together with their time and location of death or its unknown status. As with the accumulations of wooden crosses and stone slabs around Berlin Wall locations mistakenly perceived by would-be GDR escapees as especially permeable, but which proved deadly, those Stumbling Stone markers appeared in great numbers in areas of the city that had been the preferred long-term locations of its Jewish community, and also in the anonymous districts, such as Halensee, to which 'assimilated' Jewish inhabitants – Coco Schumann's family among them – had moved, especially in 1938, to avoid the dangers of Nazi-regime surveillance. Such tracings and namings of voids collect resiliently at ground level; to envision the markers of massacred Berlin bodies, the eye traversing the city looks down, as though into its multiple strata.

EXPANSIONS

In Berlin's abrupt transformation into a seams-bursting, nerve-wracked megalopolis, across the final decades of the nineteenth century and into the first decades of the twentieth, its bodies drove that expansion and its distinctive configuration: one generated primarily by corporeal obsessions, visions, gestures, acquisitions and urban swallowings. Especially in the 1890s and 1920s, Berlin projected its visions through a relentless expansiveness that prioritized the sensations and ocular demands of the body, in architectural experimentation, in innovations in performance and film cultures together with their spaces, and in the proliferation of department stores and immense, multi-storey entertainment complexes such as Potsdamer Platz's Haus Vaterland (in Phil Jutzi's 1931 film *Berlin Alexanderplatz*, the mobile film camera explores the expansive vertical dimensions and successive strata of the Haus Vaterland like an endoscopic camera scanning the interior of the human body). Berlin's self-definition in that era as a 'world city' (*Weltstadt*) intimates dual expansions: the desire to appropriate and incorporate all global cultures within itself, and the determination to raise the megalopolis's new status to a position of global pre-eminence. The accelerating dynamics of Berlin's population explosion from the 1870s – convulsively doubling, then doubling again, in a headlong accumulation that forms a contrary to the violent halving of the city's population during the seventeenth-century Thirty Years War, or its forthcoming decimation in the Second World War – vacuumed millions of workers, exiles, migrants and travellers into Berlin, largely from areas to the city's east and south, and generated the need for rapid tenement construction, notably in areas that had previously been city-edge wastelands or else industrial terrains, such as the 1880s–'90s constructions in the Prenzlauer Berg district around the Helmholtzplatz. The railway, subway and tram transport infrastructure developed during those decades was also driven above all by corporeal imperatives: to set Berlin bodies in movement, from tenement zones to industrial zones, from lavish residential areas to department-store areas, and from over-crammed space to expansive city-bordering spaces of forests and lakes which now needed to be architecturally equipped with sub-cities for vast numbers of bathers, as at the Wannsee.[5]

Berlin became a city that drove its bodies mad in those decades, almost knowingly so, as though the excessive expansiveness required to create a megalopolis necessarily had also to generate urban neuroses whose manifestations were exclusively externalized, in corporeal tics, hysterical outbursts, protests, quarrels – alongside the physical symptoms of tuberculosis that also resulted from the city's expansion into endless tenement configurations, each with many bodies packed into damp and freezing rooms, including cellar-level and subterranean strata. The construction, mainly around the first years of the twentieth century, of immense asylum sub-city complexes, such as those of Buch to the north of Berlin, as well as tuberculosis sub-cities, such as that of Beelitz-Heilstätten to the southwest of the city, anticipated expansive future outbreaks of the mad and tubercular. As Andreas Killen highlights in his book *Berlin Electropolis*, particular categories of occupations, such as telephone operators and transport-infrastructure workers, were prone to corporeally manifested urban psychosis, including intricate simulations designed to elicit payments from bureaucratic state-funded workers' insurance schemes.[6] The First World War, with its conjuring away and erasure of vast numbers of the young male bodies of Berlin, served to empty out the city to a degree which proved long-term (for the remainder of the twentieth century – apart from its saturation by refugees from 1944 –

Berlin's streets appeared far more voided and spectral than those of other European cities, having been designed for a far larger population than the one which came to traverse and occupy them). To compensate for a corporeal dearth, the surviving bodies' madness expanded. In the 1920s, war-generated traumas transmutated a significant element of the Berlin streets' eye-attracting population – often self-signalled with placards as flesh and nerves mutilated by warfare – into one that was both scarred and mad, transmitting its shocks and unbearable experiences of slaughter into street gestures, cries and self-proclamations. Visual artists such as George Grosz seized representations of that madness from those streets, and, around the end of the 1920s and in antici-pation of new madnesses to come, walker-writers such as Franz Hessel, Siegfried Kracauer and Walter Benjamin evoked Berlin's urban space as one of incessant, competing and expansive psychoses, projected from its bodies.

The expansiveness of Berlin's sensory furores positions its corporeal dimensions as being intractably mismatched or at odds with its urban and architectural dimensions. Bodies excessively overspill imposed parameters, in self-directed desires for consumption and arbitrary compulsions for gratification, as well as in ecologically oriented ambitions and visions that extend far beyond city-authority strictures. The city cannot contain its bodies, as captured in the resonant title of the film actor Hanns Zischler's 2013 book, *Berlin ist zu gross für Berlin* (*Berlin is Too Big for Berlin*). Berlin bodies' irrepressible elations, together with their shatterings and re-envisionings of urban space, generate a pressurized corporeal expansion which ruptures or negates containments, so body and city never achieve temporal simultaneity or spatial reconciliation.

In contemporary Berlin's urban space, the unprecedented expansion of digital screens and data hoardings around bodies in movement (far more engulfing, in many ways, than the 1920s culture of pervasive neon signage, along entertainment axis avenues such as the Tauentzienstrasse and the Münzstrasse, which served to illuminate bodies' transits and attract ocular attention towards the nightclubs or venues behind those signs) actively infiltrates and inhabits those bodies, so that mobile Berlin bodies in immense corporate environments may themselves form expansive markers and projectors of digital media. Such infiltrated bodies appear to form contrary presences to those momentarily still markers composed by more peripheral figures in urban space, but both presences signal incipient collapse and disintegration. Berlin bodies, once enmeshed with digital media, form expansive instruments for mapping the city against the body, in amalgams that intimate that one element of that volatile conjoining will be annulled by the other.

By contrast with the dense, expansive excess of contemporary Berlin's saturated digital screens, markers of absence and voids often vitally guided the eye of the body in transit through the city across its four postwar decades. In the summer of 1979, after East Berlin walks through the silent and apparently depopulated (and almost carless) terrain of the surface-excoriated Prenzlauer Berg streets, with their still integral missing components, I walked southwards towards the Alexanderplatz – reconstructed through the 1960s as an immense but glacially voided plaza, opening outwards into peripheral-vision emptinesses on all sides and thereby dispersing into thin air the figures crossing it – and experienced the sense of corporeal absence which that plaza's expansion imposed.

AMASSINGS

A decade later, in the identical space of the Alexanderplatz, with the immense protests, especially that of 4 November 1989, whose expansion finally saturated the plaza to overspilling and pressurized the GDR state towards its irreparable cracking – as though an awry but resilient urban psychosis offshoot from decades earlier had precipitated the official government spokesman Günter Schabowski's blurted, unanticipated television announcement of the end of travel restrictions for East Berlin's inhabitants – that urban void transmutated into a pivotal corporeal amassing. Those autumn 1989 demonstrations were filmed both by the protesters themselves and also by the Stasi secret police, adeptly experienced cinematographers of Alexanderplatz bodies, whose elevated film cameras tracked and archived, for example, the zigzagging transits across the plaza of gangs of 1980s East Berlin punks, as evidence for the prosecution of those aberrant bodies or for the issuing of edicts forbidding their future entry into the half-city's central zones.[7]

That punitive cinematography formed only one manifestation in a long-durational lineage of filmings of corporeal amassings in the Alexanderplatz, from the very first film of that space by Max and Emil Skladanowsky, shot in the summer of 1896 and projected to spectators only once during that era, showing figures traversing the square towards its centre between the paths of newly electrified trams, to fiction films and filmic documents of that square in the 1920s and '30s (such as Phil Jutzi's *Berlin Alexanderplatz*) that chart constellations of bodies, through sudden amassings and dispersals around vocal street-sellers and performers, such as magicians and acrobats. Following the partial levelling of the Alexanderplatz through wartime bombing, it remained the destination towards which processions and marches from outlying avenues congregated, such as those of young pioneer troupes and peace activists in the first years of the GDR. Even after its comprehensive reconstruction in the 1960s, which overhauled the Alexanderplatz into a visually disorientating, city-centre wasteland – vertically pinioned towards that decade's end by the 37-storey Interhotel Stadt Berlin complex and the Television Tower – it had formed an officially sanctioned location for filmed concerts and performances, often sited in its far-flung corners, so that the bodies of audiences amassed before those performances appeared perversely to reinforce the plaza's aura of an emptied-out expanse. For the first time, in that mass protest of 4 November 1989, Berlin bodies overrode the GDR-era Alexanderplatz's vacuity.

Throughout the GDR decades, memorial sites and monuments had been created across East Berlin through the designing of directly adjoining spaces for statues or sculptures and for the amassings of bodies – contrary corporeal accumulations to the systematic dispersal and expulsion from East Berlin's urban space of dissident and unruly inhabitants by its secret police agencies – in the form of official events or performances at which an intensively vocal and ocularly engaged corporeality was demanded, in order to sanction that city-implanted monument, in the form of chants, slogans and synchronized gestures. Even in the final years of the GDR, new voids envisaged for occupation by such corporeal amassings appeared, each able to hold many hundreds of bodies, such as that facing the colossal sculpted head of the German Communist Party leader Ernst Thälmann, completed in 1986 at the edge of a large park (formerly the site of industrial and gas installations) in the Prenzlauer Berg district, and forming an active performance site for only three years, before being overturned into an obsolete performance site – now utilized pre-eminently for amassings of petrified figures in states of alcoholic or drug-induced incapacitation, or by graffiti artists intent on marking cryptic inscriptions on Thälmann's head or across the bronze base of that sculpture – in the quarter-century following the GDR's dissolution.

Berlin bodies, especially in their moving-image forms filmed by twentieth-century cinematographers or by contemporary smartphone-wielding inhabitants, manifest the intricate gestures and trajectories by which corporeality abruptly amasses and evanesces in urban space, subject to dynamics of accumulation and dispersal that are never precisely repeated, each amassing of bodies existing in unprecedented volatility. Particularly when Berlin bodies amass for an instant around a performance or act undertaken in an expansive space, such as that of the Alexanderplatz, they both transmit the unique corporeal and ocular conjunction that such a gathering of bodies generates, and also constitute a new variant of endless historical strata of corporeal amassings in that same site, archived in film or memory.

Berlin bodies may amass at extreme, in-flux sites of ruination, in which acts of corporeal amalgamation and re-envisioning form precarious entities. On 18 August 1948, 30,000 inhabitants of Berlin amassed in the Soviet zone's Gendarmenmarkt plaza – which, prior to their war-era destruction, had held two cathedrals and a lavish concert hall, and now held their ruins – in order to witness an outdoor performance of Russian folk songs and energetic dance routines by the occupying Soviet military forces' Alexandrov Ensemble. The film document of the performance and its audience by Richard Groschopp and Max Jaap, *Botschafter des*

Friedens (*Ambassadors of Peace*), frames the event within sequences of the surrounding city's near-total erasure and its surviving buildings' gutted facades; the bodies amassing for the performance begin their journeys in a nowhere terrain of cancelled inhabitation, but still they cohere as an audience, scaling the cathedrals' jagged walls and caved-in roofs to create vantage-points from which to witness the performance. That audience emanates a sensorial frenzy of pleasure (especially when a soloist performs one of the songs, 'Kalinka', in German); shots of accumulations of bodies, positioned on precarious ledges and gripping gaps in pitted facades, at great heights, demonstrate oblivious elation, accentuated by those bodies' momentary siting in a miraculous coda-zone of the city. At least one cinema-tographer also scaled the ruins' summits. Other bodies stand directly at scorched ground level before the improvised stage on which the dancers and singers perform. Arenas of destruction and imminent collapse that test Berlin bodies to extremes, in the act of envisioning performance, form optimum sites for those bodies' amassings.

As those spectators watch the Alexandrov Ensemble from their elevated, unstable perches on the cathedral's ledges, as though cramponed to vertical mountainous ice walls, they often cling compulsively to one other, in part to steady themselves from the danger of falling to the ground-level ruins below, but also in exhilaration, in the act of constituting corporeal amalgams. An amassing can take the form of a solitary experience of collective isolation for which bodies have been required to gather, in pre-prepared locations, in order to incorporate or witness rituals of power and memory, but it pre-eminently constitutes an experience in which exposures to delirium, disequilibrium and sensory disorientation, body against body, precipitate new urban conjoinings.

CONCENTRATIONS

Berlin bodies form concentrated axis points for the city's contrary, in-flux movements and its multiple strata. In their filming in August 1948, the conjoined human figures of that elated audience precariously affixed to the barely-still-there facades of the cathedrals and concert hall, pitched high above the Gendarmenmarkt plaza and gripping one another in order to transmit, body to body, both the vertiginous pleasure generated by the performance and the desire not to plummet into ruination-marked urban space, distil essential corporeal manifestations in their positioning against urban surfaces. When such bodies direct their gestures of survival inwardly, thereby rendering that configuration dense and intractably carapaced, they dispel the capacity of the city to engulf corporeality through subjugating dynamics of proliferation and expansion. An act of corporeal concentration – especially one undertaken with an extreme inter-action of conflicting sensations, such as the elation and anxiety of the Gendarmenmarkt spectators – needs to be caught and imprinted, by the film camera or eye, in order for that amalgam to be registered as one which fractures the city's prevalent rhythms. It operates solely within a regime of instantaneities, before that concentration is prised apart and Berlin bodies become exposed once again to processes of urban abrasure that work to disintegrate and dispel them.

Pivotal concentrations of bodies in Berlin's urban space have often been enacted in far more constrained terrains than those of the Gendarmenmarkt or the post-1960s Alexanderplatz. Especially during the late 1970s (at the same moment when the reconstruction from their ruins of the cathedrals and concert hall of the Gendarmenmarkt finally began in East Berlin), in the neglected Kreuzberg district of West Berlin during a period of acute housing shortages, urban activists and local residents relentlessly demonstrated, in the tight confines of road junctions such as the Heinrichplatz, against the ongoing demolition of the surrounding streets' disintegrated nineteenth-century tenements. The acquisition of the resulting wastelands by property speculators from government agencies and Berlin's city authorities had already allowed them to build vast new housing complexes, such as the contested multi-storey Neue Kreuzberger Zentrum at the nearby Kottbusser Tor junction, completed in 1974.[8] Those demonstrations opposing property speculation, which used the print media of posters and leaflets to advocate the occupation of emptied-out tenements and the development of autonomous residents' networks with ecological and

collectivist preoccupations that directly opposed those
of the city's authorities, were often surrounded and
then attacked in their concentrated parameters by
white-helmeted police forces with riot shields, through
brutal manoeuvres prefiguring the more sophisticated
'kettling' techniques used worldwide by riot police in
the 2000s and 2010s to spatially subdue and petrify
anti-globalization and ecological demonstrations
around junctions, such as that of Oxford Street and
Regent Street in London. Urban bodies may intentionally concentrate themselves into resistant amalgams,
but they can also be concentrated from exterior space
by invasive forces of suppression, thereby generating
a breath-expelled crushing.

The two main junctions – the Oranienplatz, along
with the Heinrichplatz – along eastern Kreuzberg's
protest artery of dissident culture during the late 1970s,
the Oranienstrasse (where the seminal punk rock club
the SO36 opened in 1978), both became concentrated
urban nodal points for the origination of demonstrations that amassed activist figures for incursions into
the surrounding streets, to oppose demolitions and to
initiate house occupations, and also for the attempted
spatial constraining by riot police forces of those concentrations' anti-corporate virulence. The riot culture
of Kreuzberg's Oranienstrasse was accentuated and
doubled by the activist community open-air performance
culture that developed alongside it in the adjacent plaza,
the Mariannenplatz, in front of the artists' studio
complex newly housed in the former Bethanien

convent hospital, constructed in the 1840s and itself only saved from property-speculation demolition through campaigns of protest and occupation at the beginning of the 1970s, following its closure as a hospital.

Alongside activist communities and the Turkish populations which had arrived from the early 1960s in that eastern dead-end zone of Kreuzberg – 'Berlin's arse' (*der Arsch von Berlin*), as it had been caustically dubbed, and self-named, for many decades, since the nineteenth century, always peripheral and denuded, and then also oppressively up against the Berlin Wall – those dilapidated tenements whose erasure was so desired by late 1970s West Berlin property speculators also formed the homes of stranded elderly remnants of the area's pre-war community of industrial and river-port workers, now death-distilled and concentrated down to their final traces. That community formed a counterpart to that of the elderly inhabitants of East Berlin's Ackerstrasse, whose last-ditch corporeal transits of that similarly worn-out, fissured street had been documented in film in 1973. Its figures' aberrant street appearances, in infinitely slow and bewildered trajectories along the Oranienstrasse, with its new prevalence of Turkish cafés and radical-collective activist workshops, gave them the spectral appearance of the survivors of a cataclysm that had scarred and voided that street, but had also accorded that concentration of figures the enduring capacity to enact residual fragments of urban memory.

Those slow-moving, elderly figures which I watched on my first walks along the Oranienstrasse in 1979 – bodies propelled into cells of isolation among the pushing pulses of activists, punks and Turks – undertook vitally concentrated gestural movements of Berlin bodies: those of disorientation, fragmentation, repetition and opposition, as they gradually evanesced into the striated face of the city. The entire existence of Berlin bodies may be concentrated into one oblique and contrary gesture, poised for its projection between memory and oblivion. Along with street-focused photographs of Turkish children's games and of riotous confrontations, those elderly figures were haphazardly archived during that era, against faded-out pre-war shop signage and graffitied, damp-destroyed tenement facades, by the Kreuzberg photographer Ludwig Menkhoff – an itinerant figure who took his photographs on alcoholic journeys between the district's bars – in the form of obsolete corporeal strata within the area's predominant activist culture of resistance. After further eruptions in the 1980s, that resistant culture itself became petrified and edged towards disappearance by the contemporary transmutation of Kreuzberg, with that renovated district's unexpected repositioning into a more central, lucrative location after the vanishing of the Berlin Wall, finally becoming the property-value Eden of which its 1970s speculators had forlornly dreamed.

RESIDUES

The act of engaging with Berlin's urgent imperatives and disorientations, and of confronting and contesting the manifestations of city-authority strictures through interventions exerted upon its surfaces and strata, as in Kreuzberg's late-1970s riotous street protests and their accompanying performance and arts cultures, resulted across the city's cultural history in a transplantation from body to city of corporeal residues, imprinted – involuntarily or intentionally – onto urban forms. A residue's transfer from the domain of corporeality to that of the urban can imply a surrendering of the body's substances to proprietorial city archives, but such residues may also remain ligatured to the body which originally emanated them, through attachments of memory or via those residues' configuration in such an aberrant medium that it cannot ever be fully assimilated to the domain of the urban. Residues of Berlin bodies obstinately survive, even when nothing ostensibly remains of elements of the city as the result of comprehensive processes of erasure and destruction; in urban space, corporeal residues are invariably generated after endpoints, as the fragile evidence of bodies' now-exhausted contacts with the city, extending from infinitesimal glancings to engulfing re-envisionings.

Residues inscribed upon Berlin's surfaces may be the marks of fluids that initially formed part of the body or were manually propelled from it – blood, saliva, sweat, sexual fluids, paint, marker-pen ink – or else comprise digital data that spectrally traversed the body before becoming adhered to urban space. The intervals momentarily occupied by the transits of corporeal residues, propelled between body and city surface, themselves form enduringly residual space, long after all evidence of those transits appears to have vanished from it. Residues' sites are most glaringly evident at the spaces of mismatch between obsolescence and the contemporary; residues' integral surpassedness rises up from invisibility whenever it contrasts in extremity with the livedness of present-moment surfaces and screens. In Berlin's urban space, residues most prominently manifested themselves during the 1990s transition from the former East Berlin's anachronistic forms to its renovated, corporatized forms – as in neon shop signage, street lighting and architectural anomalies, as well as in the clothing, dimensions, hair and skin of bodies initially unyielding to that transition – until the jarring obsolescence of those archaisms itself became subject to dissolution across time. Disjunctures in the city attract and accumulate the presence of residues.

The surfaces of former East Berlin in the early 1990s comprised an unprecedented screen for the inscriptions of seething residues from multiple experiences of the GDR's vanishing, together with residues from polarized political contestations that pre-dated the GDR state itself. The endpoint of the GDR, in conjunction with the sudden availability in eastern Berlin of endless building-surface space for those residues' inscriptions

(notably during the interval, extending across several

years, in which the ownership of many of those buildings became voided and unknown, following the GDR's collapse, rendering them acutely exposed to residues' graffiti markings), opened that screen, supplemented by the innumerable surfaces of railway-yard buildings and of train-carriage exteriors and interiors. The immense blank brick firewalls of tenement buildings, in particular, optimized the dimensions of intricate graffiti inscriptions. In peripheral areas of former East Berlin such as the tenements of Lichtenberg and the housing-block sub-city of Marzahn, those graffiti confrontations, of neo-Fascism against neo-Communism, were directly accompanied in that era by bloody nocturnal gang battles which added their own residual fluids to graffiti surfaces. Those obsolete inscriptions, phantasmatically launched from corporeal, urban and political obsessions, soon became tightly meshed and interlayered with opposed graffiti contents, with their own styles of inscription, focused on the compulsions and sensations of the contemporary city, thereby generating entangled graffiti-strata which enabled those obsolescent residues to vividly project themselves, before becoming gradually submerged in infinite new layers of graffiti's genealogy, or else effaced entirely once the ownership of buildings became re-established. That saturation of graffiti, already partly archaic and imminently entirely archaic, even at the moment of its inscription, rapidly overspilled the surfaces of the former East Berlin and resuscitated the graffiti cultures of former West Berlin districts such as

Kreuzberg and Neukölln, which had been subdued and

neglected since the late-1960s student-riot furores and the activist cultures protesting property speculation and other contestations of the 1970s; many densely graffitied areas of 1990s Berlin took on the interconnected form of residual historical hallucinations and ongoing corporeal seisms.

Vital residues, of corporeal processes and surpassed urban-historical obsessions, are compulsively transmitted from Berlin's bodies to its surfaces, to create a framework in which the body is always in the act of being absorbed, in tension or elation, into Berlin's screens. But Berlin bodies may also themselves incorporate residues emitted by the city, in a process of the corporeal absorption of residues that accompanies and accentuates the more direct scarrings and markings inflicted on transiting bodies by the city's serrated edges. Since residues form the emanations of superseded entities, those absorbings often operate at tangents, fragmentarily, or across history's gaps, as in the infinitesimal exposure of Berlin's contemporary residents to the city's high-density nineteenth-century industrial toxicity, still ineradicably extant in such locations as the Prenzlauer Berg district's park alongside Thälmann's monumental bronze head. Such marginal exposures of the body, to obsolete toxic subterranes and contaminated groundwater leakages, gradually accumulate to form an essential component of the living body as Berlin city residue.

DETRITA

Detrital Berlin bodies form the essential, aberrant component of the city that is always subject via vilification to rejection or expulsion, or is seen as impossible to assimilate into city space frameworks that in Berlin are already too multiply shattered, in any case, for integrative processes, so that all Berlin bodies hold, to a greater or lesser degree, detrital elements, and inhabit detrital city space. Detrital Berlin bodies possess a wide range of variants, from refugee and exile bodies, to bodies subject to digital-media dynamics that assign detrital attributes to all figures and eyes which, through intractability, will not mesh in subjugation into the digital city. Detrital bodies may be jettisoned into peripheral, unseen city space, but also into its most ocularly exposed, central zones, such as those of its railway stations, notably Ostbahnhof and Zoologischer Garten, with their long histories of forming detrital terrains, and plazas and parks, such as the Alexanderplatz and the Görlitzer Park. Once Berlin bodies become detrita, they no longer occupy exclusively human parameters, and are subject to non-organic, non-combustible mutant mixings with other rejected or refused city trash materials, thereby coming to form amalgams with the non-human and the animal. As well as encountering alien presences and animals, detrital Berlin bodies also intimately frequent the city dead, and inextricably conjoin with them, notably in Berlin's immense subterranean strata, such as bunkers' ruins, heating passageways and subway tunnels, as well as in its sub-ground-level nightclubs.

Detrital Berlin bodies traverse the city just as its more 'integrated' human components do, but with a distinctive style of movement, often undertaken across groups; detrita must group and amass in order to cross the threatening city without arrest, as in the early-1980s Stasi-filmed city-centre transits of gangs of East Berlin punks heading towards their elected gathering sites at the riverside Spreepark funfair or the outlying Ulmenhof asylum grounds. Berlin bodies' detrita are integrally multiple; a lone-figure detrital presence in Berlin can potentially embody and engulf the entire city by replicating it. Detrital manoeuvres characteristically scatter horizontally, in small constellations of figures, across the face of the city, in part to elude detention by city authorities, and in part since they perceive no reason to move linearly, before then regathering in axis sites in order to pursue missions of psychosis, addiction or alcoholism. But those detrital city transits may also operate on a vertical axis as well as horizontally in descents (detrita, when not self-propelled in another direction, will fall), via slippages into cracks and abrupt abjections, through the city's surface level, or else in contrary, near-vertical ascents to its highest points, such as the alcohol bottle- and syringe-laden war monument summit of the Kreuzberg district's Viktoriapark.

Even in their exterior space gathering points in the city, in the entranceways and concourses of central

railway stations or within overlooked, neglected
wastelands, Berlin's corporeal detrita never cease to
move, unendingly enacting performances of infinitesimal, corroded gesture, with accompanying vocal
declarations or glossolalia, during the near-zero
temporal intervals between the corporeal demands
of desperation or addiction. Such split-second performances may collect over decades, for an omniscient
city eye, into an immense archive of detrital gesture
that, in its excessive amplitude, incorporates the urban
compulsions of Berlin. Alongside the adherence of
detrital figures to particular preferred sites and peripheral wastelands within the city, where they can conduct
their performative acts in unsurveilled invisibility and
anonymity, the city itself may render its inhabitants
temporarily sited, exposed and bonded immovably to
the Berlin pavements' surface, through its own accumulated detrital assets – notably the vast quantities of
chemical-based, adhesive materials used in the city's
inexhaustible post-1990 street construction and building
renovation work, which stick tenaciously to the soles
of one's shoes. Such sudden decelerations and arrests
of in-transit Berlin bodies, however momentary, transmutate those figures into motionless detrita marking
otherwise dynamic urban space. Artworks, such as
Néle Azevedo's rapidly melting multitude of tiny,
humanoid ice figures, *Minimum Monument*, installed
on 2 September 2009 on the stone steps of the concert
hall in the Gendarmenmarkt (where city-gripping
spectators witnessed the Alexandrov Ensemble's

performance, sixty years earlier), form the inverse process, of corporeal detritus leaking into the city's surface.

Berlin possesses an intricate lineage of detrital urban representations: Grosz and Döblin (and Rainer Werner Fassbinder, in his film adaptation of Döblin's *Berlin Alexanderplatz*), among many others – across art, writing and film – worked as mappers of detrital city transits and of the city stickings of Berlin bodies who may want to head elsewhere, such as Döblin's figure of Franz Biberkopf on his release from Tegel prison and journey by tram back into the packed network of streets to the northwest of the Alexanderplatz, but instead find themselves centrifugally adhered to the city's most detrital, poverty-stricken zones, in which criminality, corruption (including corruption on the part of the city authorities), acts of sexual violence and addiction, may be at their most intense. Among other areas, Kreuzberg's now obsolete role as the detrital 'arse of Berlin', stemming in part from its notoriety as one of the most denuded low-paid-workers' districts of the nineteenth-century city – that denudation still tangible in the 1970s, in Menkhoff's street photographs of its bodies – assigns that area a privileged cultural status, in a parallel way to that in which the city of Marseille and its surrounding region was (and is) both negated and perversely celebrated as the 'dustbin of France' ('la poubelle de la France'), in the contexts of poverty and historical postcolonial expulsions of populations, and also in the all-surpassing excremental squalor of its dirt-encrusted surfaces. Vitally insurgent detrita – conjoined across the human and the urban – are always ready to invert their status and stasis, and so engulf the eyes and senses of the contemporary city.

Existing beyond the still recuperable, salvageable domains of residues and concentrations, Berlin's detrita maintain and hold, in their far-gone corporeal and urban dimensions, a determining content, even a last-ditch, almost vanished one. The corporeal-detrital, in its addictions and performances, often constitutes whatever remains most visible and immediately tangible of the body, to the city and its media, once the remainder of the body has been eroded, worn away or digitally voided. The urban detrital also maintains a momentarily suspended, pre-expiration form of city space in utter disintegration – but, unlike the body, that detrital city space may still be transformed at the brink, and reactivated or revalued (for example, through processes of massive gentrification, as in the Prenzlauer Berg district), propelled beyond all resemblance to its previous emanation of the detrital. The status of detrita manoeuvres on a tightrope, as with individual human memory's status at the onset of terminal dementia, with an already life-expelled and breathless last gestural attempt at gripping to reach disappearing, obsolescent urban events and gone-before bodies, an instant before they are all erased into the dirt of non-memory.

SKINS

In Berlin bodies' extreme instance of undergoing pro-
longed abrasure from city-space contacts, they come to
form walking skins: not even detrita – since detrita have
the perverse capacity for last-gasp urban transmutation
– any longer, now beyond even negative valuation, and
reduced to skin surfaces which themselves may be fissured or split to reveal the internal corporeal material
beneath those skins. Berlin bodies as skins operate in
their urban acts under intensive, dual pressure: constantly affronted from the exterior by city-directed
influxes and assaults, and perpetually subject to interior flux as the body reconfigures itself in response
to the city's projections, which infiltrate even into the
interior dimensions of corporeality. Berlin bodies as
skins are always apertures and screens for the incoming imprintations of the city space they traverse, to the
point of an acute eroding of that corporeal facade; they
form membranes that must also outwardly transmit the
body's insurgent desires via only a vulnerable, paper-
thin medium.

Once Berlin bodies have lost their already negated
status as detrita, everything within and outside them is
concentrated into their skins, so they form skin-figures
whose sole attribute is their determination resiliently
to walk the city. Beneath that skin, their interiors may
have been comprehensively annulled – exsanguinated,
pitted out, scooped, disheartened, excoriated – so that
they constitute corporeal urban experimentations,

uniquely able to anatomize the streets of Berlin in their transits across it, in an autopsied idiom that the theorist Antonin Artaud incisively formulated and also performed, in Paris, through his final radio-media screams and texts of 1948: as 'bodies without organs'. Berlin-body skins are what remain when even the detritus of the remnant has been cleared from urban space; their form is so streamlined as to be almost invisible to city-authority surveillance and digital recording devices, but is still able to exact urban explorations, as a still living, exterior-facing, all-eyed, marked and imprinted skin surface.

Berlin's streets and buildings also possess their own contingent of skins: pre-eminently, the skin of the ballroom. The interiors of old Berlin ballrooms, from the end of the nineteenth century and the first decades of the twentieth century, hold their densely engrained skins intimately around their occasional corporeal occupants. From the many hundreds of such ballrooms constructed in Berlin in those decades, only a few survive into the contemporary moment, such as the Spiegelsaal in the Auguststrasse, reached by a staircase above Clärchens Ballhaus, preserved with its mirrors intact through its hibernation-era usage as storage space across the GDR decades, together with other semi-forgotten and darkened ballrooms, shuttered or walled in, notably in backstreets of the northern districts of Pankow and Weissensee. The distinctive skin of the Berlin ballroom can also be glimpsed in variants such as the interiors of long-derelict cinemas, such as the Stummfilmkino Delphi (Silent-film-cinema Delphi) alongside Weissensee's Caligariplatz, also dormant for most of the GDR era. During the Spiegelsaal's moment of nightlife glory in eastern Berlin around the end of the 1920s, on the far side of the city Artaud himself inhabited the interior skin of a grand, uproarious café, the Romanisches Café in western Berlin, during his film-acting stays, each of several months (playing, in one film, *Gunshot at Dawn*, a wily murderer named 'The Trembler', closely akin to Peter Lorre's murderer Beckert in *M*) in 1930 and 1932.[9] The Romanisches Café was erased from Berlin's cityscape through its wartime bombing in 1943, with all of its organs and skin-surfaces, and all the surviving corporeal detritus of Artaud, who later wrote in an insane asylum of having once encountered Hitler at the café, during his final Berlin stay in 1932, and of pursuing with him a discussion of the future of Europe which led to a violent brawl among the café's clientele.

The skin of the Spiegelsaal, holding its occupants' bodies and eyes, forms a never cleaned green, black and brown epidermis, extending from the oak dancefloor to the cracked walls and the ceiling, illuminated at night by a vast chandelier. That dense skin, accumulated over a century or more, is layered from the body traces infinitely and insistently pressed into it: the marks of ecstatic or veering hands, nicotine smoke, exhilarated dancers' breath, pointed heels, liquids thrown against it in exasperation or fury, late-night sweat in profusion, corporeal transfers, together with closed-up decades of storage dirt. Wall striations, along with apparent fire damage in the form of soot, ash and streaks of flame close to the ceiling level, were created by the detonation of a wartime bomb that struck the roof above but did not destroy the ballroom (another bomb decimated the street side of the same building). The room's vast mirrors are corroded in part almost beyond reflection, their coiled-up silver coating self-eaten away to the point of ocular cancellation; several mirrors bear the marks of bullet or bottle impacts, alongside long scratches and scrapings that loop in transits, turning in on themselves, as with the course of city-crossing footfalls. On high-summer nights in the Spiegelsaal, its skin is reactivated by its occupants' body heat and appears livid as it begins to emanate a 1920s-era reek. Berlin's ballrooms form tainted skin-mirrors able to emit infinite projections into the vision and senses of the contemporary bodies that inhabit them, but all such projections are corroded, negated ones. A skin that transmits or projects has always undergone some form of prior transplantation that now renders its content aberrant, as with the tattooed and decorated skin of the third-century Roman emperor Valerian, reputedly flayed (his skinning alive itself causing his death, according to some accounts) after his capture and enslavement by Shapur I, in order for his stretched skin to be adhered for display to the walls of that king's palace. The skin of the Spiegelsaal's interior forms an exceptional medium for the transmission of Berlin's aberrant nightlife history – and that of the city itself, from the first moments of the twentieth century onwards – into its occupants' bodies.

Urban skins and body skins always immediately disclose and reveal themselves in Berlin, as conjoined exposed media; even if they are conducting a subterfuge or enacting an aberration, its process is projected instantaneously. As Berlin-body screens, they parallel the capacity of film to project moving-image sequences of Berlin directly onto the city's own surfaces, as for example in artists' exterior-space film screenings of Berlin's cityscapes, often staged on summer nights, projected onto the 'skins' of such buildings in Kreuzberg as the Bethanien and other seminal, time-marked architectural screens. Such exterior-space film projections of Berlin's skins, despite their appearance of a profoundly wounded and traumatized corporeal form, also demonstrate that once only skins are left to survive, there is nothing left to lose, either for the city or the body.

On icy walks through the near-deserted streets of East Berlin, and adjacent West Berlin districts, during the winters of the 1980s, I occasionally noticed my skin's surface becoming discoloured, spot-marked and gradually carapaced from the smoke-smog emitted by the pervasive domestic burning in GDR apartments' heating ovens of innumerable bricks of lignate – the lowest-quality brown coal, with only very limited heating value, but immense pollutant potential – so that the bare skins of the city's traversers, and also finally the surfaces of the frozen cityscape itself, became immersed in that new, noxious skin.

TRACES

All cities, along with their architectures and voids, constitute living repositories of corporeal traces, pitched between memory and oblivion. Berlin bodies uniquely generate a city that comes into being primarily through the active tracing of bodies: searches for lost bodies, archaeologizings of anatomical remnants, excavations of urban layers to locate their corporeal detritus, interrogative viewings of city-walking skins, and tracings of new traces. That process of tracing itself forms the eye-driven flux upon which Berlin momentarily rests to reflect upon its history, in its restlessness.

Across Berlin's history, particular sites became concentrated tracing zones, such as its ruined post-1945 railway stations (especially those receiving trains from the east and southeast, such as the Anhalter Bahnhof) at which Berlin's war survivors ocularly sieved all arriving passengers for familiar traces, and amassed improvised noticeboards with inscriptions seeking links to the traces of the lost or imprisoned, during that era of mass population displacements. Since many surrendered German soldiers held in May 1945 after the Battle for Berlin, such as the telephone operator of Hitler's bunker, Rochus Misch, were dispatched to Soviet Union gulags or prisons and only returned to Berlin nearly a decade later, after Stalin's death, the process of tracing vanished bodies could be one in which its unfindable subject appeared definitely erased (as most gulag prisoners were), but then abruptly rematerialized in Berlin's urban space long after their tracing had ended, as with Misch. The tracing of bodies entails a maximal scanning of urban signals and data, since all tracing can become redundant if even the most infinitesimal particle of data eludes the tracing eye. In contemporary Berlin's streets, face-displaying notices affixed to facades and lamp posts still form the urban manifestation of tracing for missing persons who, as a result of their unwillingness or incapacity to project a cogent presence in the city – for example, through youth revolt or old-age dementia – slip below its surface into untraceable subterranes. Berlin's tracings form delicate, exploratory ocular conjoinings, of the corporeal with the urban, designed to extract lost bodies from the city's opaque strata.

Berlin bodies, through their act of intensive urban inhabitation, gradually transmit to the city, through skin contacts, the chemical elements they hold, extending from relatively substantial quantities, such as those of carbon and zinc, to infinitesimal traces of radium, silver, cobalt and gold. In its receptivity to the bodies of its inhabitants, the city readily ingests those trace elements; the more intimately it holds or constrains those bodies between its surfaces, the greater the quantity of corporeal trace elements, many of them toxic or detrimental to human life, that are invisibly projected into the city. Trace elements embedded within bone structures or organs may not willingly exit the body to form part of the city, and so only ever fall within the city's domain once the bodies that hold them join the city dead, as scattered ashes or earth-interred bones. In Berlin such infinitesimal absorptions of chemical trace elements from its inhabiting bodies entail their amalgamation with the city's own trace elements, resulting from its holdings of chemical-warfare weaponry of extermination, together with the technological trace elements from obsolete Cold War surveillance devices, alongside traces of long-obsolete industries' pollutants, and the trace elements of the obliterated dead, killed in massive numbers through technologies and chemical compounds of explosivity during warfare. The trace elements of the body infiltrate both vital and disintegrative components into the city.

The corporeal gestures of Berlin's inhabitants, in their multiple styles and transformations across time, form an invaluable element of the cultural history of the human body in that city. Each gesture – whether of work or leisure, enacted in immediacy or obsolescence, performed for a precise constructive purpose or else gratuitously, as an insult or intended obscenity or to evoke a mystery – instantly archives itself into the city's surface as insistently and irresistibly as a chemical trace element. Such gestures may be infinitesimal ones, initiated but then abandoned before they can be fully performed, or remain unseen by their intended spectators; they may involve only the most minute, hair's-breadth gestural movement of the fingers or the eyes. However insubstantial a gestural movement may appear (in contrast to expansive gestures of political power, for example) in the context of the infinite gestural languages that have vivified the Berlin megalopolis across its history, it still forms a seminal trace of the body in the city, and, in many ways, a close counterpart to barely tangible urban transmutations that may hardly register, at their moment of occurrence, in the perception of the millions of Berlin bodies, but which can still form the transmutations upon whose traces all of those bodies' future urban lives are hinged.

Urban vision in Berlin may be enacted, especially in external conditions of darkness, with unparalleled intensity, as its inhabitant's eye traces the shifting forms of city surfaces, together with the contours of nocturnal bodies, in order to extract valid data for such purposes as consumption, sexual pursuit, or spatial transit. 'Tracer' ammunition characteristically incorporates a flare or other medium of illumination into its projectiles, including those tracers composed of inflammable chemical elements such as barium or magnesium which the human body also holds among its trace elements, so that the projectiles' trajectory, from weapon to target (whether a body or architectural element, to be obliter-ated) can be clearly seen by their shooter, and the next projectile then aimed with unerring accuracy. In that sense, Berlin bodies deploy a form of tracer ammuni-tion vision, by which the searching city gaze is itself illuminated across its course and the eye interrogatively traces its own acts, so that if any act of vision misfires, the next will hit its target.

A Berlin trace – whether of a body that has been lost sight of and has slipped from touch, or of a part of the city that appears to have been almost entirely razed

– always emanates a fragility that emerges from the volatility of any entity that seeks to establish a stable permanence, in that city. In Berlin the trace is always lost. Even if the body or city element is relocated, it can never be pieced back into a framework that has become irreparably shattered or rendered obsolete in the interval since the more entire status of that body or city element diminished into that of the trace. Even to monumentally over-accumulate traces, as in Berlin's culture of memorials, such as that of the Holocaust (the Memorial to the Murdered Jews of Europe), only accentuates the role of the trace in forming a void medium leading directly into the most rending experiences of loss.

THE HUNTED DOWN

At many moments in its histories of conflicts and persecutions, Berlin's inhabitants have been hunted through its streets and buildings – by police, gangs, agents, enemy armies – for arrest, expulsion or killing. Among such hunted-down bodies are those of exiles and refugees with no valid documentation to stabilize themselves within the city; bodies – such as those of Berlin's Jewish population during the Nazi era – arrested for expulsion and extermination; bodies seen as 'terrorist' entities in the disparate contexts of the 1970s and 2010s; bodies seen as committing crimes or subversions within the GDR's urban dynamics of mass denunciation in which almost any act could be perceived as a subversion; bodies that occupied empty buildings or those assigned for demolition and formed activist communities there, and bodies hunted as targets of sexual violence. The act of hunting down implies a preparatory tracking down period in which traces of an offending body are first located and identified through that body's urban verticality and exposed visibility; subsequently, once hunted down, the body's tightrope-balanced urban orientation is altered into one of falling and loss, often through a propulsion into Berlin's sub-surface strata, for example into holding cells such as those of the Nazi-era subterranes of the Gestapo headquarters, in what was then Prinz-Albrecht-Strasse (subsequently ruined subterranes, in part now memorially excavated and archaeologized, to be viewed as voids by spectators standing above them). The act of hunting down ranges widely in form, from abrupt incursions by gangs of arresters into private apartments or activist-occupied buildings in order forcibly to subdue bodies, to written convocations for bodies to self-surrender themselves to their hunting down, by assembling passively at a particular time with their possessions in single suitcases, at a detention centre or railway station, ready for their expulsion from Berlin.

Hunting down forms an urban act which obliterates the capacity for corporeal autonomy and solitude, since it involves an imminent, intimate overpowering of one body by at least one other, and more often by a grouped gang, of riot police or other subjugators. The hunting down of bodies across and within Berlin's space forms the most corrosive, accelerated and death-inflected form of corporeal tracing; in body hunting's speed, and in the immediate desire of its executors to inflict pain or death via the tracked-down body's overturning into stasis, the city itself must form a complicit co-perpetrator, through the escapeless constraints of its buildings and streets.

The figure of the hunted-down Berlin body, frozen or in transit across city space, appears prevalently in renderings of that space across visual art, filmic, photographic and digital media, but most iconically in Lang's film *M*, in the figures of Beckert's young victims who go willingly with him to their sites of murder in the city's wastelands, once he has hunted, selected and vocally appropriated their bodies, and also in the figure of Beckert's own body, marked and hunted down in Berlin's streets by its gangs of criminals and beggars, then propelled into an abandoned distillery's subterranes for his trial and intended execution. The figure of Beckert as both slaughter-intent body hunter and exposed, hunted-down body – those identities enacted near simultaneously, separated only by his sudden mirror-recognition, in wide-eyed terror, in a shop's doorway, of his body's overturning into the status of the hunted – intimates the fragile aperture that exists in Berlin between roles of urban power. Notably, that reversing transmutation was experienced by the political leaders of the GDR as hunters-down of dissidents and Wall infiltrators, assisted by their border guards and agents, whose status abruptly mutated in 1990 from that of overseers and perpetrators of body huntings to that of corralled, imprisoned figures (as with Erich Honecker's detentions and abandoned trial before his final departure from Berlin for Chile, and his successor Egon Krenz's incarceration, alongside those of numerous border guards who had shot down death-strip transiters).

In private colour film shot in the 1980s of Honecker and his associates in the forests close to their Wandlitz compound of guarded, lavish villas, to the north of Berlin, Honecker proudly boasts of his prowess at the hunting of animals, and declares his capacity for profligate regimes of slaughter, the open ground in front of his figure blood-saturated with the displayed bodies from that day's killings of deer and other animals, most of them forcibly channelled by assistants into his hunting rifle's sightlines. The culture of hunting at the peripheries of Berlin, densely marked into landscape through innumerable wooden towers designed for covert sniping at animals, is presented in Honecker's filmed declarations as the site of his own exceptional corporeal achievement, in terms of the hunter's ocular accuracy and ability physically to traverse hunting grounds, and also in the enumeration of the sheer quantity of animals' bodies hunted down there, killed, counted and displayed to the film camera; animals' bodies in any space of Berlin are always integrally Berlin bodies, to be counted as such, alongside human bodies. That culture of hunting down also permeates the central city's history, as one of multiple variants of hunted down slaughter, from that of Spartacus League figures in 1919, to the city's Jewish inhabitants of the 1930s and '40s, to dissidents, urban 'terrorists' and activists of the 1970s, and to refugees and displaced bodies of the contemporary moment.

Alongside the act of hunting down as one of subjugation or slaughter, Berlin bodies, especially in the cacophonic arena of its nightclub cultures, also experience sexual hunting down as a set of procedures of intricate subterfuge and oscillation, as articulated in the title of Smokey Robinson's 1966 song (performed in that era by The Marvelettes, and in 1980 by Grace Jones) 'The Hunter Gets Captured by the Game'. In visual art, Ernst Ludwig Kirchner's *Potsdamer Platz* (1914) paintings of female figures undertaking acts of spectacular but hazardous prostitution indicate the seminal role played by nocturnal Berlin's urban space as the performative arena that holds and accentuates the aberrant reversals, in sexual dynamics, of acts of hunting down. But Berlin's sexual orientations and experimentations also interconnect closely with the city's more corrosive, murderous histories of acts of hunting down, notably in the 1933 arrests and concentration-camp deportations – to Sachsen-hausen, on the northern edge of Berlin – of the city's gay and transsexual figures.

THE MALFUNCTIONED

Berlin possesses special sites assigned for its malfunctioned bodies, together with locations in which madness, rage, negation and refusal propelled Berlin's bodies into such corporeal extremity that they themselves rendered the city malfunctional. The zone of madness to the north of Berlin constitutes an especially sensitized arena of malfunction, in multiple variants and traces: the Sachsenhausen concentration camp, as a site of extermination for bodies perceived by the Nazis as sexually malfunctioned, as well as of politically, racially and socially unacceptable bodies – and a site which accelerated and expanded, after 1933, in its capacity to engulf and annul bodies anti-thetically opposed to the Nazi regime, so that its momentum of extermination endured even beyond the end of the Nazi era through its adaptation into a Soviet-zone detention camp in which, among many others, Heinrich George, *Berlin Alexanderplatz*'s filmed Biberkopf, died in neglect in 1946; the lakeside Ravensbrück concentration camp, north of Sachsen-hausen, along with its many adjacent sub-camps intended primarily for women and female children; the immense Buch asylum – a Berlin sub-city in its own right, designed across multiple, ornate pavilions in the decades on either side of the twentieth century's origin, by Ludwig Hoffmann and others, in anticipa-tion of the untold numbers of the neurally city-malfunctioned, destined to be driven mad by Berlin, with the expected numbers, especially of young men, then reduced by First World War deaths – one pavilion of which also formed the location for Hitler's autopsy, conducted by Soviet army pathologists who needed to establish beyond doubt that a particular incinerated body, discovered in a shallow grave in the first days of May 1945, was that of Hitler; and the specially constructed Wandlitz Waldsiedlung ('forest community') compound, intended as a Berlin-distanced forest-surrounded refuge, in the aftermath of the 17 June 1953 uprising in East Berlin, for the GDR's leaders, whose isolated acts and filmed declarations (such as Honecker's hunting delirium) intimate a resemblance of that compound to that of Kurtz in Francis Ford Coppola's film *Apocalypse Now*. Such sites to the north of Berlin form a landscape of corporeal and architectural malfunction that signals the fragility of the membrane separating ostensibly stable performances of power and their implosion into convulsions of slaughter and psychosis: a barely detectable neural interval, across memorial time and space.

The riotous events in the avenues of East Berlin of June 1953, together with those of 1956 in Budapest, convinced the GDR's leaders that they were corporeally vulnerable in central Berlin, and needed to distance themselves even further than their encampment of grouped villas, the Majakowskiring, in the northern district of Pankow, by constructing another sub-city of the mad, still further to the north (eventually they would order the building of a guard-protected motorway exclusively to channel themselves from Wandlitz into the city centre and back). The corporeal insurgence of 17 June 1953, and its malfunctioned transit across Berlin, began on the previous day at the under-construction Stalinallee (the GDR's most prestigious urban architectural project of that era) in builders' protests at increased work quotas and lowered wages, as well as in more generalized dissent at the GDR's hapless leaders, who had been thrown further askew at that moment by the death of Stalin, and were mocked in the workers' chanted protests through their corporeal attributes, as outlandish and undesired Berlin bodies: goatee beard (Ulbricht), belly (Pieck), glasses (Otto Grotewohl).

On the following day, the Stalinallee's builders walked across East Berlin, gathering hundreds of thousands of supporters from all over the half-city in an elated accumulation of mutinous malfunctioned bodies, along Unter den Linden to GDR ministry buildings in Leipziger Strasse and to the nearby Potsdamer Platz wasteland zone of conflict, then spatially volatile in the era before the construction in 1961 of the Berlin Wall. The protest – aimed explicitly to overthrow the GDR's regime, as well as to create urban uproar through a seminal corporeal traversal of Berlin – was documented in the medium of 16mm film-camera celluloid (without synchronized sound) by cinematographers employed by newsreel organizations both in East Berlin and West Berlin; the West Berlin cinematographers either crossed into the Soviet zone to film, in acute physical proximity to the protesters and under

conditions of great danger, or else zoomed their camera lenses from the safety of the adjacent British and American zones. The protesters unleashed conflagrations around Potsdamer Platz, setting alight kiosks built for the dissemination of information about the merits of the GDR, as well as the distinctive commercial building the Columbushaus, constructed in 1932 by the modernist architect Erich Mendelsohn, across the plaza from the earlier, multi-storey entertainment complex, the Haus Vaterland, and already charred and part destroyed during wartime bombing. After several hours, that aberrant malfunction of power in the city abruptly dissolved with the arrival of Soviet tanks and riot-police snipers, who opened fire on the protesters, causing many fatalities. Onlookers from West Berlin, many of them students, crossed into the Soviet zone to throw dislodged paving stones at the tanks, or located themselves for their protests exactly at the boundary line (marked in barbed wire and paint) which tanks would not cross; many of the injured and dead were carried to West Berlin hospitals. The film newsreels projected in West Berlin cinemas two nights later, edited into the weekly programme whose projection began on Fridays, denounced the mass killings of street-exposed Berlin bodies, but the East Berlin newsreel projections' commentary attacked those same figures as justifiably killed saboteurs and provocateurs, whose crimes included setting fire to the Columbushaus, whose storeys contained offices of the city authorities in which plans for the ongoing reconstruction of East Berlin were incinerated. The East Berlin newsreels designated that moment of city-negating corporeal malfunction as Tag-X (X-Day).[10]

That 'X' in time intimates the forcibly conjured ending that needed to be assigned to urban corporeal malfunction in order for the East Berlin city authorities to enforce a reimposed normalization of Berlin's bodies. In West Berlin that day was contrarily elevated through its assignation to a public holiday which endured until the renewed malfunctions that provoked Berlin's re-unification, into a mutant amalgam-body of initially irreconcilable elements; the date of 17 June was also allocated to the space of the city, specifically to the parkland-surrounded avenue extending from Unter den Linden into West Berlin (an avenue that had especially attracted Speer and Hitler as a privileged artery for reformulation in their plans for Germania). As well as leaving historical memory traces such as film newsreel documents and photographs, that uprising's corporeal city eruption became incised profoundly into Berlin's urban space, all the more potentially resurgent for the GDR's attempts to scour and invisibilize those traces.

City-located corporeal traumas and war wounds may tangibly emerge in Berlin's streets and confront their occupants not only from the city's own fading uprisings and wars – in the way that, even at the end of the 1970s, pedal-cart-driven maimed figures from Second World War battles or urban bombings still collided intentionally with passers-by, in West Berlin streets, to wordlessly solicit money, thereby evoking war-residue artworks by George Grosz and Otto Dix – but can also be transplanted, through the city's refugee and exiled population, from innumerable other recent conflicts, such as those in Syria, Peru and Ukraine. Street-exposed corporeal malfunctions in Berlin can also be performatively self-inflicted ones, extending from facial piercings and whole-body tattoos to the self-mutilation of sexual organs (such as the dissection of testicles). A wide range of city-displayed psychotic or aberrant corporeal acts – recalling the acts viewed in the 1910s as being generated directly from the neural excess of the new 'electropolis' of Berlin, and as necessitating the dispatch of their perpetrators north-wards from Berlin, to Buch's sub-city of madness – now constitute an integral, near-normalized element of the contemporary city, notably when performed with such obsessional, unvarying gestural repetition that the city rapidly habituates itself to malfunction.

Berlin, like other contemporary megalopolises operating via regimes of habitual excess, forms a locus of technological as well as of corporeal malfunction, with frequent crashes of overloaded digital media, and fused or blanked-out image screens and hoard-ings of immense dimension attached to the facades of its plazas, such as the Alexanderplatz. Technological malfunction can exacerbate corporeal crashes, but the body itself holds the capacity abruptly to raze all tech-nologically instilled powers of surveillance and spatial prohibition, with the same insurgence that propelled Berlin bodies across the avenues of East Berlin on

17 June 1953. The contemporary corporatized city is one that both demands and depends upon a digitally regulated, complicit and subjugated population of bodies, but in Berlin sensory and historical malfunction is instilled too deeply into the city itself for the effective constraint of such ostensibly pacified bodies, so that glaring malfunction spills in profusion from the city to its bodies, and from non-compliant Berlin bodies to the city's streets.

DANCERS

A vital corporeal presence in Berlin's streets, plazas and wastelands, and within its subterranes, is that of its dancers, occupied with projecting into the city the gestures of innumerable variants of dance, drawn for example from East Asian regions such as Japan and Southeast Asian areas such as Cambodia, from South America, North Africa, the southern countries of Europe and other originating sites, but always inflected by their transplantation to the reeling, serrated urban space of Berlin. Especially in summer months, the streets of Berlin, which habitually engulf their occupants, are themselves disorientated and unbalanced by the presence of dancing figures, often accompanied by the performance of music; dance also forms one instance of the manifold corporeal manoeuvres by which dis-possessed Berlin bodies solicit money to sustain, for another moment, their precarious hold on inhabitation

of the city. Any corporeal gesture which becomes
embedded into the arena of urban movement, and
infiltrates that movement's dynamics, by unsettling
or amending them, constitutes a manifestation of city
dance. In many ways, dance forms an elated loosening
of malfunction's pervasive, repetitive gestures in Berlin's
exterior space, since dance can never be precisely
replicable, and holds potential durations from the
infinitesimal to those of extended choreographic
immersals. That gestural act of 'loosening' can appear
to engender a relaxation of urban strictures, but it may
also twist upon itself into a dance of violence, refusal
and negation. The uprising of 17 June 1953 across East
Berlin's streets appears, across the entirety of its filmic
documentation, as a form of extended dance of death,
initially self-celebratory through its capacity to incite
conflagrations, deride the physical attributes of figures
of power and conjure revolution (at least to some
degree, as a performance for the cinematographers
filming the event), but is then abruptly propelled, at the
moment of the Soviet tanks' appearance, into contrary
gestures of headlong evasion, ground-level self-flinging,
convulsions and angered one-way confrontations with
the tanks' invisible occupants.

The acts of Berlin's dancers across the twentieth
century took place in a proliferation of locations: in
dancehalls active in the 1900s such as the Central
Hotel's extravagant Wintergarten ballroom, in the
Spiegelsaal of Clärchens Ballhaus and the many
other 1920s city-wide spaces with their sexually

drawn configurations (vivified above all by Berlin's most notorious dancer, Anita Berber, whose cocaine-driven choreographing of ecstasy and provocation ended with her death from tuberculosis in Kreuzberg's Bethanien hospital in 1928), in clandestine swing clubs such as those in which Coco Schumann performed in the Nazi era, in sites of desperation-induced dancing by starved bodies in still ruined post-war venues patronized by Berlin's occupying soldiers, in the night-club Chez Romy Haag's 1970s reassertion of Weimar-era sexual experimentation conjoined with performance art, in frenzied punk rock dance halls such as the SO36 at that same decade's end, in post-reunification 1990s immense club venues, ex-cinemas, subterranean vaults and reused East Berlin industrial spaces deployed for techno, trance and Ecstasy-propelled dance excess (often obliviously traversing boundaries between public dance and public sex acts) such as Metropol, Sexperimenta, Ostgut and its mutation into the cavernous space of Berghain's generating station. Those urban locations together form an immense corporeal encounter between Berlin's bodies (and bodies transplanted momentarily from other cities into Berlin, to become its 'guest worker' dancers) and the city's buildings, strata and abysses. That intensive corporeal expenditure in dance, pursued to the point of extreme exhaustion and beyond, together with its great exudation of fluids (sweat, semen, blood), into multiple spaces across the face of the city, marks the body profoundly, across more than a century, into Berlin's surfaces.

Dance in nightclub venues, especially those directed solely with financial intent, habitually demands relentless standardization, even when its gestures are self-launched into exhausted collapse; but Berlin's nightclubs, such as the SO36, and innumerable experimental spaces over many decades, have also formed pre-eminent aberrant sites of the corporeally malfunctioned. Across the twentieth-century cultural history of malfunctional, 'badly' dancing Berlin bodies in nightclub environments, that of the Weimar-era Cabaret of the Nameless (*Kabarett der Namenlosen*, active from 1926 to 1932), forms a distinctive instance of dance gestures that overturn ossified performance forms; in that cabaret, held one night each week, hapless, deranged or corporeally impaired young performers – often self-convinced of their own exceptional facility as performers – were slyly commissioned by its director and 'master of ceremonies', Erich Lowinsky, to enact gestures (of dance, alongside those of acrobatics, magic tricks, hypnotism, recitals and other media) of such audience-perceived ineptitude that those spectators could respond with an acute uproar of hilarity, ridicule, humiliating insults and interruptions, and with physical interventions, including those of Lowinsky himself, onto the stage to curtail the ongoing performance. The Cabaret of the Nameless, with its director's impelling of Berlin dancers to enact glaring ocular and sensory disruption, thereby salutarily negating 'skilled' performance and casting the spectators' expectations into

disarray, intimates the extent to which corporeal

malfunction forms a seminal force in Berlin's urban rapport with its bodies.

Beyond Berlin's enclosed spaces of nightclubs, ballrooms, choreographic art venues and other sites designated as dance zones with particular spectatorial regimes (or with no spectators at all, in which everyone entering must only dance), encompassing locations that were once, even many decades ago, dance-inhabited and are now abandoned but still dance-marked, the gestures of dance also permeate the city's exterior spaces. A dance momentarily performed on the streets of Berlin, intentionally or through spontaneous exhilaration or despair, reconfigures the time and space of the city; it may resuscitate and accentuate its surrounding urban elements and dimensions, but also contrarily infuses and striates them with gestures of disintegration and death (as in performances, often enacted in the city's wastelands and interzones, by Berlin-based choreographers of Japanese dance forms such as *ankoku butoh*). Interrogative ocular and corporeal transits through the space of Berlin themselves necessitate a form of sensitized self-choreographed urban dancing, oscillating incessantly across eye and body movements, always subject to fragmentation, and performed both with an acquired agility (enabling the body not to crash into city surfaces or other bodies) and also an essential unsynchronized ineptitude – like that of the performers in the Cabaret of the Nameless – that allows the city to be covertly unscreened and anatomized, by an exploratory urban eye-dancing.

FOOTFALLS

The interface at which Berlin's bodies make their most direct sensory contact with the surfaces of the city is often that between the soles of shoes or bare feet in movement and urban pavements or other horizontal planes. The hands and face can also be pressed against or into Berlin's surfaces, as with fingers touching the shrapnel-subtracted voids on the Monbijou Bridge's parapet, thereby inviting momentary corporeal incursions from Berlin's ghosts, or the pressing of the mouth against a wall surface during acts of assault or sex which characteristically propel bodies, via abrupt blows inflicted on the back, against those surfaces, with so little interval of warning that the hands cannot shield the face from those violent urban contacts, which may lead to abrasures of the lips and the forcible imprintation of traces from a wall's painted graffiti or signage into the forehead or cheeks. Other variants of such direct corporeal-urban contacts are the act of sitting, for example on city-crossing public transport, and of oblivious post-collapse lying down, often performed nocturnally and naked, face down or face up, after excessive alcohol or narcotic consumption.

By contrast with such intermittent or one-off intersections between flesh and the ground-level city, the contact of footfalls with urban surfaces forms a far more habitual one, repeated many thousands of times over, on extended transits through the city; footfalls possess their own distinctive rhythms of speed or malfunction (experienced, for example, by walkers enduring foot injuries, so that one footfall will impact directly on the pavement, while the other will barely graze or painfully convulse against it), like those of dancers striking their feet in tight sequences against the oak-floorboarded sprung dancefloors of the Spiegelsaal or of the resistant concretized ground of factory-converted techno clubs. Footfalls indicate an intimacy in the conjunction of Berlin corporeality with the city's space that is almost always initiated from the body, which desires a traversal of that space; Berlin's surfaces will rarely insurge upwards to strike their inhabitants' feet, except in exceptional seisms sparked, for example, by subterranean explosions (such as those of war-era bombs whose detonation occurs with many decades' deferral, through the final disintegration of faulty fuses). Footfalls constitute a sequence of movement exacted by the body upon the city, its accomplishment surveyed from above by the attentive eye which guards against stumblings into whole-body falls.

In the uprising footfalls of 17 June 1953 in East Berlin, undertaken by rioters' shoe soles on the rough, semi-wastelanded pavements around the Columbushaus and the GDR's ministries, and documented in those events' filmic traces, the street impacts of feet accelerate and skip, in intricate arcs and aberrant trajectories, in order to facilitate the confrontations and acts of incineration of the rioting bodies; as with all exceptional impacts or 'dances' of the body against urban surfaces at moments of crisis, those footfall contacts are undertaken in concentrated bursts, which push the foot more firmly against stone or tarmac whenever a particularly strenuous act is underway, such as the overturning of an obstacle. At times, those footfalls descend onto burning tarmac surfaces and barbed-wire boundary markers, particularly in the footfalls of West Berlin-based protesters and cinematographers who hesitate to traverse that boundary, knowing that their footfalls' entry into East Berlin's Soviet zone will render them immediately subject to dangers that risk upending their soles.

Once the Soviet tanks arrive and begin to shoot at the protesters' bodies, most footfalls are transformed into emergency-velocity impacts against city surface as those unprotected bodies scatter in panic; a few bodies hold their ground to hurl missiles at the tanks, and their footfalls then pivot in near-stasis in order to support the hurling movements of stone-propelling arms, with those stones torn up from the streets' pavements. In the filmic sequences showing the final stages of the confrontation, wounded or killed protesters' soles are no longer in direct contact with the Berlin streets; they are suspended in void space as those protestors' bodies are carried or stretchered towards hospitals, and shoes have often somehow been lost from feet, as in the photographs and film footage, from fifteen years later, in 1968, of shoes, chalk-circled by the police, at the attempted assassination site of the prominent West Berlin student leader Rudi Dutschke, shot near-fatally in the head while standing with his bicycle awaiting the opening of a pharmacy at the junction of the Kurfürstendamm and Joachim-Friedrich-Strasse, and up-ended onto the tarmac, before he recovered his stance and walked for a short distance, bare or socked soles in erratic footfalls against the pavement, in shock, speaking in disorientated fragments, in front of the eyes of passers-by abruptly rendered into horrified spectators, then finally collapsed and was stretched to hospital.

Through footfalls, city-traversing Berlin bodies' feet are invariably propelled downwards, and at least one sole is always in contact with the ground (unlike the contacts of animals, such as those photographed by Eadweard Muybridge in his studio or at the city zoo in Philadelphia in the 1880s as moving-image sequences in which all feet can simultaneously be suspended in space), but are driven by a horizontally oriented intention, since those bodies are habitually working to reduce the distance to their journey's spatial endpoint. As with the walking figure bronze sculptures of Alberto Giacometti, which he occasionally installed in street environments in Paris, the entire body appears gesturally focused on achieving rapid city spanning, via abrasive footfalls and other corporeal manoeuvres. But in many twentieth-century Berlin street movements during periods of urban crisis – such as the lengthy queuings of the emaciated figures of women and children during the final phase of the First World War, anticipating the distribution of governmental bread supplies in such denuded districts as Wedding and Prenzlauer Berg – that horizontal progression of footfalls proved to be excruciatingly slow, suspended for many hours at a time, so that the soles of feet (after the disintegration of footwear) remained in stalled contact with city space, as the body and skin itself petrified in conditions of acute starvation. Footfalls can also be directionless, but contrarily rapid, during observational on-foot Berlin city transits such as those exalted in the 1920s by Hessel, Kracauer and Benjamin, in which the intentional voiding of endpoints elicits revelatory ocular occurrences.

Berlin bodies' footfalls gather unique layers and constellations of detritus onto the soles of shoes, accreted across city transits from whatever materials Berlin's strata have gradually pressed vertically upwards, over decades, to their surface orifices or pores, into the exact sites with which those footfalls intersect, thereby imprinting over time – in residual fluids, adhesives, small stones and splinters, ashes and other concentrated materials – unforeseeable fragments and variants of the city's accumulated history of construction, excess, destruction and disintegration, via body-propelled footfalls.

MEMORIES

Berlin bodies now constitute near-infinite permutations of an anatomical memory entity, rendered alive when propelled into movement through the city's streets, and whose skin, musculature, bones and foot-soles all exist most essentially to conjure or project memory, through the medium of the body, in an era in which memory has near-definitively vanished and been rendered annulled or obsolete. Every movement of Berlin bodies is striated with its redundancy as an emanation of fragments of memory. In their outbursts and struck footfalls, Berlin bodies may desire enduringly to enunciate or imprint memory – multi-generational memories of urban history, often those of exile and refugee displacement, of conflict and turmoil, rather than of sustained inhabitations of Berlin itself, together with immediate memorial histories of the lived contemporary city instant – but such articulations of memory are often made void in an urban environment in which memory is sieved away into monumental forms that cancel its extreme sensations and traumas, and in which the corporate, digitized city of spatial pacification and enforced surveillance presupposes the erasure of embodied memories as channels for urban transmutation and corporeal insurgence.

Oblivion possesses its own acute corporeal pleasures, as articulated, for example, in the flat-out horizontal proximities of Berlin's bodies with nocturnal pavements and in oblivion's seminal role in the excess of the city's nightclub cultures (notably, in the urban cultural history of forms of sensory oblivion embedded into corporeal histories of unrestrained dance movement, such as that of Anita Berber in the 1920s), as a secondary manifestation of the consumption of alcohol or drugs, following that consumption's initial corporeal decelerations and vocal slurrings, and precipitations of bodies into urban falls. But oblivion also constitutes a powerful primary urban entity in its own right, as the intimate accompanist to city space which, precisely through its own defining obliviousness, can or will not recognize memory.

The most prominent oblivion-oriented memorial to the Holocaust in Berlin's exterior space is the Monument to the Murdered Jews of Europe, opened in 2005 and designed by the architect Peter Eisenman; the shoddy, rapidly dilapidating construction process for its arrangement of steles utilized chemical 'Protectosil' sealants that were manufactured by the conglomerate Evonik Degussa, a 1940s subsidiary of which had been involved in the distribution of the 'Zyklon B' concentration-camp extermination medium, so that even in that oblivion-focused monument, memory still obstinately infiltrates the steles' cracks. But the memorials that most effectively incorporate oblivion are the twin placards displayed in the Wittenbergplatz, alongside the KaDeWe department store, and at the Kaiser-Wilhelm-Platz's triangular pedestrian zone alongside a congested street junction in the Schöneberg district (close to the 1970s apartment of David Bowie, who had then been a 'man lost in time, near KaDeWe'), enumerating the names of concentration camps as 'places of screams, that we should never forget'. Since those two placards are situated in cacophonous sites of rapidly transiting passers-by and hold no apparent historical or spatial resonance, as transplanted 'scream' sites, connecting them to the incanted names of concentration

camps, their forgetting is so readily instantaneous –
immediately discarded from perception, as though those
black and yellow raw-steel placards were nonentities
advertising adjacent fast-food restaurants – that it
reinforces the power of oblivion's own infinite duration,
as a never-remembering in the first place. The admoni-
tory inflection of 'should' in the act of forgetting, or of not
forgetting, together with the indeterminate authority of
the anonymous voice enunciating that 'should', intimates
a spectatorial option in which the incessant urban
oscillation between oblivion and memory would require
a forcible, against-the-grain push towards memory, and
in which oblivion appears to present the more 'natural'
state of response to trauma.

Oblivion may form the predominant corporeal and
sensory experience for Berlin bodies, so that memory
itself constitutes an exceptional, perverse apparition.
Through the resilient memorial aperture of that
perversity, I remember seeing the Wittenbergplatz
concentration-camp placard on my first walks through
West Berlin in 1979. The placard, or an earlier version
of it, appears from city authority records to have
been installed there in 1967, initially at a different
location in the Wittenbergplatz, as an initiative of
the International League for Human Rights, long
before the concept of extravagant, high-budget
city-centre memorials had been initiated. In that
1979 viewing, it appeared as an absence of memory
– as self-embarrassed urban signage, negligible and
arbitrary in its relationship to the concentration camps

it selectively named – which momentarily stopped dead my transit through the city.

Across the first half of the 1990s, the theorist and film-maker Laura Mulvey, together with her collaborator Mark Lewis, made the film *Disgraced Monuments*, which, among many other jettisonings of Communist-era memorials from exterior space, especially in the defunct territories of the Soviet Union, evoked the removal from its East Berlin site, the Leninplatz, of a colossal statue of Lenin (depicted standing before a wall), constructed from 1968 to 1970, in an area that had been comprehensively wastelanded by war-era street fighting and bombing. The statue was framed by newly built constellations of apartment blocks, including one immediately adjacent to it, and was equipped with extensive space for solemn corporeal amassings at its feet by East Berlin's citizens, notably its tracksuited Communist youth groups. The statue, once dismantled, was relocated in 1992 to subterranean Berlin, through its secretive burial in fragments alongside a lake on the city's southeastern edge. Berlin's sedimented memories, too, form disgraced entities, expelled from their integumented rapport with city space and supplanted by oblivion's own sensory regime, or, more pervasively, by voids.

Berlin's distinctive 'body' of memory is that held by all of its occupants, activated in transit through urban space; memory's comprehensive supplantation in the contemporary instant aberrantly accentuates memorial traces as urban detritus, that exists only as a barely-there stratum conjoined with equally detrital memories of exile in other cities, and of displacements and journeys through interzones. Berlin bodies form an in-movement corporeal archive of urban memories, with that content subject to its own integral malfunctions and footfall-propelled perils, as well as to that precarious archive's razing in digitized environments. Whenever I walk through Berlin, I hold memories, many of them no longer consciously accessible, of all of my perceptions while moving across the city over decades, starting from (or ending in) those first walks of the summer of 1979 in which, alongside sightings of East Berlin placards with their own distinctive preoccupations, I read the West Berlin placarded exhortation in the Wittenbergplatz to 'never forget', and realized – in the overarching context of city-authority exhortations to comprehensively and immediately forget – that to remain interrogatively open-eyed to Berlin's coruscating amalgams of memory and oblivion demanded tenacious in-transit highwire vision.

ABSENCES

Berlin bodies possess the capacity to fade from sight without warning and transform themselves into bodies of absence, in full view in city space, while they walk across its terrain, as though making way for their corporeal supplantation by Berlin's subterranean ghosts or as preparatory self-erasures for those

fading-out bodies' generation of their own phantoms, so that Berlin bodies often appear intensively engaged in the act of self-absenting in order to activate their own hauntings. What would appear to be dreaming distraction in other cities forms corporeality's disintegrative vanishing into absence in Berlin. First, the interior space of the body, excoriated and pitted out by its urban experiences, begins to absorb inward-facing skin surfaces, as with the actions of organs that have ingested corrosive acid; then, the outward-facing skin itself starts to deliquesce in and out of vision like a malfunctioning shoddily pixelated moving-image screen in one of Berlin's great plazas, until the skin's markings, including its assemblages of wounds and abrasions, are wiped out, and the entire body is finally swallowed into absence as though it had been eaten alive by Berlin's engulfing urban regime. All Berlin bodies appear, at one time or another, to be poised at some early or terminal stage in that process of self-absenting or impelled disappearing, from its first flickerings to the extreme moment at which almost nothing of corporeality remains, just the barest footfall or hair's-breadth gesture that still binds the absented body by a sheer thread to Berlin.

Berlin still holds all of its seminally absented inhabitants, deported for extermination, as with its Jewish population of the twentieth century's first decades, or dispatched for conflicts and colonizations, never to return. City districts which lost embedded populations, such as that of East Berlin's Prenzlauer

Berg, almost entirely evacuated to more outlying areas (or to the former West Berlin) as a result of mass gentrification processes over the 1990s and 2000s, enduringly mould themselves more intimately around the bodies of that vanished population, than around the current, negligible one. In Berlin, corporeal population absences may be compensated for through influxes of refugee or self-exiling bodies, such as those of the second half of the 1940s (from formerly German cities then mostly rendered Polish, among other originating points), or of military-service-evading students and oblivion-intent artists and musicians in the 1970s, or of new generations of refugees and transients in the 2010s, that equilibrate population holes. Berlin's dimensions as a megalopolis readily encompass oscillations between absences and profusions, voids and overspills. Corporeal absences may generate a city-authority-sanctioned memorial culture in the context of those bodies' outward-directed expulsion for extermination, which only serves to accentuate that voiding; inwardly transplanted populations also serve to reinforce those genealogy-shattering absences while still possessing their own forms of absence, articulated in exile's improvised melancholy (as in songs of Iranian or Turkish voices overheard from cafés or apartments in the dead of night while walking the streets of Kreuzberg), and often corporeally projected in dance gestures of falls, nostalgias and vanishings into absence.

Berlin's architectural absences also exacerbate those corporeal absences, especially whenever its most prominent lost buildings detritally subsist in filmic traces (such as those of the city palace's 1950 detonation) along with its city-contesting absent bodies, such as those of the elated, then terrorized uprisers of 17 June 1953. Since Berlin's buildings were predominantly destroyed or badly damaged by aerial bombing and street battles from 1943 to 1945 (and, prior to those destructions, as a city-clearance prelude, by the Germania obsessions of Speer and Hitler), to the point that the city was rendered more absent than present, never filled absences enduringly map multiple past variants of Berlin as corporeal as well as architectural entities; reconstructions of many wastelanded or semi-collapsed sites in East Berlin only began in the 1980s, so that, over the intervening decades, absence had become a deeply integral, sensorially habituated element of urban perception in that half-city. Glaring absences in Berlin's urban space also resulted from property-speculation manias and demolition sprees such as those that constellated Kreuzberg's tenement streets with voids and enraged that district's activist rioters in the 1970s, and were then reactivated with ferocity in the post-Wall decades.

In order to conjoin for maximum visibility the two 'never forget' steel placards of concentration-camp commemoration at the Wittenbergplatz and the Kaiser-Wilhelm-Platz, so that each placard could be glimpsed from the other's site – in a project of urban absence that, given enough inducement, the Berlin city authorities could conceivably sanction as they did with similar (finally unrealized) large-scale demolition projects around the Alexanderplatz in the early 1990s – the entire intervening terrain of ornate Schöneberg-district streets would need to be wastelanded, including the building that once held the Chez Romy Haag nightclub (and now holds the Connection gay nightclub), in an inverse process to that of those same streets' reconstruction, meticulously and uniquely documented in 1946 by the Schöneberg amateur film-maker Herbert Kiper, in the form of hand-titled 16mm fragments, during the course of his daily walks through the warfare-wastelanded district, and self-archived under the title *Schöneberg Rebuilds: A Cross-section of our Lives in 1946.*[11]

Such a reconfiguration would necessarily assemble into an essential amalgam the disregarded city-space traces of absence of Berlin's concentration-camp deported, even from such malfunctioned remnants, through the 'should' imperative of never forgetting, which signals that nothing may stand or intervene between those twin placards, in the same way that no digitized corporate hoarding's visibility within contemporary Berlin's ocular regime should ever be impeded. That architectural upheaval would also annul the two placards' current sightlines. Both placards are now imprinted on either side with the names of ten concentration camps, to which two new names, Trostenez and Flossenbürg, were added in 1995 to the original 1967 enumeration, as though they were destinations that had been annexed at the last moment, so that two distinct facings from different eras are apparent. In the Kaiser-Wilhelm-Platz, one side of the placard faces benches of attention-deficient alcoholics and the other faces the fast-moving traffic lanes of the Hauptstrasse, as though positioned in the style of a 1920s cinema marquee, such as those of Los Angeles' Downtown Broadway, designed to attract drivers' attention through the layered incantation of forthcoming attractions' titles; on one side, a sticker affixed to the placard reads 'we are team-mate', and an indecipherable graffiti tag is inscribed on the traffic-facing side. The walk from one placard to the other takes around twenty minutes. In the Wittenbergplatz, one side of the placard faces a wall of the underground station's ground-level hall, constructed in 1913 and reconstructed in the 1950s after wartime bomb damage (the placard's content could never be read from that side without a particular intention to occupy the empty interval from which that content is legible), and the other obliquely faces the edifice of the KaDeWe department store; on one side, a sticker has been affixed to the placard reading 'kiss me i am famous', while on the exposed KaDeWe side, nothing impedes the placard's visibility other than the gradual city-inflicted traces of erosion and abrasure on its surface.

INERADICABLES

Since an originating, engulfing absence, or an abrupt process of rendering absent, form Berlin's predominant corporeal modes, urban presence appears an endangered status subject to imminent cancellation. In order to institute a sustained presence in the city, Berlin's bodies contrarily engrain themselves into urban space as *ineradicables*: bodies that are maximally immune to all usurping urban manoeuvres, or else conjure for themselves a form of active oblivion (an inverse oblivion to that which annuls urban memory) that autonomously disregards collective absenting. The presence of a Berlin body is solely tenable if it is ineradicable and holds its ground in the city, in full, multidirectional visibility; for that inextirpable corporeality to demonstrably root itself in urban space demands a disabused, omniscient knowledge of the sleight-of-hand expulsive strategies that city-authority and corporate power deploys to absent or expel an entrenched presence of the body in the city, together with a concomitant awareness of the history-entangled urban strata, layers and subterranes into which that ineradicability of the body embeds itself.

Across Berlin's twentieth-century urban history, distinctive or idiosyncratic corporeal figures were often presented, in popular media such as newspapers and newsreels, as ineradicably associated with the city, as so-called 'Berlin originals' (*Berliner Originale*): figures seen as acutely preoccupied with public events or forms of sexual experimentation, and possessing a guileless, obsessive attachment to the city, articulated in vocal outbursts or through an aberrant or malfunctioned physicality. To infiltrate Berlin to the point of ineradicability implies the establishing of a dynamic corporeal stasis that resistantly occupies the same urban site, across decades. Among such twentieth-century Berlin 'original' bodies, the figure of Charlotte von Mahlsdorf, the transvestite proprietor of a museum in the far-flung eastern Berlin district of Mahlsdorf dedicated to the *Gründerzeit* – the historical period of affluence and intense construction activity following 1870 which generated that era's ornate apartment houses in Berlin, with their elaborate facades and internal decoration – notably holds that ineradicable status. Until 1990 Charlotte von Mahlsdorf had also been the pre-eminent advocate of East Berlin's alliances of transvestites, transsexuals and other endangered groups, but her ineradicable status became negatively inflected (an ineradicable is always profoundly con-trary, striated by contradictions) in retrospect by her apparent complicity with East Berlin Stasi secret police agents as the only viable means to sustain the existence of her museum and activist networks. Her decades-long endurance in Berlin was finally relinquished through her sudden, self-exiling departure from the city, under abusive pressure from the neo-Nazi gangs prominent in the eastern districts of Berlin in the post-reunification years. In 1993, shortly before her departure to Sweden from Berlin, I visited the silver-haired, black-dress-clad figure of Charlotte von Mahlsdorf at her museum, and she showed me her *Gründerzeit* artefacts – many of them left behind in the 1930s by Berlin's Nazism-fleeing Jewish inhabitants or else salvaged by her from bombed-out 1945 buildings, all

133

of them ineradicably marked by those scarred urban histories – and spoke too of the transvestite culture that she had determinedly embedded, against extreme odds, in East Berlin.

Other prominent Berlin 'originals' include the one-legged figure of Reinhold Habisch (known as 'Krücke'), celebrated for his obsessional devotion to Berlin's exhausting six-day non-stop cycle-race fixtures – pivotal urban events, held once or twice each year, notably in the 1920s (in *Berlin Alexanderplatz*, Biberkopf assiduously follows frantic radio reports of the unfolding contest) – at which Habisch occupied the cheapest standing area, never leaving the race arena during the relentless event, which often involved the hallucinating, sleep-deprived racers crashing violently into the trackside and being propelled over boundaries into the spectators' areas. Newsreel film footage of the six-day race's post-war reinstitution in 1950 (the first contest for many years, since it had been banned in the Nazi era) shows Habisch immediately reoccupying his old spectatorial site for the race's gruelling duration. What subsists of twentieth-century Berlin's 'original' bodies in the contemporary city is their intense involvement in ineradicably occupying and thereby transforming urban space, on their own obsessive terms, even in the face of factors that would normally annul that occupation; if they are expelled or exiled from Berlin's space, they will compulsively return to it at the first opportunity.

In order to maintain their all-exposed embedded presence in the contemporary urban arena, which sustains its corporate power through homogenized corporeality and petrified ocular regimes, ineradicable Berlin bodies must demonstrably perform acts that either annul that power or else subject it to a coruscating disregard. As a result, ineradicables, as corporeal agents of urban aberrance, emit perverse projections and create detrita of their presence that together become deeply seared into urban space. Ineradicability intimates both the resilience of the body in infiltrating and standing its ground in the city, and also its capacity to imprint corporeal traces and visual remnants that cannot then be erased from Berlin's facades and ground-level surfaces, or from urban consciousness, via the forms of bodily fluids, graffiti, personal archives, memory fragments and spaces reconfigured or reassigned by insurgent inhabitation. But the expansive multiplicity of such detrital traces can only ever be perceived when ineradicable Berlin bodies have, through exterior force or a final perverse act of self-contradiction, abandoned their embedded urban location.

In that act of vanishing, a previously ineradicable Berlin body may have simply infiltrated itself still more deeply into the subterranean zones that had formed the physical anchorings for its above ground-level demonstrations and detrital projections. In such zones, that body becomes conjoined – in the urban memory that survives of it – with the strata of bones of Berlin's city dead, as well as with its populations of ghosts. In numerous Berlin-located films, the disappearance of ineradicable city bodies may also be the result of penal incarceration, from which they finally return into Berlin's space at the films' first moments, as in Bruno Stroszek's release from prison into his usual Potsdamer Strasse location of prostitution, alcoholism and brutality in Werner Herzog's film *Stroszek* (1977), or in Biberkopf's release from Tegel prison and his veering tramride back into Berlin's Scheunenviertel district in Jutzi's *Berlin Alexanderplatz*. Ineradicable but self-exiled Berlin bodies may also return from their exile to die, as in Charlotte von Mahlsdorf's return from Sweden to Berlin just before her death in 2002, or in Anita Berber's return to the entrenched site of her Berlin-outraging sex-dance frenzies, from last-ditch performance engagements in Beirut and Damascus, shortly before her death at the age of 29 in the Bethanien hospital and her interment in an anonymous grave (later cleared, so that even her unmarked bones vanished) in a Neukölln cemetery. The death-focused withdrawal from visibility of an ineradicable body can form a subterfuge or provisional exit, performed whenever power-oriented or surveillance-enacted attempts are insistently made to extirpate it from urban space, leaving open the capacity for it to return to re-haunt – with still greater ineradicability – its Berlin site.

TRANSFIGURATIONS

Berlin bodies are incited to perform – or spontaneously enact – self-transfigurations in the exterior spaces of the city, by which corporeality is subject to a perceived extreme mutation or transformation, which can be contained within one minuscule gesture of self-display or through a vast, all-eye engulfing projection of the body's overhauling in its intimate conjunction with Berlin. Spectators or passers-by may glimpse a body or face in a condition of exaltation or abjection, consciously demonstrating an ecstatic, sexual or rapturous gestural act, or else compelled by overwhelming emotional or narcotic excess to undertake that act; equally, spectators may perceive nothing unusual at all in the behaviour of a body whose transfiguration is internally directed, or mediated so liminally that its gestures remain near-imperceptible within the cacophonous, visually overmarked urban arena.

Acts of corporeal transfiguration undertaken in Berlin's spaces often assume the form of intentional citations of art or photographic works (notably of 1910s–'20s Expressionist-era works, such as those of Erich Heckel, in which gestural convulsion or acute stylization formed a predominant element of corporeal display), or of film and film's exalted Berlin bodies, above all that of Marlene Dietrich, born in the city's 'Red Island' (Rote Insel) district in 1901, but can also be near-simultaneous viral replications of corporeal manifestations transmitted via digital media devices. A vital element of the essential ecstasy of transfiguration is its potential to be performed in full view as a secret, elusive self-mythification. As with the location of Berlin's ineradicable bodies, the enacting of corporeal transfiguration in urban space demands a stasis (a momentary stasis, at least) to enable its performance, even in the condition of transfigurative invisibility in which nothing but an unaccountably halted figure is perceived by passers-by. A body in a state of transfiguration will not necessarily generate the appearance of a city-searing provocation, placed under the insistent threat of eradication which ineradicable Berlin bodies must adeptly counter in order to exist (as in Charlotte von Mahlsdorf's defusing of East Berlin secret-police threats in order to allow her museum and activist networks to endure), and can contrarily form a fully sanctioned urban attraction, assigned to the domains of art, fashion or dance.

In Berlin's urban art and film histories, corporeal acts may constitute distinctive transfigurations only to the extent that they result from transits and infiltrations of urban space; such dynamic traversals precipitate transfiguration, even though its display is then invariably performed in stasis. The transfiguration of Berlin bodies exists far beyond the limited domain of their *refiguration*, in which they are only gradually altered or amended by external urban acts (as in scarrings marked into their skin's surface, through city space collisions or assaults), or else in which their figurative presentation is an enhanced or reworked one of past Berlin bodies, as in artworks which supplant Expressionist-era bodies with those of subsequent decades, as with the Kreuzberg-located work of West Berlin's 'New Wild Ones' grouping of figurative artists of the 1970s, Salomé among them, with their defining pre-occupations in music and nightclub cultures.

Transfiguration signals, by contrast, an extraordinary, irreplicable corporeal event in which Berlin bodies utterly determine urban representation. In Otto Dix's portrait of *The Dancer Anita Berber* (1925), undertaken during a dance tour outside Berlin but directly embodying the performative excess of the city's nightclub culture in that era, the self-displayed figure's red dress, red hair, red lips all overspill into a glaring red expanse, razing and transfiguring the body's surrounding city. Transfiguration may also indicate an abrupt elevation of the body above the city through a vertically oriented transit, as in that of the ruin-scaling, ecstatic spectators seen in the filmic documentation of the Alexandrov Ensemble's 1948 Gendarmenmarkt performance of music and dance, in which those bodies, through that act of ascent and in preparation for an act of vision, extravagantly surmount the semi-erased city.

The self-exhibition of transfiguration in Berlin's space is one that cannot sustain itself for more than a few seconds in acute exaltation, and embedded within transfiguration is its imminent fall into disintegration, as intimated in Dix's portrait of Anita Berber; transfiguration and disintegration can even exist simultaneously in corporeal oscillation, for vertiginous spans of to-be-curtailed urban time. Transfigurative pre-eminence is notably driven by sensations and transits that are rapidly exhausted and rendered disintegrative through their instilling into the body's conflagratory act of self-display. While ineradicable Berlin bodies tenaciously preserve and defend their city-sited aberrant practices over lengthy durations, across decades, transfigured bodies are ready almost immediately to surrender themselves to the city's mercy at the elapsing of their display, since there remains nothing further to be projected or worth showing, once the body has already exposed its glorious instant of revelatory self-exaltation; it can now be levelled, or consigned to detrital subterranean zones. In their burnings-out, Berlin bodies' transfigurations may form ultimately negative mutations that jolt the body far beyond its habitual alliances and frameworks, into unmappable terrains of disorientation and psychosis.

Berlin, with its uniquely corporeal twentieth-century myths and their engrained location in the city's streets, invites such mutations, and subjects its occupant bodies to far more exhaustive processes of transfiguration than in other megalopolises. The pressurized, striated urban layers of Berlin, in configuring the movements of its occupants through them, may wrench the body out of its habituations and compel it spontaneously to perform an unenvisaged transfiguration, with that body's core obsessions driven in an instant from screened interior to exposed surface, and projected directly into urban space. But extreme corporeal transfigurations, especially when positioned in the optimally oblivious, deviance-saturated parameters of Berlin's urban space, such as its plazas and nocturnal streets, cannot dependably elicit a concurrently intense response from their accidental spectators, for whom the once-only performance of monumental corporeal and urban histories, concentrated into one body's self-exalted form, presents only a supremely negligible display.

EMITTERS OF NOISE

City noise accentuates Berlin's acts of corporeal self-transfiguration. Noise itself undergoes movements which transform it, notably when it traverses Berlin's body-marked walls and perimeters to enter voided interiors. Berlin's distinctive aura of noise – meshings, concoctions and amalgams of acts, obsessions and habits – is subject to a percussive fragmenting in such transits, especially when the interiors of those buildings are semi-exposed to exterior space. In exploring still bombed-out or abandoned houses and factories at the very beginning of the 1990s, in the neglected, often-moribund nocturnal streets of the Mitte district, from debris-strewn room to room, I often heard the infiltration of noise into those spaces mutate with each spatial shift, increasing or lulling, as though inflected by the extent to which it had to traverse walls or else seep in through striations and open-air-exposed windows. Occasionally, during those spatial explorations, music and voices from a newly opened bar or nightclub would insurge into that space, or come up through the floor-boards from the subterranes directly below. The strata of debris accumulated on each floor emitted their own particular noise too, as the furniture and ornaments, left behind decades ago and partly crushed underfoot, exhaled their disintegration; houses of uprootings and death breathed their expirations. In that era, abandoned East Berlin factories, workshops, sanatoria and cinemas all possessed their unique internal regimes of noise – their ground-level ruination incessantly dislocating itself and cracking apart – conjoined with the intricately shifting currents of noise projected through the buildings' walls from exterior city space.

Numerous fiction and documentary films collect the phantasmatic, outlandish incursions of Berlin city noise into ruined buildings, from earlier decades than the 1990s. In *Die Kuckucks* (*The Cuckoos*), from 1949, an orphaned and homeless group of children occupy a bombed-out West Berlin house which they then enliven and defend, among other attempted incursions, against the residual noise of destruction surrounding it (adjacent shells of shattered houses are still falling or being detonated by ruin-clearance squads). In *Jahrgang 45* (*Born in 1945*), from 1966, bewildered figures in their early twenties, with idle time on their hands, roam the neglected interiors of ruined Prenzlauer Berg buildings, with their otherworldly soundscapes, as they attempt to annul and reinvent lives within East Berlin's strange confines. And the children of the documentary film *Berlin Auguststrasse* spend the summer of 1979 on transits through their shattered domain of bullet-holed buildings and Spree River quaysides, absorbing incoming city noise and also propelling their own vocal noise outwards.

Berlin city noise, experienced inside its buildings, is pre-eminently a corporeally originated infiltration, composed of voices, shouts and screams, gesture-propelled outbursts such as those of angrily pumped car horns, and the noise of desperately running foot-falls, striking against tarmac, late at night. Berlin bodies form emitters of noise, whose sonic traces distinctively occupy the abandoned spaces they inhabit with the status of corporeal entities in their own right, especially when those spaces – as with those of long-neglected cinemas or nightclub ballrooms, such as the Delphi Stummfilmkino and the Clärchens Ballhaus Spiegelsaal – are acutely sensitized to carrying the memories and intensive resonances (the noises of laughter, dance steps, fury, seduction, bottle-shatterings, intimacies, exclamations, as well as film sound and ballroom music) of bodies that appear vanished, but are still all residually there. Berlin's many contemporary city-sound-obsessed bodies form the transactional agents of entire worlds of noise, often operating with obsolete sound currencies, preoccupied with the dynamics and caprices of aural as opposed to ocular orifices, and incessantly juggling between external cacophonies and internal whisperings.

Across most of the twentieth century, vocal city noise in Berlin was associated directly with its anatom-ical media of projection, as *Schnautze* (focused upon the mouth-surmounting 'snout', as well as on its emitting via the lips, vocal tract and lungs): raw, caustic, abrasive, often derisive, improvisational commentaries and conjurations on city life, performed by Berlin's bodies as they moved through that city or else observed its exterior space from a position of spectatorial stasis. In Jutzi's film *Berlin Alexanderplatz*, when Biberkopf, just released from prison, is advised to make a living with his body's muscles, he responds that he will instead generate his means for life in Berlin solely via his voice, through the projection of *Schnautze*, while ineradicably standing his ground in the Alexanderplatz and emitting vocal commentaries on what he witnesses (corporeal malfunctions, derided figures of authority, children's gestures and the ongoing architectural reconstruction of that vast space), thereby ensnaring the attention of audiences who become focused upon his own, vocally driven act of urban spectatorship.

The amassing into unruly archives of 1980s West Berlin's voices and industrial noise preoccupied Wim Wenders in his film *Wings of Desire* (*Der Himmel über Berlin*) – especially in the film's opening soundtrack of vocal evocations of desperation and isolation, sieved through the film camera's infiltration of apartment-wall surfaces and subway-carriage doors, together with its sound archivings of voices autonomously reading archives, in the library-hall expanses of the Staatsbiblio-thek – and also engaged noise musicians, pre-eminently Einstürzende Neubauten, with their sonic accumulation of vocally embedded West Berlin cacophony-scapes: simultaneously a generation in exposed city space of new noise, and a selective collection from pre-existing and ongoing sources of urban noise.[12] Performances in nightclubs and other venues of urban noise, incorporating fragments of city detrita (such as oil drums and pavement shards) as instrumental sources of sound to be beaten with hammers, in order to create unforeseen emanations of West Berlin, formed a distinctive element among the proliferating sonic cultures of that semi-forgotten mid-1980s half-city.

The emission and reception in Berlin's urban space of automated noise without any immediate corporeal source forms a longstanding experience, from that of the emergent city's pervasive factory and transportation sounds, to detonations during urban warfare, and contemporary digitized emissions from iPhones and city-plaza corporate image-screens. Berlin's inhabitants of the twentieth century often perceived unrelenting noise from industrial installations and factories, together with toxic smells such as those emitted by Prenzlauer Berg's inner-city gas and chemical plants, as a sustaining urban presence, notably welcomed by those (as in 1950s East Berlin) whose political convictions led them to regard such noise as demonstrating an invaluable element of enhanced productivity for five-year industrial plans. The shrill trajectories preceding explosions of wartime bombs and incendiary devices habitually elicited extreme attentiveness, since not to hear them subtracted an instant from the precious time which an under-attack Berlin resident had to rush towards a sheltered space. Contemporary synthetic noise, devoid of tangible human intervention, possesses an ambivalent status. Its dehumanization and potential to be danced to hold intense attractions for city-engulfed Berlin bodies, especially in nightclub environments. But automated noise, in its repetitions, can also be instantaneously consigned by its intended auditors to unexplored oblivion in contemporary cityscapes, in corporate zones around the Alexanderplatz and Potsdamer Platz, even when its tone is that of an incessant urgency, since it carries no compelling corporeality, but will still persist, with ever greater saturation and resilience, in response to that spectatorial dismissal.

ENACTORS OF SILENCE

Silence in Berlin's urban space may be enacted as a repudiation of the intensity and excess of noise, but it can also be engendered by an abyss-directed, sudden fall of the body – self-generated via ecstasy or narcotic blackouts, or else resulting from epileptic or narcoleptic bouts, unexpected slippages into unconsciousness, and other factors – that invariably possesses a pivotal rapport with the experience of urban space. Berlin bodies' silences are closely enmeshed with perceptions of the city, and even the profoundest fall into silence within Berlin's space remains imprinted and contaminated with the city's compulsions and cacophonies.

No silence in Berlin is ever an innocent silence. Often, the enacting of silence intimates a readiness of Berlin's bodies to be endlessly infiltrated, through the apertures of the ears first, then via the eyes, and finally throughout all corporeal strata, by that city's history of acts and falls that created silence or constituted enforced silencings. Within that history, and especially during Berlin's many eras of persecution, hunting down and conflict, silence held the potential to generate a hair's-breadth barrier of protection from death or physical maltreatment, as in the need for concealed bodies to remain utterly silent in order to avoid arrest or assault by police agents or enemy soldiers. In Robert Siodmak's 1962 film *Escape from East Berlin*, a woman pursued by border guards after an abandoned Wall-crossing attempt is hidden in a bombed-out upper room of a house by its occupants, so that she stands in vertiginous silence and terror on the narrow ledge of flooring still remaining around that otherwise decimated room, feet poised at the burned and cracked floorboards' precipice, only a footfall away from a lethal plummet down through numerous storeys to the cellar, while the border guards search the house; when they eventually force open the locked door to that voided, near floorless room, they conclude that nobody could conceivably inhabit it and so fail to detect the woman's body concealed in silence at the edge of their field of vision. In East Berlin, under the mass-detection surveillance sound regime of the Stasi secret police, an entire culture of silence and of elisions and razings of noise averted that surveillance and its instruments of sound recording, of words, noises or actions whose emitting bodies risked being allocated to the domain of criminal subversion, if recorded. In assembling a cultural history of Berlin bodies' silences and silencings, across the twentieth century and into the contemporary moment, a distinctive status could also be assigned to anonymous figures (and their hands) in the act of finally turning off all-engulfing, durational cataclysms of city noise, in innumerable power plants and industrial installations across Berlin, along with the nonchalant fingers disconnecting, in extreme exhaustion – the last of the sweat-sodden, dehydrated, ears-ringing clientele now emptied out – the skeletally jarring, maximum volume sound systems of 1990s hardcore techno sessions in such nightclubs as Ostgut held in former air-raid bunkers or derelict factory basements and other abandoned subterranes, after non-stop full-on durations of several days and nights, and thereby plunging those nightclubs into a silence still deeper for its abrupt annulling of cacophony.[13]

Attempts in contemporary Berlin to counter raised noise levels combatively, and to suppress events that erupt with sonic frenzy into urban space (such as building-seisming parties or motorcades of horn-blaring cars transiting avenues to celebrate Turkish-community weddings) are often presented as ecologically or humanly justified demands for the right to live without intrusive noise – effectively, a 'right to silence' which mirrors the right accorded in numerous countries to the arrested to disregard police questioning, and say nothing. That demand implies the generalized legitimacy of access to a descent into deep silence, at any moment and for any inhabitant of any city. But to claim and attain that demand often necessitates a contrary, sustained sonic antagonism – shouted out in fury – in order for it to be established in the cacophony-abused dimensions of Berlin. Having secured the stilling of urban noise, silence-immersed bodies may then discover that the human ear exposed to corporeal silence can be still more fractured by noise than that exposed to Berlin's city noise, since silence wildly accentuates the body's own internal sonic regime generated both by the pulsings and malfunctions of internal organs and by the buzzings and hissings of the auditory organs themselves, which have often already suffered long-term damage, as a result of their engrained exposure (as a habitual element of Berlin's inhabitation processes) to street-located noise furores and hearing-splintering performances of white noise. Berlin's bodies possess variants of a vast range of auditory faculties, from the most sonically oblivious to the most neurally sensi-tized organs of hearing, and the city's regimes of noise and silence fluctuate intensively from one extreme to the other to probe those variants. The ear in Berlin explores the pervasive saturations of noise and frag-mentary, barely-there sonic traces of urban space as interrogatively as the eye, and aural interrogations hold their own sensory memorial histories of Berlin noises that have now vanished, or are heard once more after many years of silencing, thereby precipitating resurgent memories.

Just as Berlin city silence is never innocent, the city's residues of corporeally generated or exclaimed noise, implanted into its buildings' exposed surfaces over many decades, can form tainted detrita, as in the speeches of prominent figures of Nazi power, such as Goebbels, given in the 1930s and '40s in extant Berlin auditoria, such as that of the cinema preferentially used for numerous Nazi film-industry premieres and other events, then known as the Ufa-Filmtheater (originally, at its opening in 1925, named the Olympia-Filmtheater, and still in operation as the Filmtheater am Friedrichs-hain), and remain inextricably embedded as acoustic content, among infinite other contrary contents amassed over decades, in the material fabric as well as in the histories of such auditoria. The violent act of silencing, especially in instances of political street fighting and fiercely contested activism in Berlin around the end of the 1920s, such as the interruption or termination of ongoing chanting and speeches – by Communist activists of Nazi activists, or by Nazi activists of Communist activists – indicates a refusal of noise as the projection of perceived maleficent power and the mutation of that noise into bloodily exacted silence. The enduring dynamics of the forcible transformation of vocal sound into silence, imposed in oscillation by one opposed faction against another in contexts of street demonstrations, as in contemporary ecological contestations of the abuses of Berlin's open spaces, wastelands and other resources, intimate the desired necessity accorded to silence as the forcible razing and absencing of city-located voices.

The performance of silence in Berlin's urban space may equally form an act or experience undertaken without contestation, in solitude, even at the heart of the megalopolis, with the intention to create a maximal concentration by which to reflect on manifestations of the intersection between corporeality and the city. That silence can be a contingent event that exists only for an instant before it is shattered, and it may also be up-ended from quietude into acute cacophony, bringing down upon the body that enacts it all of the hidden noise-histories of the streets of Berlin, simultaneously, from urban facades, voids and subterranes; that silence can also overturn its own status as overseen and experienced by one isolated figure, in stasis or in transit in Berlin, to take on instead the status of a familiar collective before-the-storm silence whose ominous resonances prepare the city for new catastrophes.

CONJURATIONS

Berlin's visual arena is one inhabited by acts and processes of conjuration, as a hallucinatory, death-determined megalopolis terrain in which events so extreme and impossible once (or recurrently, and enduringly) took place, that the physical occupation of that space now entails aberrant projections, precarious envisionings and striated visualizations. In any ana- tomical surveying of bodies transiting Berlin's plazas and streets, those figures simultaneously emanate their supreme capacity for self-conception together with their torn-open exposure to conditions of acute, petrifying constraint. Berlin bodies could not exist in city space unless they were obstinately self-conjured – out of, and against, the void surfaces, strata and subterranes that would otherwise constitute bodiless Berlin – and also arbitrarily *conjured up* by envisioning forms of media, including corporate and authoritarian media, whose intentions may be as maleficent as they are capricious. Berlin bodies, and Berlin itself, are never neutrally 'imagined'. The tightrope-walked interstice between those two opposed and oscillating dimensions of exist- ence – the self-generated and the forcibly constrained – imparts to Berlin bodies their pivotal precarity. An integral element of the body of work assiduously under- taken by Berlin's city dead – to sustain the city, and to maintain open their own conduits back into it – is to conjure the living into phantasmatic life and move- ment, and then to infiltrate, into the bodies and eyes of the living, through an abrupt grafting, the implanted memories and driving obsessions that sustain visions of the city; the Berlin city dead hallucinate and conjure the living as spectral entities in their own right, while the living accord to the Berlin city dead their bodies.

Since Berlin was subject across the twentieth century (and is now) to incessant desires to transform it, but cannot readily be transformed because of its own intransigent resistances, transformation misfires and turns haywire. Transformation is mutated by its own malfunction into conjuration, escaping from the intentions of its instigators. Once conjuration is running rampant across urban space, it enmeshes Berlin bodies. Many Berlin artworks of the early twentieth century that interpose mis-conjured urban space with the bodies occupying it, such as George Grosz's paintings and drawings, formulate Berlin's bodies in the grip of a profound uncertainty whose attempted probings are themselves wild conjurations. Since it can never be established how far conjurations will extend in their revisualizations of urban space and its bodies, corporeal parameters are indeterminable; organs, facial features, voices and gestures all become dislocated. Spectatorial responses to the first celluloid film-projections in Berlin (those of Max and Emil Skladanowsky, onto a screen installed in the Wintergarten ballroom of the Central Hotel, in November 1895, following glass-disc projection spectacles of the preceding years, by Eadweard Muybridge and Ottomar Anschütz, in other Berlin venues), documented in newspaper reports, emphasize the corporeal mutations integral to eye-focused technological conjurations; the bodies held in film's sequences, and experienced in their unknowable uncertainty as spectral or diabolical conjurations by their spectators, underwent a vital malfunction of vision in their emergence.

Conjurations often appear as innocuous sleight-of-hand manoeuvres, and possess pre-filmic worldwide projection histories in magic-lantern events, often in the forms of conjurations of fantasized cities that abruptly deliquesce or are destroyed, and of bodies (including ghost bodies) that proliferate, shift dimensions in time and space, or undergo fabulous adventures. But a Berlin body's conjuration, by contrast, is invariably negatively inflected by the overheated conjurations that the city itself was subjected to, across the twentieth century: pre-eminently, in the conjuration by Speer and Hitler of Germania, as a city so outlandish in its formulation that only the wartime deferral of its plans' realization could preserve intact the ecstasy of its conjuration, evident in accounts of Hitler's addictive returns to his scale models, in the final months of his power, even when the actual Berlin around him had been largely erased by aerial bombing and its population driven by fear into subterranes. Other misfired architectural conjurations include the East Berlin city authorities' formulation in the early 1950s of the Stalinallee – the madly accelerated building process for which backfired so badly that it served to generate the 17 June 1953 uprising – and the West Berlin city authorities' plans, in the 1970s era of property speculation and its attendant financial inducements, for districts such as Kreuzberg to be constellated by voids and defined by demolition, thereby enraging that era's rioting activists. The lineage for such architectural conjurations then intensified into the 1990s post-reunification envisioning of the dehumanized Potsdamer Platz's vast corporate towers and hotels, and Berlin's swathes of mega-memorials. Urban conjurations in Berlin often occupy disparate parameters to corporeal conjurations, since their formulation elides the dynamic physical occupation of space, as the location for the performance of corporeality's acts and gestures; but those urban conjurations, when realized, may attain such grandiose dimensions that they spatially subjugate and overrule the transits of Berlin bodies.

The excoriated precarity of Berlin's bodies in their exposure to urban conjurations is expanded to an unprecedented magnitude of corporeal destabilization in digital media's deployments of power and projection within contemporary city space. Digital media are themselves distinctive variants of conjuration, and integrable into cultural histories of conjurations' relationships to urban bodies and their sensorial and spatial perceptions, and also into histories of conjurations' malfunctions; the conception of Berlin as a digitized corporate city, and its city authorities' imperative demand for Berlin as an entity to fulfil and spatially realize that role, is itself in many ways a misfired conjuration, articulated in the compacted, historically oblivious naming of eastern Berlin's expansive riverside technology zone project of the 2000s, 'Mediaspree' (notoriously protested by its buildings' vast-scale graffiti inscription with countering imperatives, such as: 'Fuck Off Media Spree'). Digital media, in their operations within urban space, are habitually orchestrated into petrified systems whose self-delineating conjurations

rigorously preclude malfunction and thereby invite
their own engulfing by malfunction.

DATA

What is definitively known about Berlin bodies
constitutes data, which can be added to, amalgamated,
subtracted and deployed for predictions on the future
of urban corporeality. Berlin bodies interrogatively
generate city data, and are themselves rendered into
corporeal data. What is unknown about Berlin bodies
constitutes negative data, infinitely vaster in scope than
the data of what is known, since Berlin bodies are perpetually involved in processes of mutation, obsolescence,
vanishing and self-obscuration that proliferate with
each approach that gauges those bodies. Knowledge
of Berlin bodies and their histories forms an immense
entity of provisional, contrary data, annulled with each
new corporeal and urban malfunction. Securely known
data may appear limited to the mineral, liquid and toxic
components of each Berlin body in its relationship to
corresponding components of urban space, but such
cross-readings themselves are subject to corporeal
flux and to incessant shifts in Berlin's terrain, as its
strata and subterranes emit unforeseen toxins as well
as resurfacing memorial detrita. All-encompassing
data on Berlin bodies would optimally enumerate
quantifications of gestural and ocular movements
and encounters, across and against urban space, in

the contemporary instant, together with data-recorded traces of all such movements in reverse time towards an initial moment (an always-conjured moment) of urban origin when, for instance, an ambitious eleventh-century margrave ruling an obscure sandy plain of northern Europe first conceived of scatterings of riverside huts as a 'city', which would become Berlin; in such quantifications, lost data invariably forms the predominant element of knowledge about Berlin.

All artworks, film images and writings that envision Berlin and its corporealities also constitute variants of raw data for urban knowledge of the city, even when they work to accentuate opacities and anti-representational acts, and form oblique tangents, experiments and fragments in relation to the city. Such contrary sources of data form an unsteady amalgam with cultural-historical data, anatomical and biological data, topographical and ecological data, and other subdivisions of Berlin's data, in the establishment of what may be knowable of the sensitized connective tissue stretching between Berlin and its bodies. Those bodies comprise integrally mysterious, elusive configurations that are often seized in ways that annul known data; the overturning of known data itself forms a pivotal approach to anatomizing corporeal acts in the streets of Berlin, especially since such acts often seek (and sought, across the twentieth century, in intermittent, volatile histories) to upend – with revolutionary or activist aims, or in the course of undirected sensorial upheavals – what is ostensibly known of the body.

During the course of several years of sustained Berlin transits, on foot and by public transport, from 1990 to 1993, in which I did little else but track the gestures of Berlin bodies and absorb the rapidly transforming fragmentations of urban space, especially in East Berlin districts such as Mitte and Prenzlauer Berg, and in the interzones between the two former half-cities, now multiply splintered, I unintentionally accumulated an archive of data in the form of ocular body observations and urban excavations, and in my own body's gradually engrained experience of relentless city traversals. Each instance of urban exploration precipitated the gathering of an infinity of data. For most of that time, I noted down and photographed nothing of what I saw, preferring to allow the seminal gestures and urban surfaces to foreground themselves in my ocular memory, with all other data eroded across time into oblivion. But when, in the final months of that period, I finally wrote, in a concentrated burst, the experience of that intimacy with the dynamics of urban transformation, it was often the oblivion-consigned data of acts and observations that insurged into memory and inscription, and the ostensibly seminal incidents and locations that were abandoned. The accumulated ocular, memorial and sensorial data I was handling possessed its own convulsive life, that imposed and projected itself.

Digital data of Berlin bodies – in its comprehensive capacity for anatomical and online surveillance, location and intrusion, pre-eminently for corporate and city authority priorities of visual power – forms an unprecedented exposure of corporeality that resonates with conjuration's dynamics. Digital data cannot be fabricated, contradictory or self-obscuring; its profiling intention, extending across individual city inhabitants and entire urban (or global) populations, is to be omnisciently maximal. The consumption habits and medical histories of citizens, as well as their activist involvements, obsessions and manias, are all readily data-accessible. The exhaustive digital profiling of a body may retinally and anatomically scan it to the last muscle and secretion. But when digital data reaches that maximal level of knowledge about Berlin bodies, and acquires just one more fragment of data, it excessively mutates into the domain of conjuration, since nothing is definitively known of Berlin bodies; it remains always within the capacity of such bodies to void all fixed physical and urban knowledge. Corporeal entities in Berlin's space possess a data status that is vitally unknown.

PROLIFERATIONS

Proliferations of Berlin bodies occur whenever a mass desire to evacuate one populated space and instead occupy another space, with urgency and an oblivious disregard for the dense, face-to-face and intense proximity that will ensue, overwhelms the city's occupants; proliferations entail the movements of multiplicities, and incorporate the rushed velocity of corporeal influx as well as the static, tense condition of crushed-together bodies once they have amassed into a proliferation, boundaried by the facades delineating a plaza or else by a building's interior surfaces.

In Berlin's nightclub spaces – from the licentious venues of the 1920s such as those in which Anita Berber performed her provocations, to more contemporary, vaster venues located in former energy-generating plants and air-raid bunkers in which bodies strip to emit heat as well as corporeal fluids – proliferations exist primarily to transmit sexual infiltrations, danced body to body. Proliferations in immense exterior spaces in Berlin, such as the post-1960s Alexanderplatz and the 1936 Maifeld alongside the Olympic Stadium, by contrast, are driven by political determination or intended subjugation. Since it takes an extraordinary influx of Berlin's bodies to constitute a proliferation in such expansive spaces, each event's dynamic corporeal compulsion (such as that which propelled East Berlin's bodies in their many hundreds of thousands into the Alexanderplatz on 4 November 1989, in protest against the sclerotic GDR regime, or that which compressed incoming bodies for Nazi rallies and sports events on the Maifeld, able to hold at least 200,000 bodies and aerially filmed from above in 1936 in Leni Riefenstahl's *Olympia*) appears an irresistible one; consumer frenzies may also propel bodies into momentary exterior-space proliferations as they approach department stores or fairs. Berlin bodies' proliferations habitually gravitate towards specially designed gathering zones such as the Maifeld, but they can also reconfigure and overrun sites created for other purposes, as in contemporary music festivals held on the vast space of the disused Tempelhof airfield. Proliferations only become apparent in contrast with street-level corporeal scarcities, equally prevalent in Berlin's urban-space histories through body-voiding events of depopulation such as that of young male bodies during the First World War and of the population's self-concealment in cellars during the hard-fought arrival of the Soviet army in April 1945.

On late-night walks though the streets of the still-disintegrated, ill-lit Mitte area in 1990, the entire city district often appeared to me to be outlandishly emptied out, with figures rarely sighted, as though an abrupt deportation or panic-impelled urban fleeing from imminent disaster had taken place, thereby inciting explorations of the abandoned detrita of the lost city of East Berlin.[14] The distinctive resonance of corporeal proliferation's spatial influxes in Berlin is that it contrarily unfolds in a megalopolis site defined by its mass-extermination-driven expulsions and vanishings of bodies.

Along with its role as a spatial arena for corporeal proliferations, Berlin also holds proliferating urban obsessions with its own figures (figures born in Berlin such as Marlene Dietrich, transient figures such as David Bowie, figures of totalitarian power and invented figures) and sites. Such obsessions often originate in isolation in an ostensibly once-only, irreplicable corporeal or ocular experience, then become magnified and transformed by proliferation's aberrant momentum into urban *propositions* that are incessantly projected, and pre-eminently function via repetition. In Berlin, everybody is obsessed with something, and corporeality is frequently mediated via the unsilencably vocal or glaringly visual articulation of that obsession. Through spatial or online social media convergences, the isolation of an urban fixation is rapidly supplanted by an onrushing proliferation of allied, intersecting obsessions. City-venue exhibitions devoted to documentation around Berlin's figures or sites form channellings of obsessive proliferations into institutional spaces, into which (if the collective preoccupation, cohered around exhibited material traces, is strong enough, as in the Martin-Gropius-Bau museum's 2014 exhibition of Bowie's inhabitation of Berlin in 1976–9) corporeal proliferations of spectators then flood. Through proliferation, Berlin as an entity is itself transfigured into a focus of collective elation, but remains always rawly striated, via the city's overturning manoeuvres, with that elation's imminent negation.

Since digital technologies are conceived by their corporations as maximally global, spanning cities worldwide, their proliferating apparition in Berlin (for example, in spectators' mass documentation as digital still images or moving-image sequences of ongoing concerts taken by smartphones held at arm's length, as though in an arcane collectivized ritual whose non-performance would be anomalous) is, in many ways, identical to that in other urban spaces. The experimental use of proliferations of cameras operating near-simultaneously to animate the same act or event first emerged with the moving-image recording of animals and human bodies – with those bodies often choreographed into obsessional repetition, or into aberrant gesturality – in Muybridge's work of the 1880s in Palo Alto and Philadelphia. Muybridge, on a Europe-traversing tour, projected the results of his experiments via glass-disc media at Berlin's Urania scientific hall, on a vanished site close to what is now the city's main railway station, on 9 March 1891, for an awed, packed audience that appears to have perceived them as less spectral and diabolical than the celluloid-film projections of Max and Emil Skladanowsky in the ballroom of Berlin's Central Hotel, four years later. A numerical proliferation of digital images recording bodies at any moment in Berlin's urban space may pass from the saturated to the negligible in abbreviated spans of time, as technologies advance, accelerating numbers from a million each second to ten million, for example, so that manifestations of proliferation are rendered near-immediately obsolete; the visual entity of proliferation itself forms an always insufficient, mismatched medium for the seizure of urban corporeality. Instead, a unique, blurred or skewed image, such as those that often accidentally memorialized figures deported from Berlin – enmeshed within mass expulsions or as solitary deportees – will more tellingly render that city's bodies.

The immense neon signs and electrified letterings that proliferated from the 1960s in the rebuilt Alexanderplatz, attached to the facades of buildings

such as the multi-storey apartment towers newly
constructed for the GDR's elites, and exclaiming the
merits of the plastics and elastics industries as they
rhythmically illuminated East Berlin at night, were
dismantled in the early 1990s, but were then only hesi-
tantly replaced by downscaled variants of the arrays of
digital image-screens that constellate many European
city-centre plazas, as well as those of such cities as Tokyo
and Bangkok. During the years in which Berlin's city
authorities hesitated as to whether to raze without
trace or else overhaul the GDR-era Alexanderplatz, the
gutted emplacements and trailing, redundant wiring of
that extracted signage remained visible on the edifices
high above the Alexanderplatz (especially from vantage
points such as the highest storey of the former Interhotel Stadt Berlin), still projecting the voided neon
ghost-data of their previous transmissions; some of
the signs' immense neon letters were warehoused after
their removal and eventually enclosed in a museum
of obsolete technologies. Digital screen technologies
only began to appear, already as obsolescent as their
neon-lettering predecessors, on the Alexanderplatz's
summits from the end of the 2000s, enabling the magnified transferral of Berlin's bodies – digitally filmed by
high-definition surveillance cameras in their real-time
transits of that plaza – as spectrally proliferating 'live'
images on the screens of moving-image hoardings
alongside pre-shot corporate animations, as those
bodies abruptly oscillated from city space to screen
and back again.

DIGITIZED PRESENCES

Beyond Berlin bodies' enmeshing in digital urban culture, they possess their own networks of surveillance and ocular crashes, of decay and disintegration, of excess and saturation, of proliferation and voiding, and of contemporaneity and obsolescence. The status of the human body's presence in Berlin outside digitization already holds many of the dynamics associated with transmutational effects of digitization upon corporeality. Berlin bodies also possess arrays of wounds and markings projected from the city's history, and are intricately bound to urban strata and surfaces in ways that cannot readily be rendered in digital media, or even by images at all; such processes may require a delicate linguistic unskinning which also invokes the slaughters of Berlin bodies. In the propulsion of Berlin's corporeality into the domain of digital culture, initially over the 1990s while in temporal synchronicity with Berlin bodies' bewildered or ecstatic reelings from reunification upheavals, then more intensively and irresistibly across the following two decades – until the zero point in which all digital traces vanish through total habituation, or terminal malfunction, into invisibility within the city – a contrary sense of release is palpable, that corporeality is no longer alone with the city. Digital media's interventions in the interzone between body and city serve to appropriate that rapport, in a potentially liberatory, merciful *thieving* of space that can either compact urban corporeality into one entity or else generate distantiation between body and city.

For Berlin bodies to attain presence in the city demands ineradicable self-rootings and incessant conjurations, undertaken to avert the always imminent fall into absence which is corporeality's default mode of Berlin inhabitation. Corporeal presence often appears culturally wary in its guarded tension towards the attachments that integrate it into Berlin's city space, which may resemble capitulations and subordinations, or else outlandish obsessions (such as those displayed by Berlin 'originals'); in absence, especially during city transits, the body can preserve its vertiginous oblivious- ness that generates the pivotal elation of the inhabitation of Berlin. Protest, from street-focused demonstrations to all-out furies of rioting, forms a variant of absence or of active self-absencing, in distancing its bodies from the contaminations of city-binding affiliation and in its negating of city-authority corruption. While the merging of absence with digital culture can only intensify spatially voided elations, Berlin's corporeal presences are destabilized still further in their attempts to establish themselves within the digital domain that, notably in its alliances with city-authority processes of control, itself insists on spatial alignings and surveillance-monitored delineations of the city's bodies into restricted and authorized zones. Berlin's corporeal presences will not cohere in that digital domain; their multiple flaws and dysfunctionality, already manifested to their ostensibly last detail by other media such as film and visual art, are still further exposed in corporeal presence's unremitting intersections with digital culture. When Berlin bodies become digitized presences, they form distinctively *other* entities to the manifestations of corporeality mapped against Berlin by film and art, across the twentieth century. On contemporary urban screens' pixelated surfaces, such bodies can appear flawless, but concealed in the unmediated, unedited image-strata beneath that carapace, seething virtual histories of subjugation and violence torn from Berlin bodies' endless affrontments with city space will be unleashed.

Digitized corporeal presences are glimpsed for an instant, over the shoulders of passers-by or of passengers on trams holding iPhone screens and fixed on a still image or a moving-image sequence, so intently focused that the passers-by are often obliviously stalled into inaction, thrown out of their habitual velocity, in a rhythm of image-generated urban jump-cuts, even in environments of proliferation, causing other figures to collide with them. Frequently, screens have jammed or crashed, and the eyes of those passers-by and passengers are intent not on images of bodies, but on image-generated malfunctions of bodies. The bodies contained in those images or sequences may inhabit other dimensions, and possess only the barest recognizable contours of a human form if they have been rendered into images in movement, as in wild nightclub dancing, but they may also recognizably be Berlin bodies, simultaneously projected from one city location to that exact site of intent gazing, or frozen for near-instantaneous memorial scanning. Over-the-shoulder accidental projections expose secrets in split-second vision to eyes that must perpetually scan their surrounding space and its screens or else risk body-to-body impact – or to eyes which are always drawn to secrets. Over-the-shoulder envisionings of screens form momentary overseeings in which the body exposed is reconfigured or reimagined by its accidental proprietor, all corporeal history and narrative concertinaed into that momentary spectacle before the screen is abruptly switched off, or the image vanishes into dissolution with the disentanglement of that dual-body over-the-shoulder ocular rapport.

Digital images corrode along with the presences they project. Berlin, as a city of corporeal vanishings and hard-fought resistances, is uniquely sensitized to the transformations and obsolescences of digital culture. Mappings of the city that guide the transits of smartphone users hold urban representations that deliquesce in their hands. If, as digital theorists such as Lev Manovich and Paolo Cherchi Usai have argued, material fragility and an exposure to the all-annulling corruption of data characterize digital culture in ways that directly parallel *corporeal* culture (as well as film), the image-located memories of Berlin's bodies will in the future require painstaking extraction by hand from obsolete digital-media repositories of archival traces – in an assiduous re-archiving of disintegrated archives and of their genealogies of archaic technologies – and to be carefully scraped from the blown-out pixels of images of Berlin bodies still attached, in conflagatory fusings, to the urban image screens at the summits of the Alexanderplatz and Potsdamer Platz corporate towers. The detritus of such digitized presences of Berlin's bodies, after all recoverable traces are amassed and innumerable lost presences cast into oblivion, can then be spread out and displayed, as dispersed fragments oscillating between the material and the hallucinatory, over the pavements of Berlin, impossible to touch or pick up, but open to ocular scrutiny – as salutary media signals, and holdings of a strange era's subjugation and elation – by future eyes of future Berlin bodies.

IMAGE-RENDERED ENTITIES

An image has the capacity to infiltrate, traverse and transform a Berlin body, since Berlin's images – as with city-dead spectres – are infinitely in flux in all dimensions apart from their seminal attachment to the corporeal: Berlin's images invariably aim to seize and render the corporeal. Two-dimensional images, such as paintings and photographs, endure no hierarchical disadvantage (of being positioned 'below' moving images, for example) in the corporeal infiltrations of Berlin's images, since historically they were often generated in conditions of extreme instability – as in Kirchner's paintings of Potsdamer Platz prostitutes and Meidner's paintings of bodies seismically up-ended in apocalyptic Berlin cityscapes, or in photographs of the 17 June 1953 riots in East Berlin and photographs of uproarious, mythic nightclubs such as Chez Romy Haag or the SO36 – that instil them, in their split-second cracked-open unfore-seenness, with a further dimension, formatively voided, but always offering an enticement for inhabitation by Berlin bodies. Whenever two-dimensional images attract or infiltrate Berlin bodies, that process of corporeal rendering may be enacted via the eyes or the skin, or through a mysteriously blurred, barely conscious enmeshing in which, before its subject realizes it, that body has become a Berlin image, exposed to the perceptual oscillations which such a profound transmutation entails.

While a two-dimensional image holding Berlin's bodies can be caught abruptly in transits through the city – as with images inscribed, stencilled and graffitied onto facades' surfaces or else glimpsed on iPhone screens – and becomes all the more resonant for that sudden and transformational unforeseenness which encompasses both the body within the image and the eye of its spectator, moving images, contrarily, hold other bodies. Filmic sequences, such as those shot on celluloid stock by the Skladanowsky brothers in 1894–6 in central Berlin plazas and avenues such as the Alexanderplatz and Unter den Linden, and in northerly areas of the city such as Prenzlauer Berg and Schönholz, as Berlin's first filmic corporeal renderings, are always oriented towards the act of projection. Simultaneous and spatially fused to their

desire to film Berlin bodies was the Skladanowskys'
desire to project those bodies, as image sequences,
as soon as possible, in venues closely adjacent to the
images' capture, such as the Cafe Sello in Prenzlauer
Berg and the Central Hotel's ballroom, adjacent to
Unter den Linden. Moving-image sequences of Berlin
bodies are habitually fixed in their temporal and
spatial capture, as the carried-through and filmed
performance of anatomical acts in identifiable Berlin
locations, thereby forming antithetical corporealities
to those two-dimensional images of bodies in art
and photography that are caught in raw suspension
and spatial flux by Berlin-transiting eyes. But in film's
projection of Berlin bodies across the twentieth century, their spectators always perceived the temporal
abyss between the moment of the image-capture of
bodies which could readily be their own, shot in Berlin's
identifiable spaces, and the moment of those bodies'
projection. The space of that filmic capture (such as
that of Unter den Linden) remained constant in such
projected sequences, but film's corporeal time had
always slipped. The Skladanowskys attempted to
reconcile that temporal slippage by shooting and then
projecting their films of urban bodies and cityscapes as
immediately as possible, as with their final film, from
March 1897, shot at a crowded and readily identifiable
quayside location in the port city of Stettin, to the north
of Berlin, and intended to cram as many proliferating
bodies as possible into the film's duration of a few
seconds, before being developed and projected to its

audience (at Stettin's Zentralhallen venue) on the evening of the same day.

Across the following decades, that disjunctive temporal sensation experienced by film's spectators in viewing spectrally past Berlin bodies was stratified and made coherent, especially through the medium of newsreels, whose voiceovers announced that the filmed events were only just past, having occurred at most a few days ago. That narrated temporal proximity could itself be unnerving, as for example with the projection for cinema audiences of the newsreel footage showing the vast, specially selected crowd of amassed bodies, including the actor Heinrich George and numerous war amputees, attending Goebbels's infamous 'total war' speech at the Sportpalast venue in Berlin's Schöneberg district in February 1943 (a speech gesturally performed by Goebbels against a time-focused banner announcing 'total war – shortest war!' and intimating for the first time that Nazi Germany, along with Berlin itself as an urban entity, faced the danger of erasure if the all-out war strategy were to misfire). The Sportpalast newsreel showed images of just-past bodies now anticipating an imminent, all-engulfing destruction. Although Goebbels's speech also announced the summary clos-ing down of the city's remaining nightclub culture, the immense auditorium of the Sportpalast itself, as the location of that declaration of Berlin nightlife's total annulling, survived its subsequent aerial bombing and later hosted rock concerts over an extended period until its demolition in 1973. Those concerts included events that generated their own frenzied corporeal turmoil, in violent clashes between spectators and police officers, notably at a concert in October 1958 by Bill Haley and His Comets; the film footage of that concert riot was contrarily inserted both within cinema-projected newsreels shown to Berlin's inhabitants only a few days after the event, intended to denounce the rise of American-music-inspired youth culture aberrations in the city, and also in experimental art-film contexts, as in its later incorporation into Herbert Vesely's 1960 Berlin film, *Die Stadt*, alongside more reflective sequences, intimating film's ability to capture insurgent corporeal striations in the time and space of Berlin.

In the digital era, Berlin's bodies may now be seized by moving-image sequences in intimate spatial and temporal simultaneity to their acts, especially in conditions of mass turmoil and elation, such as the crowd celebrations stretching along the Strasse des 17 Juni following the 2014 World Cup final, performed in wild nocturnal exhilaration along the course of that avenue whose perimeters were continuously lined on either side with vast image screens that (once the game was over) exclusively transmitted live renderings of the exultant bodies poised within those image walls. The celebrants' own vision switched incessantly from incoherent fragments of ongoing crowd furore in their immediate vicinity to surveillance-oriented, panoramic image sequences of that same corporeal turmoil, clarified and projected from the screens enclosing them. Similar dynamics of corporeal uproar and its simultaneous moving-image rendering are projected from screens prominently displayed in Berlin's many large-scale nightclubs and concert venues; Berlin bodies amassed in crowds form sensitized corporealities for such digitized spectacles.

Digital images possess far greater technological capacity for the anatomical infiltration and simultaneous projection of Berlin bodies than art, photographic and filmic images, since their remit is to scan corporeal entities exhaustively (many digital moving-image technologies were developed by medical conglomerates to transmit images from body-interior traversals of miniaturized cameras during operations), in their totality, and to fix and monitor boundaries in urban space for the movements of those bodies. Digital images anatomically occupy bodies. As a result, the act of spectating image-rendered bodies projected from Berlin's exterior-space screens – such as those installed high above the Alexanderplatz in the sites where 1960s multicoloured neon signage was once illuminated – often entails a sense of viewing bodies *torn* from urban space, even when the 'live' sequences shown are those depicting bodies currently inhabiting the surveyed space below those screens. Even in ostensibly conjoined simultaneities between images and bodies, in contemporary digitized environments, time is ready to fracture, and the coherence of space plummets in anticipation of its own vanishing.

TRANSACTORS

Every negotiation between Berlin bodies and the urban environments they inhabit, undertaken for visual, textual and oral pre-eminence or for the inscription of corporeality upon city surfaces, forms a transaction in which something is invariably lost or sieved out from the body and, at the same instant, something *else* becomes consolidated into that body and thereby amends its parameters. Body time and body fluids will be lost in urban encounters, while city detrita and city visions will concurrently be grafted into the skin and eyes of Berlin bodies; almost the entirety of those bodies' contents can be extracted or subtracted, leaving only the barest of traces to identify them still as 'Berlin bodies', while they may absorb such all-engulfing new corporeal contents and image reservoirs (as with the overhauling of many of East Berlin's bodies in the rapid-fire mutations of 1989–90) that they appear transformed almost beyond recognition. Berlin bodies' tongues and vocal tracts may emit words that can never be spoken again, while they remain exposed to the multiple infiltration of urban noise that amasses inextricably in aural membranes and nerves.

Berlin bodies form transactors that are incessantly engaged in exploring, determining and signalling corporeality's position within the interzone between body and city; since that same zone is now simultan-eously contested by digital media – in their stratifications and surveillances of physical presence in corporatized, privatized urban space – it forms a seething terrain of intensively embattled transactions and traversals, from the delicate to the violent, in which the imposition of corporeal vanishing and annulling may form a supreme goal. Berlin bodies as transactors, in their veering losses and gains, contest the city in last-ditch street-located affrontments that resonate aberrantly – for the at-stake status of corporeality – with those between April 1945's urban defenders and Soviet army urban invaders, whose aim was to constrict Berlin's Nazi-controlled space until nothing remained. Trans-acting visibility itself now constitutes a preoccupation for Berlin bodies; they may head underground – into spatial subterranes or virtual zones – as an adroitly transacted condition, or strategic capitulation, that anticipates the eventual re-emergence of enduring corporeality into ocular prominence. Berlin bodies' spectrality itself constitutes a transacted entity.

To view Berlin bodies' transactions, in a state of exposure on the city's streets, necessitates interrogatory acts of moving across urban space, on foot or by public transport, that instigate the display of ripped open, frag-mentary instances; transactions seized in their entirety are rendered static, and voided of the vital mutations that are integral to their process. Transactions may be undertaken in offhand silence and accomplished relentlessly, as in narcotic transactions observed in the Görlitzer or Hasenheide parks, or else accompanied by exclamatory sonic outbursts first heard as echoes from several streets away, as though a distant gang warfare confrontation were taking place, as with the cacophonic Turkish market adjacent to the Yorckstrasse S-bahn station. An infinitesimal or gratuitous transaction undertaken by Berlin bodies can readily assume a more gesturally intense form than a transaction envisaging wide-scale upheavals of urban space and its corporeal markers.

Transactions, especially those envisaged by Berlin's property speculators, often instigate the summary razing and vanishing of significant elements of the city; transactions striated by opaque events or corruption, such as those surrounding Berlin's new airport plans of the post-1990s period, generate vast building projects whose utility is spectacularly annulled even within their process of design and construction. Whenever Berlin bodies' transactions overheat, as in disputes over the valuation of corporeality or city space, their gestures may expand unstoppably into an excess that ignites live currents, as with those issuing from the generating stations that power Berlin's apartment complexes and factories, and whose obsolete predecessors dot the city's eastern wastelands, as malfunctioned, overloaded urban organs. The sensory or electrical charge released from corporeal transactors and transactions, once exempted from immediate imperatives, may acquire a contrary life in which urban entities themselves initiate and multiply corporeal transactions, as in the architectural form of the Berghain nightclub, its building constructed in the early 1950s as an electricity-generating substation to heat apartments in the adjacent Stalinallee (its architectural style signalling its role as an annex to that avenue and the surrounding housing complexes), then stranded in exposed obsolescence in the 1990s in the wastelanded interzone between the Ostbahnhof station and the renamed Stalinallee, before eventually inciting – in the building's resuscitation in the 2000s as an immense, globally notorious nightclub sub-city – infinite corporeal transactions, of overheated cacophony-inflected elation, between its sex-fevered mass of occupants, once channelled inside, specially selected from intently scrutinized waiting lines after transiting the residual wasteland around the generating station via networks of awry metal fencing.

All transactions undertaken covertly in Berlin, notably those underpinned by corruption, historically resonate with the culture of 'black market' transactions pursued in the city on a wide scale in the years of denudation following 1945; those illicit transactions (often denounced in that era in public information newsreel films, projected especially in cinemas in the Soviet zone of the city, where the desire to oversee and delimit transactions was especially urgent) encompassed all media and artefacts of consumption and survival, extending to Berlin bodies themselves. Following the collapse of Eastern Europe's Communist regimes at the end of the 1980s, and into the contemporary moment, a vast reactivation of those black market corporeal dealings pivoted particularly on Berlin as the destination or transit point for prostitutional and sex-industry transactions (habitually directed westwards, in the opposing direction to the Nazi regime's predominantly eastward-oriented deportations of their enemies' bodies, to be transacted into ashes, from the Grunewald and Anhalter stations) originating in countries such as Moldova, Albania and Bulgaria, as though those prostitutional bodies needed to be channelled via the urban space of Berlin – and nowhere else – in order to be maximally exposed to Europe's pre-eminent power of corporeal transaction.

ACTORS

Berlin's seminal actors undertake no transactions: they possess no extraneous elements or artefacts to deal or dispatch in shipments to Europe's contemporary internment camps or sex venues, no projects in corruption or speculation to conjure and realize, and no exchanges of vision and noise to negotiate in ocular and cacophonic urban turmoil. All they hold are their own bodies, in the streets of Berlin, and the gestures that project those bodies, with no return. In that sense, Berlin bodies can take distinctly insular and separated forms, even when their gestures resonate globally, through film, performance or digital media. When a Berlin body conducts zero transactions, that body constitutes an *actor*, exposed in urban space.

That body may still publicly speak, with immense amplification, as for example with the Berlin mayor Ernst Reuter's short speech (delivered from fragmentary, cryptic handwritten notes) from the shrapnel-pitted Reichstag building's steps on 9 September 1948 in front of an oceanic proliferation of Berlin bodies – a large percentage of the entire city's population, amassed once again in the month following the body-saturated open-air concert in the Gendarmenmarkt's jaggedly vertical ruins and this time filmed by newsreel cinematographers in such a way that the assembled bodies appeared to horizontally overspill all urban space, extending across the war-defoliated terrain of the Tiergarten park and beyond. Reuter's halting words incited a global eye to survey the western zones of Berlin in their vulnerability to being seized by the Soviet-controlled eastern zone, then denounced the prospect that the USA and its European allies would imminently give speculative 'prices' to those western Berlin zones for sleight-of-hand transaction and delivery to the USSR. Reuter's words themselves transacted nothing and had nothing on offer, either from his own body or from the voided, wastelanded space of Berlin's western zones; his act of global appeal for Berlin (spoken during the ongoing Berlin Airlift of 1948–9) not to be abandoned required the erasing of any prospect of exchange. Berlin actors must possess nothing, and be situated in terminal isolation.

Since Berlin actors negate transaction and hold voids, they can project and gesture only their own bodies, from their location of separation, either via their voices (as in Reuter's broken-voiced speech) or through other corporeal fragments. Such projections may not be intended for any specific audience, but, when emanated with urgency and intimating a crisis, of the conjoined body and city, they irresistibly propose that Berlin bodies, and the city itself, are so unique in their topographical configuration and historical solitude that they must be gifted non-transactional attention. The exterior eye focuses unreservedly on the self-directed acts of Berlin bodies.

The 'Red Island' (Rote Insel) forms a triangular strip of land dividing Berlin's Schöneberg and Kreuzberg districts, located between the two deep cuttings of the S-bahn lines that diverge at Yorckstrasse and bordered at its southern perimeter by the Ring S-bahn line that circles central Berlin. During the nineteenth century, part of that island was used as a ground for military manoeuvres, and long north–south streets of tenement buildings for workers – whose entrenched affiliations to socialist parties gave the island its name – were constructed in that century's final decades; cemeteries were opened on either side of the main street, the Kolonnenstrasse, that horizontally bisected the island, and an immense gasometer was added at the island's southern extreme in 1908–10. Many artists and Berlin 'originals' inhabited the Rote Insel, in self-willed internal city exile. Spatially and sensorially cut off from the rest of the city (accessible only by bridges), it possessed a distinctive, legendary aura in the topography of Berlin, as the 'lost-in-time' urban component that would never integrate or transact itself with the surrounding city, and held only itself and its bodies. In their autonomous annex of Berlin, the inhabitants of the Rote Insel had nothing to project but their own embodiment of directly contested intersections between corporeality and the city. To transect the Rote Insel on foot, from its southern to northern end, forms a transit in which the fluid status of urban traversal is countered by the obstinate immovability of the island itself, so that you appear phantasmatically to be crossing the island, while it acts upon you.

At the southern end of the Rote Insel, in a tenement building on one of the streets that vertically striate it, Marlene Dietrich was born on 27 December 1901, and spent her first years inhabiting that beyond-the-city island. In her combative, unremitting approach to Berlin – interrogating or opposing all of its political, cultural and corporeal regimes – that generated a loving antipathy between her and the city, and in her eventual exile (to the USA, then to Paris) and solitude, Dietrich emanates the sense of focus of the Berlin 'actor' who will not trans-act or capitulate, and has nothing to project but the sensational aura of her (or his) body. The yellow-painted facade of the building holds two plaques; to the south, the street is rapidly curtailed by the Ring S-bahn tracks, but to the north, it stretches out along the island, with near-deserted pavements and silent, unrenovated build-ings – their upper windows often populated by intently gazing faces – whose ornate entrance halls are constel-lated by faded stained-glass decorations.

Walking the space of the Rote Insel demands an irresoluble journey located in a contrary dimension to habitual Berlin city transits. At the island's northern end, the crumbling Alter St Matthäus cemetery slopes down towards the Yorckstrasse S-bahn station; during the manic prelude of demolition in the late 1930s prior to the envisaged building of Speer's Berlin-supplanting Germania, curtailed by warfare, a northern part of the cemetery's terrain was razed in anticipation of forming part of the course for one of the new megalopolis's grand avenues. The cemetery had been a fashionable one in the nineteenth century, for industrialists and entrepreneurs, artists and writers, whose cracked mausolea and crypts are now being reassigned and repopulated – in Berlin's excessive city-dead regime – by the newly dead, especially AIDS activists. The core group of conspirators who attempted to assassinate Hitler at his Wolf's Lair headquarters in 1944, including the corporeal agent of that malfunctioned assassination plot, Claus von Stauffenberg, were interred in the cemetery after their nocturnal execution by firing squad, but then disinterred almost immediately, their bodies incinerated and the ashes scattered, as though the Rote Insel's cemetery had proved too volatile a terrain to absorb those bodies. Bruno Schleinstein, who appeared as an extraordinary figure (as though conjured in a story by the Brothers Grimm, also buried in the Alter St Matthäus cemetery) in Werner Herzog's films under the name 'Bruno S.', forms a corresponding presence, as an autonomous Berlin actor, to that of Marlene Dietrich at the far end of the Rote Insel. Although Schleinstein – abandoned at birth and incarcerated in many institutions before pursuing his solitary, combative life in Berlin – only appeared in two of Herzog's films in the 1970s (including the Berlin-located *Stroszek*) and devoted far more of his time to his work as an itinerant street musician, his tomb on the Rote Insel is marked with one word below his name: 'actor'.

PERFORMERS

Berlin bodies as *performers* of the city and its space habitually envision more engulfing and far-reaching work than either its adept transactors or its insular actors. Berlin performers' gestures aim to incorporate the entire city and entail the deployment of the entire body, since their work is to constitute a collective, amassed performance of Berlin's urban space, even when their performative desire to manifest that space results in the form of the most shattered fragment, and even when that performance's process is a misfired one, disassembled as it is delivered. Berlin performers always almost succeed in embodying the city, but their acts diverge irresistibly at the last moment into haywire malfunction or else are unceremoniously usurped – as with von Stauffenberg's attempt at the Wolf's Lair to detonate Hitler's body, derailed at the final instant by the nonchalant kicking aside of the bomb-containing briefcase, and with the history of his own post-execution body, interred then jettisoned from its assigned Rote Insel location. The entire population of Berlin – at any given moment, and especially at instants of extreme crisis – holds the impossible corporeal task of performing the city, as a supreme urban mission that overrules and absorbs all other habitual gestures, lusts, commitments and manias, but that is itself overruled by performance's integral aberrance.

To perform Berlin corporeally entails an envisioning of how the city will appear after that performative act is accomplished – an act of urban performance necessarily unleashes a transformation of some kind – even if that transformation is already annulled in its formulation. Performative aspirations for Berlin take vastly divergent forms that intimate the flux inherent in the rapport between corporeality and urban space, ranging from the most infinitesimal act of performance – a convulsive, momentary gesture enacted in a hidden courtyard, subterranean space or peripheral wasteland, tracked by no spectatorial eye – to a vast and media-scanned undertaking of urban performance, such as the decades-in-preparation project by the artists Christo and Jeanne-Claude of wrapping the Reichstag building in panels of aluminium and polypropylene fabric, finally accomplished in June 1995, for spectators – amassed in exactly the same space as those for Reuter's speech of 1948 – whose eyes, in an ocular performance still veering and displaced by the previous half-decade's immense mutations of Berlin's space, fixated on the gaps and cracks between the shifting panels, or upon the cranes that manoeuvred them. Sitting among those spectators,

I watched the performative urban transformation of the

instant of the Reichstag's re-emergence – identical, but now spectrally cast askew, its power and history momentarily annulled – as the panels were drawn away. Whatever transformation had been incited immediately sank into Berlin's dense strata. The focus and targets of performative acts in Berlin's space oscillate wildly between corporeal and urban forms, deploying the malleable integument between body and city as their performative medium, from acts of killing (or preparations for killings then carried through elsewhere) enacted on a massive scale at ground level, to the performative granting of a gift – as with the air-lifted gift of West Berlin's survival non-transactionally requested by Reuter, and delivered to those inhabitants of Berlin assembled before the Reichstag ruins in a performance of precarious transits through the skies above the city to the Tempelhof airfield.

Whenever Berlin bodies perform the city, they render its elements into new forms, for potential projection and consumption, as in slaughterhouse processes that rigorously extract from animals' bodies those elements that initially appear useless but can be mutated, often by violent means, into consumable by-products. Berlin itself forms a by-product of its amassed bodies' aberrant performances that render its apparent uselessness or incapacity as a megalopolis (periodically intent on precipitating self-erasure, impeded by opaque city-authority transactions, and always notoriously financially 'ruined') into vital visual and sensorial urban material. For over a century, from

the 1870s, a great expanse of eastern Berlin's Friedrichshain district was given over to a slaughterhouse sub-city, encompassing a range of rendering processes, among numerous other technologies (Döblin's novel *Berlin Alexanderplatz* enumerates the sheer scale of those technologies of slaughter), eventually forming the principal slaughterhouse serving the population of East Berlin before itself being rendered obsolete in the 1990s, with its many ornate sheds gradually demolished or renovated into commercial spaces over the following two decades. Before that sub-city's redundancy, the East Berlin artist York der Knoefel inhabited it over a period of two years, across the last phase of the GDR's existence – when the slaughterhouse was known as 'Fleischkombinat Berlin' – in order to create a photographic art installation, *Slaughterhouse Berlin* (*Schlachthaus Berlin*, 1986–8), in the form of a labyrinth of large-scale image-embedded zinc panels into which spectators performatively entered on foot, rapidly becoming disorientated, in an experience of intimate, inescapable contact with an iconography of Berlin's slaughters. Those spectators finally emerged from the installation with their own bodies overhauled and sensorially 'rendered' by their non-linear transits. The original *Slaughterhouse Berlin* performance installation was recreated in 2012, a year after der Knoefel's death.[15] With the redundancy and razing of Friedrichshain's slaughterhouse sub-city, the resulting absence of processes of transmutatory rendering in contemporary Berlin's urban topography accentuates the need for its inhabitants themselves to envision their own performative renderings of the city, via cuts and fragments.

Berlin's body performers animate the city, through the gestures of durational inhabitation or in unconscious, instantaneous collisions. Those gestures are least in evidence in the city's auditoria of performance, apart from those auditoria consigned to abandonment, but are virulently at stake over Berlin's external spaces, on its plazas and wastelands. For bodies that expend a lifetime's span in Berlin, embedded in the city's strata and subterranes, and equally for bodies undertaking only an abrupt, oblivious transit of a momentary duration across the city's surfaces, all rapports with Berlin's urban space constitute performative enmeshings that, in their amassing, impact in gestural movement upon the city, firing it with the multiple malfunctions and re-envisionings that sustain it. Those bodies receive in turn the labyrinthine experience of the performance of Berlin itself – as urban history, as fissured architecture, as city-conjured exhilaration – that constitutes a profound sensory and ocular infiltration.

BERLIN BODIES

For a cultural history of the body in Berlin, the exploratory urban transits of human figures form a vital element in the city's corporeal dimensions and strata. The following parts of this book will look especially at such figures' urban infiltrations and traversals, notably in their sensory dimensions of vision and sound as well as in their revelations about city life and in their urban apocalyptic disintegrations or voidings. As a result of the pre-eminence of the moving image as both a visual and urban medium across the entire course of the twentieth century and the twenty-first century's first decades – carrying traces of Berlin bodies in urban space from the Skladanowsky brothers' first films of 1894–6 to digital sequences (handheld smartphone sequences, as well as sequences projected digitally from immense image screens in Berlin's great plazas) – the phenomena in particular of amassings of Berlin bodies, together with their movements across the city, notably in turmoil, conflict or activist protest, have especially seized the attention of the urban eye as it absorbs and transmits the unique status of corporeality in Berlin and its intersections with the city's space.

Particularly in the late 1920s, and into the early 1930s, when experimental film-makers and newsreel cinematographers became captivated with tracking the spectacular impulsions of vast crowds across the city, and their gatherings in tenement courtyards and in plazas, the direct confrontation and oscillation between Berlin as corporeality and Berlin as urban entity became a source of fascination too for the city's own inhabitants. They were able to view sequences holding their own street-located physical forms (or forms near-identical to their own), projected in cinema spaces, in such films as Siodmak and Ulmer's *People on Sunday* (*Menschen am Sonntag,* 1930), and László Moholy-Nagy's *Berlin Still-life* (*Berliner Stilleben,* 1931). Those body traces were memorially seized by film for future Berlin explorations. Berlin as corporeality and Berlin as urban entity work to affront and transmutate one another, most probingly in such filmic sequences, in which Berlin bodies amass and separate, move through subterranes and tunnels, and across bridges and traffic intersections. Teeming crowds traversed Berlin in that era for political or revolutionary aims, in the form of demonstrations or journeys to attend rallies in outlying areas of the city, but also crossed and exited the city for leisure activities, especially on Sundays, and towards Berlin's lakes (to the close-by Wannsee in *People on Sunday*, but also towards lakes, such as the more distant Motzener See, then closely associated with preoccupations with nudity, health and physical training that often held affiliations to fascist, left-wing, pacifist and anarchist groupings). A formative shift occurs in those filmic sequences around 1928, from chaotic public-transport struggles and impasses around overpacked trams and subway trains, to more streamlined, accelerated transits, with the overhauling – largely the work of Reuter – of Berlin's fragmented city-transit system into an integrated form as the Berliner Verkehrsbetriebe (BVG). Berlin bodies were filmed in that era on foot too, speeding across or aimlessly wandering in the city.

Film also seized the manic intensity of amalgams of Berlin bodies, especially at moments of urban up-heaval and above all in the newsreel documentation of Goebbels's 'total war' speech at the Sportpalast venue, whose sequences focus as much on the amassed bodies of the audience poised against the hall's cavernous space and on their convulsive reactions – instantaneously and repeatedly propelled from their seats to assert their readiness to support or pursue 'total and radical' acts that will conflagrate their city – as on Goebbels's own delivery of his incitations. Film also enduringly imprints upon urban space the extreme contrast (one beaten incessantly into Berlin's terrain, and into the vision of its traversers) between such filmed historical moments of acute corporeal intensity and their contemporary vanishing into contrary traces or monuments, and into voids, as experienced in a walk along the now run-down avenue the Potsdamer Strasse, from which a turn along a pathway leads to an isolated metal placard embedded incongruously in a terrain of dirt, at the entrance to a disintegrating, forlorn housing complex, marking the location of the Sportpalast as the site of Goebbels's filmed speech.

While sequences of amassed Berlin bodies – in movement against the exterior background space of plazas and ruins, or highlighted against the internal space of auditoria and ballrooms – were recorded frequently over film's century or so of visual pre-eminence as a city-recording medium, film was able on only two occasions to trace such immense accumulations of Berlin's inhabitants that they could be seen as *embodying* the city (notably through the participation of overwhelming percentages of the population): in the filming of the demonstration in the Alexanderplatz on 4 November 1989, for East Berlin's population, and in the filming of Reuter's speech, on 9 September 1948, for the population of the entire city, emerging from all of its contested zones. Reuter's previous incarnation as the devisor and implementer of Berlin's integrated public transport system, twenty years earlier, appears in the context of that filmic sequence as the prescient act that enabled his immense audience to reach the speech's site in front of the Reichstag (despite the damaged form of that transport system in 1948), just as his still earlier incarnation, thirty years previously, in 1918–19, as a Soviet commissar in Saratov dealing directly with Stalin and Lenin and signing death warrants for executions, gave his speech's semi-improvised evocation of West Berlin's threatened obliteration (avertable only by the Berlin Airlift, and by the focusing of a global eye on the city) its persuasive razor's edge.

Although only filmable in dispersed fragments, moving-image sequences of the yearly riots on Berlin's May Days also carry that aura of populations – Berlin's activist or riot-attracted populations – engaged in an insurgency of bodies that substantially coincides with the city's space. The recorders of such actions can only seize momentary rushes and blurs of bodies, or instants in which activists and riot police directly confront one another; often, moving-image devices are knocked from the recorders' hands by batons or other hands as they move at speed, or their lenses are shattered. The devices can be seized and confiscated by the city's authorities, and their contents used as physical evidence to prosecute rioters. Such sequences of Berlin bodies in excess – propelled into aberrant or spectacular acts by sensory and ocular excesses, and excessive too in their sheer spilling beyond filmable space – demonstrate the interventions through which corporeality engulfs urban space.

The free body culture (FKK: *Freikörperkultur*) of the 1920s and early 1930s, whose divergent political affiliations allied its factions spatially to particular lakes around the peripheries of Berlin, endured across the GDR era, in part as a repudiation of state-authoritarian control that extended to the domain of corporeality. In her celebrated song 'Du hast den Farbfilm vergessen' ('You Forgot the Colour Film'), East Berlin's mid-1970s teen idol Nina Hagen wryly complained of her own FKK body's lack of luminescence in its representation by the mundane black and white photography that character-istically evoked East Berlin's monochrome cityscape. At sites such as that of the grass-covered terrain at the eastern shore of the Heiliger See, across the lake from the Cecilienhof Palace in which Stalin, Churchill and Truman met in 1945 to formulate the topographies of post-war Europe, FKK adherents spent decades of summers, gradually metamorphosing from the young, lithe bodies of the first years following East Berlin's disappearance in 1990, to bodies mutated across time by age, illness, accident and excess consumerism, and were joined by new bodies, so that such locations of naked, amassed Berlin bodies disclose an urban corporeality in transformation, at each contemporary instant, with its distinctive elements and markings: the scars, the wounds, the scored lines, the puncture points, the abrasions, the sexual organs, the abused zones, the hair, the skin, the deformations, the swellings, the emaciations, the rashes, the bones, the nails, the tattooings, the mouths, the undersides, the subterranes, the histories, the eyes: Berlin bodies.

2

FRAGMENTS TORN FROM A HISTORY OF THE HUMAN BODY IN BERLIN

ONLY FRAGMENTS . THE CITY VIA CORPOREAL FRAGMENTS

ONLY FRAGMENTS

In Berlin, only fragments exist. To create an aperture by which to project itself, a Berlin body must disassemble, disorient, upend, blur, cut down, concentrate and dislocate its corporeal elements, so that they align themselves with the urban fragments that constitute the city's cultural history and its contemporary conjurations. Berlin is not a whole city, and while no cities worldwide form coherent presences, especially in the global domain of digital cultures, Berlin's coherence is relentlessly subtracted and unstitched in a unique way across its urban history, as well as across individual sequences of ocular transits of its space. Urban fragments are sensitized to being seized in fragmentary forms, as Berlin's writers, artists and film-makers of the first decades of the twentieth century perceived (most presciently, Franz Hessel and Siegfried Kracauer), but the seismic dynamics of urban fragments and of textual or visual fragments always form vitally irreconcilable, deeply disparate entities. While there are *only fragments* in Berlin's domain, fragments delineate and propel themselves multiply, and the renderings of fragments, from urban and corporeal raw materials, take on infinite manifestations. The volatile intersections across which corporeal and urban fragments collide, and attempt to infiltrate one another, form essential Berlin zones of perception and re-envisioning. Urban fragments are torn from cultural histories of the city, in writing, film-making, art and performance; no element of such histories integrally adheres to any other, and those histories more habitually form annullings, reversals or razings of one another when positioned in intimate rapports. Urban fragments are concurrently torn too from the processes in movement of their ocular interrogation and capture by Berlin's spectators.

Fragments hold their content in time by a precariously veering eye's focus – as on a split-second opening of a lipsticked mouth poised against a wall surface of overlayered graffiti and shrapnel impacts, or a blurred running figure against the conversely moving course of the river Spree, or a celluloid frame of Berlin rooftops embedded within a digital image. Fragments will always imminently lose that content and revert to a voided entity, in time. But such Berlin fragments also hold their spaces, together with the vanishing histories of those spaces. The immense expanse of the Treptower Park memorial and burial site for the USSR's soldiers killed in their 1945 assault on Berlin – the spectacular space part-assembled from granite taken from Hitler's ruined Chancellery building, incorporating a sequence of sculpted friezes of battle action with commentaries by Stalin, and surmounted by the statue of a Soviet soldier crushing a swastika underfoot – formed the location across several hours in 2014 for a choreographic work devised by Boris Charmatz of fragments of bodies, in which twenty solo dancers performed in delineated zones of that terrain of memory and death, separated from one another by invisible spatial membranes and often undertaking infinitesimal gestural fragments only minutely distinct from utter stillness.[16] Spectators moved between those zones as though transiting a suddenly populated sub-city within Berlin, its elements abruptly projecting themselves in fragmentary outbursts that then deliquesced in the retinas absorbing them. The city dead of that space – many thousands of young bodies collected by war from distant originating points but amassed at that memorial space by the intensity of acts of urban killing, and interred beneath it, thereby becoming pivotal Berlin bodies until the future moment when they will be summarily disinterred and the site razed, via history's caprices – themselves formed a subterranean element of the performance, infiltrating and inflecting its gestural fragments from below.

In an invisibly detached zone within that memorial space, adjacent to one of Stalin's friezes, the Japanese dancer Ko Murobushi (the first *ankoku butoh* choreographer to perform in Europe, in 1978) undertook a dance of arduous gestural fragments, each separated from all of the others and interconnected solely as a projection of shattering corporeal transmutation, that inhabited that space as a spectral Berlin-body variant. Murobushi accompanied his abbreviated dance, towards the moment of its abandoning, with a gasped commentary of vocal fragments which his spectators moved closer to hear, and in which he noted that, in Berlin, in dancing, he was thinking of someone who had died, and that his fragments of dance projected a plethora of dead bodies or spectres that were unable to move, manoeuvre or manifest themselves, except through that dance, expelled from their incapacitation into the space of Berlin through the medium of his body, which simultaneously resisted those spectres but served as a transitable aperture for them. Since his dance was suddenly abandoned – exhausted, Murobushi exited his performance, curtailing its vocal commentary too, and wandered over the cracked memorial ground to recline and recover his breath on a marble bench alongside Stalin's frieze – those projected spectres could not re-enter it (even if they had wanted to), and themselves became perpetually transient inhabitants of Berlin, accumulated in their isolation into its excess population of the city dead. Murobushi's abandoned dance, among and invoking Berlin's city dead, was one of his last, since he died the following year.

Berlin's bodies irresistibly tear out fragments from their corporeal histories, to manifest those extracted, exposed elements to the city's eyes. A corporeal fragment will never assimilate itself, nor become pacified; even in its most intensive affrontments with other fragments, it will not conjoin or reconcile itself with them, and – as with the spectres emitted from Murobushi's fragments of dance, enacted in solitude on the Treptower Park memorial ground with its own subterranean population of ghosts – it cannot re-enter the body that expelled it (at least, not until that body itself joins the Berlin city dead) so that it exists in limbo in the urban space of Berlin, tangible to transiting eyes especially in the city's most abandoned zones, wastelands, ballrooms and auditoria. While Berlin's monumental, stratified forms of petrification are effortlessly dispersed, only aberrant fragments remain embedded in its space.

THE CITY VIA CORPOREAL FRAGMENTS

Berlin often emanates the sense of being so densely layered and duplicitous in response to its imageries and archivings as to form an immensely unknowable zone, into which urban cultural histories unable to engage with its integral aberrances and contrary strata soon melt. Criteria developed in relation to other cities are carapaced away from Berlin's space: nothing exists that is *like* Berlin, and art, film and writing can never act *as* Berlin in a documentational form, since Berlin's surfaces are ultimately resistant to all assimilations, actively dissolving and transforming their attempted documentation while undergoing only surface markings, or at most momentary incisions, from their recordings, archivings, sequencings, scannings, envisionings and re-envisionings. If Berlin can be known, as a knowledge-exceeding and knowledge-annulling urban entity, it is known corporeally and via fragments. In order to exist, corporeal fragments need to project themselves, even when that projection is so inwardly directed that its discernible trace is in shadows, virtual spasms and light-leaking subterranean acts. Fragments – as with concentrated outbursts of physical materials and fluids unleashed in Berlin's streets – are constituted too from corporeal subtractions and withdrawals, in apparitions against darkness that need to be read in negative. Fragments are also the embodiment and residues of processes of urban abandoning, in which an ongoing inhabitation of Berlin has been abruptly curtailed, through an engulfing cataclysm or overturning, and fragments of the building or body which still subsists in ruins simultaneously emanate those forms' current dissolution and the life they once held. Since such momentous collapses are everyday, habitual occurrences in Berlin, fragments of corporeal abandoning comprise a pervasive debris that sensorially spills into urban space in a parallel way to that in which wreckage, shards and toxic detrita from demolition processes exacted on Berlin's buildings sprawl profusely across pavements, gutters and wastelands.

In Berlin, the eye, in anatomizing transits through streets and plazas, amasses fragments and attempts to convert sensorial and ocular content into knowledge. That capacity – even when it is an immediately annulled capacity – to *generate* knowledge of the excessive megalopolis may be deployed even against the will of Berlin's passengers, who would often prefer instead to experience the bliss of oblivion than to be subjected to urban fragmentations, but it will still operate and accumulatively archive itself into those passengers' ligaments, bones and apertures, amending their forms, so that fragments themselves create distinctive, autonomous Berlin bodies within the corporeal domain of the city's witnessing. Urban knowledge optimally uses the human body for

its transmission, in the same way, on the Treptower

Park Soviet army memorial terrain, that the spectral infiltration of the dancing body of Ko Murobushi by the city dead – literally right there, in their many thousands, directly below his convulsed feet, in their subterranean burial vaults, as well as vocally and gesturally conjured via his own memories and hallucinations that transported distant city dead, from Japan or elsewhere, into the space of Berlin – operated solely through a corporeality sensitized and attuned by its shattering. Urban knowledge transmitted in fragments holds a precarious status; its process of transmission has no secure space of diffusion and no fixed receptacle, and its physical 'hosts' may not want to be inhabited by it, but it remains all that is known of the great mystery of Berlin. That precarious, liminal status of the fragmentary knowledge of Berlin's bodies – poised in suspension between corporeal and urban entities, and subject to imminent annulling from either side – takes on a *seminal* dimension, in instigating and propelling visions of the city, precisely through that precarity, so that it has to be instantly seized before it slips into its loss, discrediting, negation, or petrifaction.

Among the most tangible instances of the transition between what is precariously known of Berlin, and that knowledge's cancellation into a definitive unknowing, is in the abrupt vanishing of its buildings. Sites and surfaces that have been erased, along with the bodies that occupied them, intimate that nothing was ever there in the first place. The authority to erase – often accorded by city authorities to arbitrarily powerful

'developers', via opaque processes, notably in the first
years following Berlin's reunification – assigns the
unowned histories of the contents of now-razed spaces
to a condition of unknown-ness in which only detrital
fragments remain (traces of wreckage, as well as
scatterings of surviving images of such sites). As with
processes of abandoning, those of razing can never be
totalized, and seep resuscitatory fragments. Especially
in outlying northern districts of Berlin, such as
Weissensee and Pankow, whose neglect across the
GDR decades led both to the wide-scale endurance of
late nineteenth-century buildings such as ballrooms
and entertainment halls and to their ostensible obsolescence in the present city, the experience of viewing
an intact building on one day, then viewing a flattened
terrain of demolition on the next (with strewn fragments
of oak dancefloor and of clientele-enticing handpainted
lettering on cracked plaster), was a frequent one during
my early 1990s transits of Berlin's peripheral zones. Often,
I stopped for a few moments, along deserted, bullet-
striated ghost streets, to examine and then sieve those
now-desiccated fragments between my fingers, so that
blurred residues of the lettering – extolling, for example,
those ballrooms' dimensions or the innovations and
luxurious quality of their design – imprinted themselves
as Berlin-knowledge deep into the skin of my hands.
Abruptly inflicted absences, vanishings and voidings
of bodies and buildings, in the forms of wastelands,
still-prevalent bombsites and terrains of demolition,
together with the left-behind fragments they contain,

all serve to constitute such a pivotal experience of Berlin's space that the absorbing of absence itself becomes a vital form of urban knowledge, and the visual sequencings of absences – by the eye, or by film and digital media – make tenable the location and collecting of vanishing's spectral traces.

The precarious knowledge that is transmitted into thin air, from Berlin's accumulated or isolated urban and corporeal fragments, is a duplicitous one that can be instantly overturned into its opposing form, or else inextricably amalgamated into concoctions of documentations and fabrications. Notably, archivings and monumentalizings in Berlin often form fraudulent spectacles that generate sleight-of-hand anti-knowledge fabricated to further the agendas of state and corporate entities. In all instances, fragments of knowledge of Berlin bodies – seized accidentally or intentionally by the city's passengers, as they transit Berlin's spaces in flux – need to be intensively excoriated and rendered, in order to extract whatever they will reveal, of lost corporealities and lost strata, and of Berlin's animating detrita in the contemporary moment.

3
BERLIN'S PASSENGERS: TRANSITS, ENTRIES, EXITS

INFILTRATIONS . TRANSPIERCINGS . EXUDATIONS .
EXPULSIONS . PASSENGERS

INFILTRATIONS

Berlin is a city of passengers on a precarious ride;
they may be carried along by the megalopolis in
a state of oblivion and ecstasy, and given refuge
from encroaching calamities, along with a rider's
spectacular viewing point into Berlin's corporeal
and urban history, but on either side of that ride,
Europe's abyss and Berlin's own scorched-earth
wastelands are avidly ready for bodies' tipped-out
falls. To *enter* Berlin, as an open-eyed passenger,
requires an act of adroit corporeal infiltration, that
unskins or grates or scars or imprints or transforms
the transiting body in that process of entry, whose
demanding or impossible imperatives were historically most tangible during West Berlin entries, via
train or autobahn corridors through the GDR, during
the city's division, and remain tangible too for
contemporary refugees and outcasts. Infiltration,
for those who enter Berlin, may form an initiating,
fast-moving act that irresistibly propels its passengers
into its haywire momentum. Berlin has visually and
sonically announced itself globally as no other city
has, resonantly offering raw, seductive enticements:
of a half-city to hide in, for 1960s bodies in West Berlin
avoiding legal pressure or military conscription, of a
wild nightclub-city of nightmares, ghosts and crashes
for those drawn to West Berlin by the 1970s music of
Bowie and Iggy Pop, and of a reunified city embodying
the evidence of destroyed histories, while conjuring

endless obsessions and sensations, for its contemporary passengers. Infiltration into Berlin often entails an act of all-consuming corporeal overturning.

To infiltrate West Berlin at the end of the 1970s, and through the 1980s, eastwards at ground level from other countries, demanded a traversal by train or autobahn through the GDR's western lands. By autobahn, across two or three hours of daylight transit, West Berlin-bound cars passed under bridges emblazoned with banners extolling the merits and aspirations of the GDR state, and on nocturnal transits, travelled along-side chemical factories and metalworks working at headlong capacity, illuminating the night sky in acetylene bursts. That eastward-directed transit by train, when I made it for the first time in 1979, gathered a sensation for its passengers of momentous corporeal propulsion and anxiety that is also instilled into the opening train-journey sequence of Berlin's infiltration in Walter Ruttmann's 1927 film *Berlin: Symphony of a Metropolis* (*Berlin: Die Symphonie der Grossstadt*), with flashes of trackside destination signs announcing the imminence of Berlin and its Anhalter station terminus. Once the train had exchanged its crew and locomotive, it passed beyond the Helmstedt border crossing, as though precipitating its passengers' bodies into unknown, vertiginous zones; before dawn, that express rattled over bridges spanning lakes and rivers, and the immense dome of the St Nikolaikirche abruptly appeared on the left above Potsdam's razed palace sites and the prefabricated glass-and-steel tower of the state-run Interhotel Potsdam, before the train halted at the Griebnitzsee crossing point into West Berlin, and the GDR crew and guards disembarked for the short final stretch through the Grunewald forest, until West Berlin's radio-transmitting tower and Teufelsberg listening-station domes appeared above the trees, and the express gradually slowed over the elevated section through the Charlottenburg district to its principal West Berlin halt, with a scream of brakes, at Zoologischer Garten station (expresses heading into East Berlin, Poland, and further east, then resumed the journey, re-entering the GDR after a few minutes at Friedrichstrasse station). Exiting the station beside the zoo into the city, in silence broken by animal cries and those of hustlers and addicts, and standing in the dawn light of near-deserted streets below the sheared-off church steeple of the Kaiser-Wilhelm-Gedächtniskirche, instilled an outlandish corporeal sensation of urban infiltration, into a void.

That infiltration of West Berlin, as a journey by train which took only several hours but involved an indefinite, time-annulled corporeal inhabitation of precarious interzonal space, had the elating, repetition-impelled soundtrack of Kraftwerk's 'Trans Europa Express' (1977), with its accompanying promotional film of the four waywardly elegant and lipsticked figures seated in a train compartment, gazing out at the neon signage of passing night cities in hypnotized pleasure, as the red-and-cream liveried streamlined

high-speed international expresses of the Trans Europ Express (TEE) network – at the peak of their operation in the 1970s, but largely rendered defunct by the following decade – propel them across Europe (but not via Berlin, too anomalously obstructed by changes of locomotives and visa checks for smooth TEE-transits, so that, as Kraftwerk narrate 'Trans Europa Express', Iggy Pop and Bowie must travel from West Berlin to Düsseldorf to meet their train).

The GDR possessed its own trans-Europe evoking network, Mitropa, but in the form of a railway catering company rather than a medium of propulsive corporeal transit. The Mitropa network also existed on either side of the GDR's history, but was operated under that name solely by the East German Deutsche Reichsbahn system across the decades of the GDR's existence. Mitropa's name and distinctive insignia – with its prominent M evoking Fritz Lang's Berlin of child-murder in his film *M* – remained imprinted on Berlin's facades, such as the shrapnel-incised arcades below the railway overpass to the east of Friedrichstrasse station, long after the GDR's dissolution, and is still seen on the sides of derelict carriages marooned in overgrown railway sidings on Berlin's eastern peripheries. The Danish film-maker Lars von Trier drew his film production company's name, Zentropa, from that of Mitropa, and shot the exterior scenes of his feature film *Europa* (1991) about a sleeping-car attendant's journeys by train between the razed post-war cityscapes of 1945 Germany, including that of Berlin, just across the Polish border from Berlin at the vast railway-locomotive roundhouse and war-destroyed brick cathedral of the town of Chojna. The location of that town, previously a German one, was seen as so close to Berlin in the twentieth century's first decades that plans were made to link it into the city's metropolitan train network.[17] *Europa* begins with a sequence of spoken and visual hypnotism shot from the front of a locomotive as it passes over railway tracks outlined against darkness (the promotional film for 'Trans Europa Express' uses parallel, repeated sequences), intimating that the infiltration of cities, Berlin above all, extending far into subterranes and zones of precarity, forms an act of profound ocular hypnotizing, edged with hallucination, that has to be countered with active imaginary re-envisioning in order to avert an utter visual subjugation.

Iggy Pop's song 'The Passenger' (1977) evokes his late-night West Berlin transits of infiltration between Schöneberg-district nightclubs such as Chez Romy Haag and the Dschungel, and also his S-bahn network journeys along dead-end lines, along with Bowie, during the era in which – after an initial stay at the luxurious Schlosshotel Gerhus in the Grunewald district on their arrival in West Berlin – they rented an apartment together in the street-facing part of a building on Schöneberg's Hauptstrasse, before Iggy Pop was consigned after quarrels to another apartment, in the building's back courtyard, where his
companion Esther Friedman photographed the

blank firewalls, along with streetscapes of that wide, run-down avenue with its small bars (where she and Iggy Pop drank) and Turkish stores. Those transits were retrospectively perceived by Iggy Pop as subservient ones to Bowie's rigorous nightclub and art-museum itineraries, just as the two albums he made in 1976–7 during his West Berlin period, *The Idiot* and *Lust for Life* (recorded in part at the Hansa studios, then stranded directly alongside a wasteland adjoining the Berlin Wall), were overseen and their preoccupations infiltrated by Bowie.

In tension with corporeal infiltrations of initiation into Berlin's space, such as those into 1970s West Berlin, the city itself insistently infiltrates its occupants' bodies, against their will or with those bodies' open complicity, in urban excavations, interrogations and piercings, from its serrated facades and edges, of corporeal vision and exposed skin surfaces. Berlin's infinite archives of urban images, including those uneasily poised between scarred memory traces and sleight-of-hand fabrications, also infiltrate, hypnotize and beguile the eyes of those transiting the city, or, with an equal virulence of transmission, those located far beyond its perimeters. Berlin's own infiltrations reconfigure the bodies that enter it.

TRANSPIERCINGS

At the interzonal subterranean crossing point for
foreigners into East Berlin, within pale-blue-tiled
forensic hallways abruptly barriered by opaque glass
partitions, the bodies of that noise-muted space's
transiting occupants, in the subterranes of the labyrinthine Friedrichstrasse station, were positioned
already half-infiltrated into that half-city, after taking
a short subway ride from West Berlin through intervening abandoned 'ghost stations' on the underground
network. At that mid-transpierced point of entry into
East Berlin, the transit held its own distinctive performance of endlessly repeated gestures and questions
from the GDR border-control officers interrogating
those in-limbo 'foreign bodies'.

On my journeys into East Berlin in 1979, and into
the 1980s, I soon learned that at the other crossing
point, on Zimmerstrasse, the capricious officers scrutinizing the bodies and dress of the queued transiters
could curtly instruct me, even within the apparent
momentum of that traversal, to leave the crossing
zone and return back into West Berlin, but that at the
Friedrichstrasse entry point into East Berlin, I would
always get through. Although foreigners holding
day visas had to exit East Berlin again by midnight,
Turkish 'guest workers' from West Berlin, entranced
by the East Berlin women with whom they danced
at Clärchens Ballhaus – and thereby exposed to the
irresistible propulsions of Berlin's transpiercings –

would habitually leave that ballroom shortly before midnight and walk the ten minutes' interval from the Auguststrasse to East Berlin's one-way exit building (the 'Palace of Tears' pavilion, constructed in 1962 on a wasteland interval between the river Spree and the Friedrichstrasse station) before buying new day visas an instant after midnight and then re-entering East Berlin via the station's subterranes to head back on foot towards the ballroom's all-night seductions. That movement of irresistible city-traversing repetition (sharply evoked in 'The Passenger'), undertaken by figures propelled eastwards in transpiercing manoeuvres, through obsessions with East Berlin's bodies or its urban space, held a contrary dynamic to the desired movements and relocations of GDR inhabitants into West Berlin's space: movements that were often stalled, and became irreplicable whenever (usually after bureaucratic delays of years) they could be realized.

Once border-crossing foreign bodies passed through that interzone into East Berlin, they were immediately exposed to the glacial transpiercing aperture sensation of entering the petrified half-city of razings and fragments. Directly adjacent to the Friedrichstrasse station, a moment's span into East Berlin's space, those bodies encountered the voided site that had once held the luxurious Central Hotel, where the Skladanowsky brothers undertook the first projection in Berlin of celluloid films in 1895, before its destruction by bombing in 1943, the ruins then cleared in the following decade to create an

enduring wasteland. East Berlin's buildings lay under a thick carapace of lignate coal dust emerging from its chimneys, as well as being blackened by many decades of industrial pollution. Although wide-scale reconstructions of gutted or vanished buildings and immense new construction projects – pre-eminently, that of the Stalinallee's monumental avenue of housing blocks – were well under way in East Berlin by the beginning of the 1950s, lauded in films and newsreels of that era with titles such as *Wir Bauen Wohnungen* (*We're Building Apartments*, 1952), and accelerated in the GDR's final decade, that half-city still transmitted a tangible aura of dereliction to its infiltrators at the end of the 1970s, together with the emanation of occluded subservience experienced by many of its inhabitants. The heart-transpiercing sensation provoked, with delicate suddenness, by amalgams of longing, melancholy and nostalgia, and generated in its most unadulterated form in corporeal transits on foot through waste-landed or scarred cities of subjugated inhabitants, was embodied in Bowie's piece 'Subterraneans', from *Low* (1977), evoked by Bowie as holding fragments – such as its insurgent saxophone element – intended to convey 1970s East Berlin inhabitants' nostalgia for urban experiences that had disappeared or were now cruelly withheld (though many East Berlin inhabitants certainly experienced no trace of such sensations, and possessed their own distinctive cultures of music, performance and art). In walking northwards from the Friedrichstrasse area, through the Mitte and

Prenzlauer Berg districts, that transpiercing melancholy – as a projection from, and upon, East Berlin's urban space of excoriated, striated tenements, and of abandoned industrial buildings and workshops whose eroded signage indicated their near-forgotten previous incarnations – only intensified.

Berlin bodies are most thoroughly transpierced – to and through the corporeal core – as well as ocularly transfixed and reconfigured, on such bewildered city transits, propelled via an interrogatory and potentially expulsive act into urban space (rather than through a habitual inhabitation); such transits entail the sense of a pivotal loss of urban orientation and itinerary that was so lauded by early twentieth-century on-foot transiters of Berlin such as Hessel and Kracauer. At moments of deep disorientation, when the prevailing sense of topographic loss has faded out and been rendered obsolete, Berlin manifests itself as a network of corporeal impulsions and illegible indicators, that insistently requires the body to transpierce it.

Berlin bodies are transpierced, too, by skin-surface infiltrations, as with the narcotic syringe-puncturings (never fully traversing the veins and arteries, and never resoluble) that made the western side-exits of the Zoologischer Garten station, together with its passengers' toilets, notorious around the end of the 1970s and the early 1980s through the experiences in West Berlin of the teenaged heroin addict Christiane Felscherinow ('Christiane F.'), as narrated in her book, which was later made into a film, and also by the necessity, in the corporeal affrontment of the contemporary city by young Berlin bodies, of pervasive self-infiltrations – via tongue studs and tattoo needles, and by metal rings traversing and encircling the skin, musculature and ligaments of sexual organs and facial features – that overhaul the status of corporeal apparitions in Berlin via the accumulation within its sites of metallic 'foreign bodies'. Such new elements transpierced into Berlin bodies cast the visual rapport between corporeality and urban space into unprecedented forms, in a parallel way to that in which other foreign bodies – passengers of the 1970s manoeuvring their way through interzonal terrains of alien scrutiny – finally pierced through the urban skin-boundary of East Berlin before plummeting into its streets' compelling voids.

EXUDATIONS

Berlin's passengers – pre-eminently those transpierced by rings, tattoo needles and studs, and conducting frenzied all-night manoeuvres by S-bahn train or in taxis between nightclubs (manoeuvres prefigured obliquely by those narrated by Iggy Pop in 'The Passenger', and in 'Nightclubbing', 1977) often sited in subterranean or peripheral terrains, such as the wastelands around the Magdalena and Berghain nightclubs – transmit distinctive city-inflected corporeal exudations of the sheer exertion demanded by Berlin for such rigorous nocturnal transits: exudations of body fluids and sexual fluids, hand-carried narcotic and alcoholic accessories, perfumes, the septic aura of unhealed piercings, the raw emanation of scars and woundings, and cold transpirations. Those bodies may also project exudations from extreme sensations directly provoked by topographical traversals of Berlin, such as anger and desire, or outbursts of frustration at painstakingly entering a wasteland after a lengthy transit, and discovering that the nightclub destination once located there has been abruptly razed or closed down (consigned to the near-infinite genealogy of obsolete Berlin nightclubs: Chez Romy Haag, Fischbüro, Exit, Maria am Ostbahnhof). Bodies transiting Berlin to initiate riots, or returning from riots, propel their own unique exudations into S-bahn carriages and wider urban space: the tang of blood from heads battered by riot-police weaponry, or the transmission of exhilaration. Such exudations are accentuated by the city space that grated or deposited their content into the skins and apertures of Berlin bodies, as the embedded, abraded traces of a glacial envelopment of those bodies by the engulfing city, to enable those exudations then to be projected outwards, notably to other passengers, who may receive them obliviously, as they conduct their own transits and emit their own regimes of exudation.

Exudation possesses an exceptional status among Berlin's projections, since, in its externally directed propulsions of corporeal elements, it operates

erratically and eruptively, and in unforeseen and often
invisible ways, and thereby carries a seminal manifestation of the process by which Berlin bodies expend
and enact themselves. Exudations, such as those
from Berlin's nocturnal S-bahn passengers, constitute
(alongside their outrages) a subtly infiltrating projection
that can possess minuscule, fragmentary components,
which may be impossible to defuse or resist in their
oblique, non-linear overcomings of other Berlin
passengers' bodies. Exudations, with their infinite
gradations and amalgams, hold and disclose almost-
lost memories and delicate, barely subsisting corporeal
sensations, and are notably transmitted (as well as
from the skins and piercings of living, moving bodies)
from Berlin's filmic sequences and photographs,
such as those of early twentieth-century bodies
documented in now-vanished districts of the city
such as the Scheunenviertel and the Fischerinsel,
with their constricted alleys, whose density instilled
those bodies with the need compulsively to exude
vocal sounds and physical gestures. From moving-
image screens and photographic surfaces, elapsed
or erased Berlin bodies can still transpierce the 'skin'
of their medium to re-enter the city, in the form of
corporeal exudations that infiltrate and inhabit the
eyes of their viewers. Filmic sequences and photographic residues of the street-located apparitions of
bodies in Berlin's once-central districts that are now
utterly disappeared, such as that around the Petriplatz

(a core square of the Middle Ages era for Berlin's

historical expansion), part-destroyed during the Soviet forces' capture of the city in April 1945 and then comprehensively razed across the following two decades by GDR ruin-detonation and clearance squads, form vital exudations (and city dead exhumations) of corporeal and urban presences so obliterated that they can now only be transmitted and animated in such delicate, tangential fragments.

The departures of bodies from Berlin may form sleight-of-hand corporeal exudations as well as more spectacular exits and ejections. Crossing points during the GDR era such as the Glienicke Bridge formed locations in which occluded city-edge exchanges or releases of bodies (spies, dissidents) could be conducted in covert nocturnal dealings, so that bodies were mysteriously exuded – as momentary interstitial passengers – into another zone. The subterranes of the Friedrichstrasse station formed a space into which bodies unwanted by the GDR authorities could be surreptitiously propelled, beyond its border, into that labyrinth of interpiercing spaces, and left to find their way into West Berlin. Whenever a body leaves Berlin behind, its city-inflicted constellations of skin-imprinted sensations and scarifications accompany it, exuded into the beyond-Berlin space which that body then enters; the absence of such bodies, having interrogatively transited Berlin and now vanished, also forms a pivotal source of enduring exudations within the city, only reinforced in their spectral projections by that defining corporeal voiding.

Bodies may slip out of Berlin as a result of
unenvisaged stumblings and spatial malfunctions;
the city's veering terrain can tip or jettison bodies
in such a liminal, obfuscated way that such corporeal
mishaps form exudations, rather than exits. An exudation possesses no clear itinerary; a stray Berlin body
may have become enmeshed in the city's subterranean
strata and never re-emerged, or have entered a peripheral, wastelanded space from which paths of re-entry
into those elements of the city overseen by surveillance
media are foreclosed or cannot be located. In a parallel
way to that in which miraculous, inexplicable corporeal
appearances in urban space cannot (at least immediately) be accounted for – from Kaspar Hauser's sudden
manifestation in Nuremberg in 1828 to the notorious,
fraudulent 'Forest Boy' Robin van Helsum's mediatized
entry into Berlin in 2011, claiming he had been living in
forests south of the city – exudations of bodies out of
urban space also form mysterious, untenable transits
in which the body has vanished but, via its emitted
traces, is still there. The display in the 2014 exhibition
of artefacts and projections from Bowie's archives
held at the Martin-Gropius-Bau museum, of the never-
returned set of keys for his rented apartment in the
Hauptstrasse, intimates a limbo process of liminally
hovering disappearance from Berlin, across 1978–9,
in the form of a corporeal exudation, rather than a
categorical decision finally to leave. In a manoeuvre
of exudation, the body is zonally blurred, oblivious

to time, half-in and half-out of Berlin, and still

ineradicably attached to the city by the markings into urban space of that body's exuded, accumulated detrita.

EXPULSIONS

Movements of Berlin's bodies take the form also of violent, intentional, systematic expulsions from urban space, as contrary transits to those of delicately poised exudations whose originating impetus is often obscured and whose destination is unknown. Expulsions may be so rigorously planned and scheduled, with relentless reiteration, that even the medium of expulsion itself and that expulsive movement's destination constitute Berlin's elements in movement and material annexes, as with the wagons that transported the Nazi-era city's lethally abjected inhabitants to extermination camps, notably Sachsenhausen on the northern periphery of Berlin, and, further to the north, alongside one of the Havel lakes, the Ravensbrück camp intended primarily for women (deported from many other cities as well as Berlin), so that those wagons duly returned to their originating stations for the expulsions of the next day or week, and the camps in proximity to Berlin effectively became 'sub-cities' of Berlin, in a parallel process to that in which satellites pivoting around large-scale extermination camps, such as Auschwitz, formed 'sub-camps'. In any act of expulsion from Berlin envisaged and planned by city authorities, political factions or autonomous, covert entities such as criminal cartels, a particular instance or manifestation of corporeality is determined to be aberrant, alien and dangerously antithetical to a fixed functional conception of urban space and its operations, and so must now be expelled, as with the way in which the GDR city authorities of the early 1980s conceived of the bodies of East Berlin's punk rock gangs as unassimilable to central city space (notably in their drunken, erratic traversals of the Alexanderplatz, tracked by surveillance cameras) and ordered that they needed to be expulsively confined to the urban peripheries or else dispatched to military camps and prisons.

Expulsions, in their often obsessional performance, are intended as expungings that will leave no detrital trace; once a body has been expelled from Berlin, its site of urban habitation may be immediately dismantled or razed with a parallel violence to the act of corporeal expulsion itself. Since the targeted body is perceived as a contamination of the city, the media and artefacts of that urban despoliation need to be subtracted from its visual arena too; not even the ashes of expelled bodies can subsist in Berlin's city-dead subterranes, and those bodies are either distanced from urban space before their annulling or else rapidly disinterred from its subterranes (as with the executed bodies of Claus von Stauffenberg and his core group of plotters, disinterred from their location in the Alter St Matthäus cemetery as soon as Hitler learned of their 'dignified' burial, and then incinerated, before those ashes were expelled to an unknown site, perhaps aerially dispersed onto wastelands beyond Berlin's limits). In all cases, the journey of expulsion also cancels the characteristic elations associated with the sensorial and ocular regime of Berlin's passengers, whose own inner-city journeys oscillate between insistent repetition and flux. Journeys of expulsion from Berlin transform and overturn the status of corporeality itself, as with that in 1943 of Coco Schumann, whose transits of the preceding years between nightclubs – playing swing guitar at several different venues, often covertly, during the course of one night – had emblematically been those of a Berlin passenger (over three decades before the nightclubbing transits of Iggy Pop and Bowie), and whose intended one-way extermination-camp deportation, initially to Theresienstadt, once his physical presence in Berlin – as a half-Jewish inhabitant born there – was determined illicit, simultaneously comprised a corporeal expulsion from Berlin and a journey intended to raze all trace in the city of his vanished body, its cultural history and its gestures.

The covert entries into Berlin of refugee bodies, and their inhabitation of outdoor camps of shacks – such as that constructed in 2012 in the Oranienplatz area of Kreuzberg, then razed by riot police in 2014 in an operation which involved the violent ejection of activists and protesters from the site – form the optimum target for city authorities' contemporary expulsions of Berlin's provisional, precipice-hanging bodies into occluded spaces (such as hostels and 'shelters', often located beyond Berlin's limits). Camps such as that in the Oranienplatz – in an area closely associated with 1970s occupation movements and with riots against spatial appropriations by city-authority-sanctioned developers, among many other contest-ations – with their improvised, ragged tarpaulin coverings and openness to rain and ice, entail an acutely exposed condition of corporeality in which refugee bodies are positioned in perpetual affrontment with urban space, and in which the sustaining, even momentarily, of refugee existence demands physical endurance along with incessant negotiations to suspend imminent expulsion. In all such provisional-space affrontments, as with activists' occupation and squatting initiatives, Berlin's spatial expulsions intractably ensue.

An act of urban expulsion can also be undertaken against and within the city, as a refusal or negation by Berlin's bodies of unbearable urban space with its constraints and fissurations, or of the intolerable conjunction which that space ignites with corporeality or psychic space, often entailing a self-willed or psychotic act of falling, from a tower or point of elevation. On a number of occasions, on nocturnal transits of Berlin on foot across decades, I saw screaming figures threatening to propel themselves from the summits of monuments or multi-storey constructions they had just scaled, or the immediate residues of such acts of plummeting; a sequence in Wenders's film *Wings of Desire* presents the city-expulsive suicide fall of an earphoned teenager from a prominent West Berlin tower as a near-oblivious disabused gesture of urban disdain. Such falls also form a desired summary expulsion of all trace of the city from the body, in an extreme instance of the ways in which Berlin bodies may attempt to expel or excrete noxious urban engulfings or infiltrations, as with the inassimilable mineral components accumulated in those bodies from exposure to the engrained toxicity and emissions of the city's terrain, especially in former East Berlin industrial sites. Those self-willed falls hinge, after a vertiginous interval, on a hard collision with urban space itself, since the endpoint of such a plummeting transit returns the body to the city's unforgiving ground-level surface. Once such a fall has been expulsively launched, the body's own velocity transports it back to the city. But urban self-expulsions can also, less terminally, extend the domain of the passenger's transits into freefall beyond Berlin's space.

PASSENGERS

Berlin's passengers ignite and revivify the city, annulling its petrifactions and its expulsive capacity. A Berlin body in excessive movement cannot readily be located or appropriated for regimes of expulsion. The status of Berlin's passengers projects a countering city ownership to that already enforced in complicity or corruption between city authorities and developers (that pre-existing ownership manifested in razings, surveillances and engulfing malfunctions such as that of Berlin's new airport of the 2010s, and implying the supreme authority to expel inhabiting or refugee bodies). The passenger may then even assume a proprietorial pre-eminence, as in the line from 'The Passenger', emerging from nocturnal ocular trans-piercings of the windows of taxis and S-bahn carriages during Berlin nightclub transits: 'all of this is yours and mine'. That collectively proprietorial status of the Berlin passenger is anomalous, shattered in its asser-tion: the passenger never owns, or even drives. Such a proprietorial rapport with Berlin's space is conjured directly from a corporeal and ocular experience gener-ated via the momentum of that act of nocturnal transit with its seminal, incanted repetitions and demands; once the passenger's body exits Berlin's transit zones, and its propulsions are stilled and its eyes' input is drained and walled, that urban-proprietorial compulsion deliquesces.

Berlin's passengers are transported through the city in containers – in the late 1970s era of 'The Passenger': decades-old, juddering S-bahn carriages with dilapidated, bare wooden seating and never-cleaned windows, and cigarette-smoke-filled taxis often driven in approximate directions by Turkish and Iranian exiles – that themselves contribute nothing to the transit other than in perceptually concentrating it, as the passenger screens out the cracked S-bahn seats' discomfort or the taxi radio's high-volume tulum or

Googoosh music. Contemporary passengers, on Berlin's S-bahn trains, also have their own narratives contested by those of itinerant figures narrating, in desperation and for donations, individual histories of calamity, expulsion or falls – with relentless repetition, those histories perpetually re-launched, via rapid transits to another carriage's space, at successive stations – as though such recitants require the propulsion of their medium of transport in order to pin down their near-unseizable narratives of corporeal disintegration. Passengers exist only in the velocity and interzonal space of the transit itself, focused on the screen window whose infiltration by the eye interrogates the city and, in fragments, reveals it to them.

The window-focused moment of sudden illumina-tory self-interrogation of 'The Passenger' ('what does he see?') embodies the mid-transit juncture of reflection that precipitates all of the evocations, explorations and transmutations – across music, art, performance, writing and other media – that amass fragmentary, momentary traces of Berlin's cityscapes and the bodies inhabiting them. That vision may be of blurred pre-dawn emptied-out streets, from a taxi's window, in which the neon signage of a final nightclub will imminently veer into focus. From an S-bahn carriage window, fragments of the envisioning of Berlin mani-fest themselves in more rapid sequences: the S-bahn line's transit directly between the shrapnel-indented walls of the Museum Island's exhibition rooms, with insights into the bodies in the museums' spaces and the river panoramas on all sides; the transit (one filmed from an adjacent highway in Siodmak and Ulmer's *People on Sunday*, to intimate the exhilaration at their momentary escape from overheated city space of the S-bahn carriage's occupants, who have wrenched open all windows and doors so that no intervening medium now exists in their contact with their propulsive transit itself) through the Grunewald forest towards the Wannsee; the transit across industrial zones and corroded sidings of eastern Berlin, with glimpses of voided GDR plazas for corporeal amassings in front of the Memorial to the Socialists in Lichtenberg and the Thälmann memorial in Prenzlauer Berg, and transits alongside firewalls and tenements in whose windows bodies are abruptly exposed to the city-infiltrating eyes of passengers. Such transits possess the sense of an infinitely expansive dimension, potentially reeling into ocular freefall or exhaustion, and extending via peripheral wastelands and urban edges beyond Berlin's space.

At the same time, those transits hold their own limitations imposed by the finite number of Berlin's S-bahn lines, so that they encompass a constrained archive of buildings and edge-lands potentially to be scanned, and a boundaried, constricted sequence of corporeal visions. During the late 1970s era of the S-bahn transits invoked in 'The Passenger', that sense of constriction had imposed itself far more intensely, with many S-bahn lines closed or transected by Berlin's internal boundaries, and with the ownership of the entire S-bahn network (then operated, even across its West Berlin stretches, by the GDR transport authorities) itself contested, together with the immense disused strips of birch-tree-covered railway yards whose potential for spatial experimentation began to engage West Berlin's urban ecologists in that same era; acute infrastructural neglect and station shutdowns, together with passenger shortages resulting from West Berliners' disdain for the S-bahn system, led to many carriages running near-empty, as ghost trains passing through ghost stations. The closest S-bahn station along the line transiting the Schöneberg district in a deep cutting behind the back-courtyard firewalls of the Haupt-strasse building inhabited by Iggy Pop and Bowie (so that those trains' irregular passages, jolts and misfiring engines would have been audible there), Kolonnen-strasse station, had been destroyed by aerial bombing in 1944 and remained closed, the overgrown ruins of the old platforms enclosing the rusted lines which still traversed that station's site.

The passenger forms an aberrant, contrary entity in Berlin's corporeal cultural histories. That figure is invariably entranced by the repetition and flux of its transits, and is able to transmit its ocular and sensorial perception of Berlin's cityscapes and bodyscapes, viewed in fragments through the windows especially of S-bahn trains, into illuminating re-envisionings and new fragmentations of urban and corporeal space, notably in art, music and writing. But, at the same time, the passenger is a figure who always stubbornly eludes becoming immersed or embedded in the city, with its teeming confrontations and activist dilemmas, such as those over its bodies' expulsions and the appropriations of occupied space. The passenger never durationally inhabits Berlin, and only incisively *glances* the city, corporeally and visually, in immediate collisions and conjunctions, riding and riding . . .

4
THE EYE
OF BERLIN

OCULAR BODY-PROPULSIONS . EYE-FOCUSED
SENSATIONS . FILM . CINEMAS . PROJECTIONS .
VISIONS . EXPOSURES . GUIDING BLIND BODIES .
BERLIN ART

OCULAR BODY-PROPULSIONS

Berlin possesses and is envisioned by its own, unique and contrary ocular regime: the eye of Berlin is an entity of fragmentation that contrarily binds corporeality and urban space. In formative contacts with Berlin, such as those experienced at first sightings after a traversal via autobahn lanes or transit-corridor train-tracks across boundaries of exudation and expulsion, as surrounded Berlin in the 1970s, and also those experienced in the contemporary moment, the city operates a distinctive overhauling of the incoming eyes of its passengers. That experience may, in its extreme instance, result in a fundamental anatomical transformation of the eye – especially in the ways in which it perceives the projections of urban surfaces, as well as sequences of film images and digital-media images in their representations and embodiments of those surfaces via an intensified and flux-inflected focus on corporeality – through physically exposed contacts, interrogatory engagements and exploratory infiltrations of Berlin's strata. Notably, the eye itself then constitutes a dynamic source of propulsion for the bodies of Berlin's passengers, whose journeys may remain ridden in perpetual elation across the awry and striated tracks of the city's surfaces, or can eventually become deeply embedded into Berlin's contestations and inhabitations – or else oscillate fluidly between those two antithetical forms of ocular journeys. The eye is an unstuck medium in Berlin.

In 1957–9, in their film *Hauptstadt Berlin* (*Capital City Berlin*), the British modernist architects Alison and Peter Smithson envisioned the construction of an immense eye at what they conceived as the city's very centre, as the pivotal element of their architectural plans (also formulated in extravagant topographical designs, drawings and mappings) for the then-ongoing reconstruction and replanning of the entirety of Berlin.[18] In that era, Berlin held its *Hauptstadt* status solely in the eastern half of the city, with Bonn assigned the role of capital of the Federal Republic, for which West Berlin formed an increasingly stranded and spectral annex. The late 1950s frenzy of international architectural competitions and invitations for projects to reconceive Berlin as an entire entity (rather than redesign particular areas, such as the Hansaplatz or the Frankfurter Allee), with many of those projects documented in promotional films, abruptly halted in 1961 with the Wall's construction, which would have situated the Smithsons' eye in East Berlin if it had actually been built; Berlin's wide-scale reconstruction continued, notably in the Alexanderplatz, but with more focused imperatives.

In Peter Smithson's spoken commentary for the *Hauptstadt Berlin* film (assembled by the Smithsons' collaborator John McHale), whose moving-image sequences show traffic flows in London rather than in Berlin, he emphasizes the necessity to disregard 'historic spaces' in order to prioritize the 'specific poetry' to be generated by new forms of urban and corporeal movement, such as rapid cross-city expressways and pedestrian escalators that converge in locations of 'maximum intensity, of maximum experience' and pre-eminently around 'a Great Eye'. The eye at Berlin's heart, for the Smithsons, would take the form of a vast all-encompassing museum of future technologies with an ovular construction, to be 'suspended' high up on pillars over the junction of the Friedrichstrasse and the Leipziger Strasse. That museum's ocular emanation would then activate and resuscitate the ruined city, rendering it an unceasingly innovative technological megalopolis. The Smithsons' 'Great Eye' for Berlin constitutes an aberrant medium of vision, as though primed to capture future urban catastrophes along with technological advances, as well as a vital precursor of the contemporary digitized city of innumerable surveillance camera-lenses and watchful urban screens, attached to buildings in Berlin's plazas and avenues, that together form one engulfing eye of corporeal scrutiny and potential negation.

The eye (and its avatars: photography, film, digital media) comprises a multiplicitous revelator and anatomizer of cities' arenas, assigning an infinite range of inflections and projections into urban space. In ocular cultural histories, the urban-focused capacities of the eye became a topic of concentrated investigation across the decades around the beginning of the twentieth century that encompassed the activation of photography into moving-image forms, almost invariably with a focus on re-evaluations or recastings of cities. Such investigations encompass, for example, that of the city

as a dangerous context for the oncoming bodies of
murder-weapon-wielding assassins or of executioners,
in the terminal eye-images extracted from the retinas
of the city dead, in Wilhelm Kühne's science of optography, in 1880s Heidelberg and Berlin; the city as a
visually attuned medium configured optimally for the
projection to the spectating eye of image-sequences
of urban bodies, including malfunctioning bodies,
in Muybridge's construction of the first space (his
'Zoopraxographical Hall') designed exclusively for
the projection of moving images to public audiences,
in 1890s Chicago; and the city as a delirious, perverse
space receptive to ocular experimentation, expanding
from film to new capacities for urban transmutation of
the eye itself, in Dziga Vertov's 'kino-eye' projects and
theories in the 1920s cities of the Soviet Union. Such

experiments in re-envisioning global city space underpin and in many ways already pre-emptively surpass those being developed in contemporary urban arenas (notably in cities experiencing conflict or very rapid technological innovation) with their focus upon ocular capacities, such as body-triggered moving-image surveillance systems and physically or neurally sensitized handheld and retinally implanted devices.

In its cultural histories, the eye forms an exposed, active receptor and reconfigurer of urban environments, most acutely so in Berlin, during its period as a world centre of innovation in moving-image capture and projection, oscillating between the eye and the city, in the 1890s and 1900s, as well as during its 1920s period of experimental preoccupations with urban vision in film, with works such as those of Ruttmann, Moholy-Nagy and Lang, and also in the contemporary moment, especially with anonymous and compulsive ocular acts rendered in moving-image media from Berlin's external spaces. A cultural history of ocular Berlin – as opposed to a wider one of corporeal Berlin – is necessarily constituted of fragments that are read from the eye-marked strata and surfaces of the city itself and its transiting bodies, as intersecting and isolated visions, inscriptions, damagings, apertures, blindnesses, revelations and corporeal movements.

Such a cultural history of the Berlin ocular – which could, with parallel validity, take the form of an abandoned fragment of an eye-focused act or a comprehensive survey of every event and moving-image sequence ever archived, recorded or documented (accelerating far beyond all accumulative archival capacities in the digital era) that infiltrates the urban into the ocular or the ocular into the urban, in Berlin's space – encompasses the eye's dual rapport with Berlin's bodies and with Berlin's cityscapes. In tracking corporeality in Berlin's space, across the span of a transit or over decades, the eye's acts amass a content that signals bodies' intimacies and collisions with that space, in their mediation via gazings, glancings, peerings, starings, weepings, poppings, winkings, tics, eyelid-closings and other ocular gestures. In its focus upon urban corporeality, the interrogative eye is often drawn first to scan the eyes and ocular manoeuvres of Berlin bodies; the eye is compulsively adhered to the eye, as the primary organ of urban perception, before (even only a split second later) investigating the sonic and aural domains of Berlin's inhabitation, or its other sensorial dimensions.

In tracking Berlin cityscapes, the eye isolates the elements of those surfaces which impel corporeal movement: propulsions through fascination (including the permutations by which figures are activated into urban consumptions of all kinds), fear, desire, obsession, in sleepwalking oblivion, or through the anger of protest. Those surface-located elements in Berlin may take the forms of displays and inscriptions, veering from the obsolete and near-invisible to the technologically innovative and eye-seizing. Across Berlin's ocular cultural history, such media formatively include the

announcements of free-standing paper-based hoardings (installed widely in Berlin's streets from the 1850s on, and still present, as the eye-oriented postered circular columns known, after their Berlin-based inventor's name, as *Litfass-säulen*, which, in their many variants, announced ongoing entertainments as well as deaths, murders, injunctions for Berlin-disqualified inhabitants to amass at particular locations for expulsion, and the faces and details of the war-lost) and the prominently displayed contents of digital moving-image screens – as well as the negated non-contents of such media as blown-out neon signage, effaced graffiti, expired monuments, near-wiped children's pavement chalk drawings, and other instances of voided eye-media which direct the body into nowheres and wastelands. The eye in transit in Berlin amasses and archives sequences of ocular propulsions of bodies across the city's space.

EYE-FOCUSED SENSATIONS

If the eye looks away from Berlin's prominent surfaces, it is still gazing at the city, in peripheral vision: at ground level, with its imminent collapsings via neglected tarmac or long-fissured paving into subterranes that may contain the ruins of obsolete nightclubs or shelters from wartime fire-bombings; at wastelands constellated with the residual debris of their abandonment or scorched-earthing, alongside traces of the more recent experiments (often with ecological, performance- or art-oriented preoccupations) undertaken there; at the neglected inscriptions, codes and friezes that distinctively endure in the details of GDR-era buildings and factories, often caught only at unlooked-for tangents; at swathes of overgrown railway tracks, leading from now-vanished termini such as the Stettiner Bahnhof and the Görlitzer Bahnhof, from which passengers were expunged many decades ago, replaced by profuse growths of birch trees; at stumbling stones; at strata of signage, in eroded paint or in blown-out neon letterings, layered over one another above shops, stores or ateliers that were once crammed with intently working Berlin bodies, and are now emptied out; and at blank or graffitied firewalls that stretch far along the sides of entire buildings, in the form of hundreds of thousands of bricks (sometimes cemented over, sometimes left rawly visible) painstakingly accumulated by workers' gestures a century or more ago, to generate an immense void facade on which Berlin's sensations ignite and transmutate. The eye's direct or oblique, fragmentary, occluded, veering engagement with Berlin's urban surfaces uniquely generates such sensations which, in their flux-driven amalgams, notably in transits across the megalopolis, constitute incessantly renewed Berlin corporealities.

Ocular sensations incited by dynamic contact with Berlin's jagged, excessive urban surfaces are often so corporeally infiltrating and inundating that they lead contrarily to meltdowns and petrifactions, during which the body visually enmeshed in Berlin must stand still and gaze in apparent hypnosis at the city, in order to absorb other, hybrid and unknown sensations. Such sensorially provoked corporeal rootings in urban space take on multiple variants, encompassing the sensation that the body is located *elsewhere* (one noted in the 1920s by Kracauer as a seminal mid-transit experience of Berlin, and undergone still more intensively in the up-ended locations of Berlin's contemporary terrain), the sensation of a pinioning, vertiginous hallucination generated by a minuscule urban detail, and the sensation that all of the proliferating histories, memories and archives of Berlin are abruptly insurging – with incapacitating simultaneity – in one site and around one body. A status of oblivion or unknowing directed towards Berlin's histories only exposes the body still more acutely towards such sensory stillings in urban space. Since Berlin's space is immense and reeling in its dimensions, with relatively few overpopulated plazas (even its great axis points, as with the Alexanderplatz and Potsdamer Platz, possess diffuse, vacated zones across their expanses), such visually captivated standing-still bodies often perform that ocular act, of rendering the city's contents into sensation, in a condition of isolation.

One evening of summer storms, I took the lift to the summit of a 27-storey apartment-tower: one of a sequence of eight (four adjacent, interconnected pairs of towers) running eastwards along the south side of the Leipziger Strasse's wide avenue, then onto the adjacent Fischerinsel, and designed in 1972 for inhabitation by the GDR's elites, in a misfired attempt, during a period of acute architectural sclerosis in the GDR, to envision an ocularly seizing 'showcase' boulevard whose city-animating urban dynamic would parallel that of the Stalinallee's riot-fraught but spectacular construction twenty years earlier. The tower was only a short distance from the planned location of the Smithsons' unbuilt 'Great Eye', formulated around fifteen years before the tower's construction, and still suspended as a phantom absence over Berlin at a height approximating that of the tower. Before making my ascent, I had covertly explored the derelict salon that extended across almost the entire ground floor of that tower, with its semi-collapsed ceiling and flooring and its gouged walls scattering low-grade masonry across the plastic armchairs and drinks tables; the tower's original residents had met, danced and socialized in that salon, but its use had become obsolete with the post-GDR reassigned ownership of the tower and subsequent departure or expulsion of many of those residents. At some point soon afterwards, work had begun to overhaul it into a restaurant or gymnasium (as with almost all of the other ground floors of that sequence of towers) but had been abandoned with evident suddenness, as though through the intervention of an outlandish urban petrifaction, leaving that salon in ruined suspension. From the summit's balcony, oriented to the east and southeast, I gazed out in a skewed arc from the Zeughaus building alongside the Spreekanal, then across the site of the razed Petriplatz directly below and up towards the Alexanderplatz, then southeastwards across Friedrichshain's steeples, factory chimneys and towers, and over the river to Kreuzberg and Neukölln, then on towards the light-blurred urban peripheries. At that instant, Berlin appeared a city of diabolical, elating fragments. All around and above, the sky was rapidly darkening and lightning flashed behind Ulbricht's Fernsehturm, but that panorama remained obstinately unilluminated, so that my eyes had to exploratively search low-lying, duplicitous contours for attempted spatial orientation and identification, as though scanning an elusive body, in a film-inflected act of ocular surveillance that generated its own sensations of tactile urban assembling, editing, manoeuvring and dissection, before being exposed, in that act's moment of impasse, to the engulfing, eye-transpiercing sensations projected back from that cityscape.

Often, walking through Berlin, I traverse locations multiply transformed across my ocular contacts over time with them, such as the Prenzlauer Berg district's Helmholtzplatz: a haunted East Berlin square of striated, excoriated tenements assigned for demolition and largely populated by activists and dissidents, alongside the immovably elderly, in 1979; then an in-limbo, part-vacated, thin-air interzone of momentary art galleries and bars, in 1990; then a massively renovated, gentrified property hub with an entirely new population of bodies (its 1979 and 1990 residents' bodies almost all gone), in 2017. Memory itself generates sensations from those simultaneously present experiences of urban space, in volatile compactings that may supplant one moment with another or else carry all of them together in dense ocular and sensorial strata. Those eye-focused experiences of Berlin's space also absorb sensorial resonances from the expanses of time not memorially experienced, and recuperable primarily via photographs, as for example from the Helmholtzplatz's initial construction out of an infernal industrial terrain of furnaces and smelting across the 1880s and '90s, its overspilling tenements' swarming inhabitation by factory and brewery workers in the 1920s, its terror-inciting destructions by bombing and street fighting in 1943–5, and its subjecting to the GDR's urban and architectural imperatives in the 1950s and '60s.[19] Such sensorial amassings from fragments of memory and of city-trace projections, sieved and rendered by ocular processes, themselves generate infinite eyes of Berlin.

FILM

Film carries, substantiates, fabricates or replaces memory, as in its capacity to hold its own sequences of Berlin's locations and bodies resonating with individual memories of the city's corporeal space, as it existed moments or many decades ago, but it also forms a special entity of urban encounter for Berlin's eyes. In many ways, film's origination is centrally a Berlin phenomenon, with the demands for innovation and vision-oriented technological resources of the

1880s–'90s city enabling the moving-image experiments of the Skladanowsky brothers and Ottomar Anschütz (as well as the televisual experiments of Paul Nipkow), and their projection innovations of 1894–5 in the auditoria of the Friedrichstrasse's Central Hotel and the Oranienburgerstrasse's Postfuhramt building; other moving-image pioneers, Muybridge above all, visited Berlin in that era and demonstrated their experiments to avid eyes in the Urania lecture hall. Berlin's locations and amassings of bodies invariably provided compelling materials to be filmed, and its artisanal workshop culture, in areas such as Prenzlauer Berg and Pankow, enabled adept solutions (albeit momentary, imminently obsolete ones) to be implemented for impasses in projection technologies that had derailed many inventors' projects over the previous decade. Alongside Paris and New York, 1890s Berlin created film as an incandescent urban medium that seized and transformed bodies in city space and vitally activated Berlin's eyes.

Film possesses an intimate rapport with the eye in envisioning and image-sequencing Berlin's corporeality and cityscapes, from the 1890s to the final moments of the twentieth century, but that rapport also encompassed a fierce contestation for pre-eminence between film and the eye as urban media. Film usurped the eye through its speed and revivifying capacity to transpierce time and spatial constraints, but it also rendered Berlin's streets as spectral zones of the city dead, while the eye's visions, even at their most habitual, were instilled solely in the lived immediacy of the current moment. Film captivated the eye with intensity for its sequences' duration but then lapsed, while the eye continued enduringly to scan city space and its bodies. Berlin's city-focused films of the late 1920s and early '30s demonstrate obsessions with the role of the ocular and with anatomizing the figure of the eye in its perception of urban space, in that era when film was often perceived as supplanting or extending the eye's capacities. But once film's experimental era had ended, at the moment of the rise of totalitarian regimes across much of Europe, it retreated into a documentational domain as the eye's surrogate in searching Berlin's space for evidence of proliferating architectural ambition (as with the 1930s filmings of buildings and stadia intended to form part of the Europe-dominating megalopolis of Germania), and then as the eye-replicating recorder and verifier of Berlin's destructions and razings, as in the sequences shot from aerial transits in 1945 of the most decimated parts of the city, such as the areas around the Frankfurter Allee, in which the eye of Berlin witnesses its own engulfing erasure via film. The eye often guided film's focus on urban space, its retina intimately posed against glass apertures, as with handheld Super-8 cameras of the 1960s, as though film risked being nullified without ocular orientation; that acute proximity between eye and lens, in rendering Berlin bodies, endured until the development of mobile devices held at arm's length in registering digital sequences of corporeal acts. But the eye could also contrarily induce film into fragmentation, distortion and aberration, in its seizing of Berlin's bodies.

In the cultural history of Berlin bodies, film often served, from its first decades, as an effective means by which city inhabitants' eyes (especially the eyes of those who had entered Berlin's industrial domain from rural communities, in its immense expansions) learned how to manoeuvre themselves purposefully through the city in straight lines, to use transport systems and to conduct acts of leisure. Newsreels, in particular, directed the eye towards Berlin bodies' gestures and spectacular feats, and also demonstrated the city-exiting movements of troop columns marching along avenues such as Unter den Linden, towards railway stations from which they would be transported in westward and eastward directions for massacre on First World War battlefields. In that conflict's aftermath, during Berlin's chaos of the winter of 1918–19, pacification-oriented newsreels showed the lines of police moving to quell revolutionary riots. Throughout the four decades of the GDR, and up until its last moments, films of mass corporeal spectacles staged in the avenues of East Berlin, such as those adjoining the Alexanderplatz – often to exhibit weaponry and to mark anniversaries, with intricate arrangements and processions of synchronized bodies moving and marching in formation – served to habituate the eyes of its inhabitants to mobile corporeality as urban linearity.

Conversely, film also worked as a medium of urban subversion and aberration to expose Berlin's eyes to the many ways in which the body in city space convulses or protests and negates linearity (as film itself does, especially in its experimental forms), from Expressionist film depictions of the 1910s–'20s with their emphasis on acts propelled in spasms by insanity and irrationality, or murderous acts driven purposelessly or out of obsession, to films documenting the student protests of the 1960s–'70s in which West Berlin's streets became the out-of-control arena of haywire, disorientated pulses and zigzags of protesters' bodies, and experimental or sexually dissident films of that same era, such as those of Rosa von Praunheim and Frank Ripploh, in which West Berlin's habitual corporeal parameters and ocular delineations were elatedly dissolved. Film's insistent seizing of 1970s gestures of urban repetition – in which an addict's body waits interminably for a narcotic transaction and then re-enacts that stasis, or in which a desperate figure unendingly cruises West Berlin's nocturnal avenues, night after night – intimated to the city's eyes that urban movements could also be interrogative, obstinate ones that tested ocular as well as social confinings. In many ways, those filmic non-linear corporeal manoeuvres were able to transmit themselves into the eye's contemporary alliances with digital devices in their capture of image sequences in Berlin's space, in awry outbursts of bodies whose acts are cut, then resurge to be performed for the eye and cut again.

CINEMAS

Berlin's cinemas, especially those surviving from film's first decades, form distinctive ocular and corporeal spaces in which urban culture is enmeshed, in a concentrated form, into the eyes of Berlin bodies as they simultaneously absorb and project acts of vision. In those spaces, which generated the pre-eminent instance of Berlin bodies' experience of the city's transmutations, across the twentieth century and up to the contemporary moment, the eye is confronted both with film's sequences and with the sensorial intimacy (also in hearing and in smell) of other Berlin bodies, often engaged, in conditions such as those of all-night cult-film screenings or experimental events in which the spectator's status is integrally unhinged, in rapports of touch. Especially during moments of emergency and danger, such as those of imminent destructions by aerial bombing in 1943, darkened cinemas in Berlin would have been sites of intensive sexual contact, as well as forming relatively well-protected shelters, and resilient ruins, for inhabitation by desperate bodies. Along with providing screens for Berlin's eyes, across the twentieth century, to gauge visions of their surrounding city and of corporeality's presences and transits within and across it, Berlin's cinematic space also conveyed to its inhabiting bodies the tactile and sensorial emanations of its own architectural grandeur, together with that grandeur's dilapidation and cancellation across the second half of the twentieth century and into the digital era.

Berlin's first spaces of moving-image projection were not purpose-built. Although Muybridge's 1893 Zoopraxographical Hall in Chicago signalled for the first time that the spectatorship of moving-image sequences demanded a special architectural conception with a screen-focused seated auditorium, divided from the adjacent city but readily infiltratable from it (and marked on its street-facing facade with eye-attracting hoardings and exclamatory enticements indicating the timings of screenings), Berlin's first moving-image events of the first half of the 1890s occupied pre-existing buildings: Anschütz's postal building hall, the Skladanowsky brothers' hotel ballroom, Muybridge's scientific lecture hall. Restaurants' back rooms, notably those on Unter den Linden, became improvised screening spaces on a durational basis from the end of the 1890s. But by the second half of the 1900s, hundreds of small, purpose-built cinemas had appeared in Berlin, especially within urban neighbourhoods, often through the spatial adaptation of the ground-floor level of tenement buildings constructed in the preceding decades; such cinemas were often equipped with a bar for their waiting clientele, as at the Tilsiter Lichtspiele in the Friedrichshain district, opened in 1908. Entire streets began to proliferate with cinemas in that era, such as the Münzstrasse, located close to the Alexanderplatz, whose dense turmoils of bodies entering and exiting cinemas captivated Kracauer on his Berlin walks.

Far larger cinemas with vast auditoria and spacious seating, architecturally luxurious and styling themselves as 'palaces', appeared in the following decades, especially in the Charlottenburg district around the Kaiser-Wilhelm-Gedächtniskirche and Zoologischer

Garten station, such as the Zoo Palast (1925; the location of *Metropolis*'s 1927 Berlin premiere) and the Delphi Filmpalast (1928); outlying districts in southern Berlin such as Steglitz and Friedenau gave more space for expansive cinemas' architectural experimentation, as with the Titania Palast (1928) and Roxy Palast (1929). In many cases, cinemas' role of providing ocular arenas for corporeal image-projections could mutate in such film palaces into spaces for apparitions of 'live' bodies, notably for music performances such as Coco Schumann's swing-guitar performances at the Delphi Filmpalast, as well as Goebbels's delirium-propelled vocal performances of exhortations, framed either as introductions for the premieres of Nazi-sanctioned films or else as solo vocal performances, directly in front of the screen, as at the Titania Palast and the Ufa-Filmtheater in Friedrichshain. That capacity of cinemas to become live corporeal spaces endured after the wartime ruination and razing of many Berlin cinemas, notably through Marlene Dietrich's legendary vocal performance, her film image transacted into an already semi-ghostly manifestation of loved, loathed Berlin flesh, close to her birthplace on the Rote Insel and after many years of absence from the city, at the Titania Palast in 1960.

Berlin's film palaces transmutated from the 1960s when the entranced film spectators that had occupied them for decades abruptly evanesced and their locations on urban arteries rendered them obsolescent as the bodies streaming along those streets, especially in newly wealthy West Berlin, demanded other spectacles. Such transmutations of cinematic spaces invariably retained traces of film's resonant aura but uprooted those spaces' previously seated bodies into mobility, as the cinemas now often operated – architecturally unchanged, apart from their signage and lighting – as vast, cacophonic nightclubs. In their extreme instance, such spatial upheavals veered into incendiary, body-endangering ones, as in the occupation of the Roxy Palast's auditorium, after its lapsing as a cinema in the 1970s, by the La Belle nightclub, that space detonated (in a collaboration between Libyan and GDR state-security operatives), at 1.49 am on 5 April 1986, the bomb's blast fatally injuring three people, including two U.S. servicemen, and ripping open the wooden dancefloor so that many of the surviving dancers were sent plummeting into the former cinema's cellars. Eventually, its status as a nightclub erased, that cinema's auditorium was reoccupied in the 2010s by an eco-supermarket (as happened too with the auditorium of the notorious Eldorado nightclub, at the heart of the Schöneberg district's 1920s sexual experimentations, in which Anita Berber provocatively danced in a tuxedo and leather boots, before its closure at the first moment of the Nazi era); the auditoria of many other Berlin film palaces became warehouses or shopping complexes, or were simply abandoned and demolished.

All cultural histories of Berlin's visions and corporealities are distilled into the surviving spaces of the city's cinemas of the twentieth century's first decades.

To inhabit the elongated auditorium of the Tilsiter Lichtspiele (which operated from 1908 to the early 1960s, when the opening of the technologically advanced Kino International on the nearby Karl-Marx-Allee rendered it redundant for the remainder of the GDR's existence, until it reopened in the 1990s), Berlin bodies leave the sloping neighbourhood street of cracked-facaded tenements, enter the foyer below the facade's neon signage and traverse the cinema's decrepit bar. As with other surviving cinemas from that era, such as the Kino Pionier in the nearby Polish city of Szczecin – also opened in 1908, in what was then Berlin's port city of Stettin – the sensory traumas, vanishings and elations of film are engrained profoundly into the Tilsiter Lichtspiele's space, permeating the eyes that enter it, even before the film starts. In Berlin's few surviving film palaces, still in operation and archi-tecturally intact, such as the Delphi Filmpalast, the emanation of close to a century of Berlin bodies' amassings in intimacy, together with the spectral, eye-generated residues in that space of their engage-ments with film and its corporeal seizings, also forms a sensorially direct infiltration into Berlin's filmic envisioning.

But in the auditoria of Berlin's abandoned cinemas, especially those in far-outlying districts of the former East Berlin, their buildings too neglected or consigned to oblivion even to be converted into budget super-markets or demolished and turned into wastelands, that sense of an active corporeality and ocular residue still vitally marked into space is voided. The foyers' floors are covered in broken glass and their interior walls inscribed with already decades-old, fading graffiti; the rows of auditoria seating have buckled and collapsed as though under crushing pressure, and the screens are ripped or gone; the resilient 'Weimar-3' GDR-manufactured projectors, too obsolete to be stolen or dismantled, are still ready to operate but the celluloid reels left behind on rusted shelves, alongside near-illegible posters for early 1990s films, are now too damp and deteriorated to transit the projectors' aperture gates. Any bodies or eyes still detritally traced in such cinematic spaces – retaining their annulled status only by a hair's breadth – are exposed and disintegrated by urban abandonment's power of corporeal fragmentation.

PROJECTIONS

Projections are at their most vital and exposed when they malfunction, casting space and corporeal rapports into disarray and revealing their dynamics, as in the gaps in time – precipitated by projectors overheating or celluloid ripping, pivoting spectators' bodies abruptly face to face in anger or laughter – that formed a funda-mental experience of Berlin's cinemas across many decades, and especially in small neighbourhood cinemas, in districts such as Friedrichshain and Pankow, in which the same antiquated projection equipment often

traversed almost the entire cultural histories both of
film and of the surrounding streets' twentieth-century
forms. Finally, a worn-out projector becomes inopera-
tive, its white-hot aperture gate convulsing and its
sprockets unhinged, so that it slices sequences of
images of Berlin's cityscapes and bodies into fragments
that may be edged in fire; the eyes of the audience, in
cinemas such as the Tilsiter Lichtspiele, then perceive
such fragments of bodies wildly veering across or
propelled into Berlin's space, until both corporeality
and cityscape are subject to the conflagrations that
even the most infinitesimal, momentary petrifaction,
in projection's sensitized locations, can unleash.
The entirety of Berlin's urban configuring, across the
twentieth century, appears as though it had transited
a malfunctioning projector, obsolete and now inassimilable to the digital era, still fiercely illuminated even when
its historical demons appear momentarily to have been
subdued, and always ready to process more and more
Berlin bodies through its apertures.

Projection in Berlin forms a two-way process,
hinged on the eye: the city projects its preoccupations,
malfunctions and imperatives onto the bodies that
occupy it, via its screens and the engulfing histories
which its surfaces transmit, while the body also
correspondingly projects its own preoccupations
as infiltrations into the city, notably while in transit
through its space. Those projections of Berlin's passengers are often formulated in utter deviance to those
emerging from the city, which are only peripherally

those of its contemporary overseers (whose banal corporate imperatives barely project any content at all, as in the conception of the 'Mediaspree' development) and overwhelmingly those, still relentlessly projected into Berlin's space, of its twentieth-century political extremities and ambitions, as well as its experimental urban reconceptions in architecture, art and philosophy. The absence or annulling of a projectionist's figure never cancels the ongoing act of projection itself, as long as it has been fully launched; Berlin's seminal projectionists – including formative city planners such as Ludwig Hoffmann and Hermann Blankenstein, who envisioned its insane asylums and slaughterhouses, as well as the architectural teams who reformulated Berlin's 1945 ruins into new urban configurations, as with Hermann Henselmann's layering over of razed terrains with the Stalinallee and other key East Berlin constructions – are themselves vanished corporeal presences whose ongoing projections onto Berlin are transformed by the city-viewing eye, along with many others, into the contrary, compacted image-strata that Berlin transmits to its inhabitants at each instant.

The formulation of Berlin as a fine-tuned, operational projection of megalopolis-spanning dimensions had, from its origins in the 1870s, to contend with and incorporate the individual psychotic or malfunctioning projections onto urban space of large numbers of its population, accommodated in Hoffmann's architectural design of the Buch sub-city of asylums for driven-mad or overstimulated Berlin inhabitants of the twentieth century's first decades. As well as formulating Berlin's rational self-projection as a homogeneous, fully functioning city – as with Reuter's implementation of its integrated public-transport system in the 1920s and mayor Willy Brandt's development of a rapid inner-city autobahn system for West Berlin at the end of the 1950s – figures of power in Berlin also had to rationalize, in their projections of the city, the moments when its space abruptly and madly insurged into political or activist-driven violence. Those projections were always at their most demanding, and subject to malfunction or delirium, when political figures of East Berlin and West Berlin were compelled to rationalize their divided forms, to the half-cities' inhabitants and for eyes beyond the city, leading to awry urban projections such as Schabowski's improvised interpretation at a press conference about newly introduced transit-regulation changes that led unexpectedly to the Berlin Wall's immediate westwards corporeal mass-traversal on 9 November 1989. Projecting with rationality the construction of an entity which, in its realization, critically and self-evidently malfunctions in urban space – as with mayor Klaus Wowereit's new airport of the 2010s – forms a predominant, enduring trait of Berlin's city-authority figures. Among those volatile projections of figures of power onto Berlin's space, and for the eyes of its inhabitants, notably via grandiose architectural re-envisionings, Speer's Germania plans are unique in being projected simultaneously with rationality (as intricate models pored over by Hitler, and with sensible provisional tests conducted in urban space, such as the 'Heavy-load-bearing Body') and with hallucinatory, destructive delirium, as a lucidly mad projection for Berlin.

Beyond projections of urban power through architectural anomaly and via the medium of corporate image-screens, projections in Berlin also take the form of moving-image sequences or animations projected in exterior space at night onto its buildings and facades from remote or occluded sources, as with the projections of filmic sequences of figures of children being deported from Berlin towards internment camps, screened onto the facades of the Dom cathedral in 2012; such urban projections' conception may initially take the form of specific named artists' initiatives but then appear instead invariably to be generated anonymously, as spectral apparitions that the city itself irrepressibly exudes through fissurations in its buildings' surfaces, for the eyes that glimpse them in mid-transit through Berlin. Nocturnal projections at summer open-air programmes, as in the courtyard of the Bethanien building in Kreuzberg, often materialize filmed images of Berlin bodies in intimate proximity to the locations at which they were captured on film. Such projections possess an originating moment in Berlin's festivals of urban illumination, notably the Berlin im Licht light festival of projections from and onto its facades in 1928. The projection of light itself, without content, as with a projector's operation after all filmic sequences have ceased traversing its projecting beam of light (often in the absence of the projectionist's gone-astray figure), is instilled with urban resonance or voiding when it is directed onto and across Berlin's sites, as with the light projections around the Berlin Wall's topographic course on the 25th anniversary of its annulling, in November 2014. Berlin eyes and amassed Berlin bodies may witness such projections in acts of intensive engagement, which release corporeal and ocular components as projections onto urban space with such velocity that they are irrecuperably swallowed into those voids and surfaces, and never seen again.

VISIONS

Visions both illuminated and striated twentieth-century Berlin, engendered through an immense body of ocular work; they attained moments of concentrated formulation at particular points across that century, then abruptly lapsed, as though subject to subterranean seismic dynamics of focus and diffusion, often unleashing violence and their own extinguishment. Visions possess their contrary manifestations in ocular obliviousness and nonchalance. Berlin's visions are never subject to the dualities or volatile ambivalences that its projections transmitted, in incorporating and overlayering the city's space and bodies; a Berlin vision is integrally a unitary form that resists duplication (there are no two visions at stake, or both will collapse) and even annuls its own representation, so that film is an inadequate medium for registering Berlin's vision, and its traces need instead to be located in urban detrita or in the corporeal exhaustions and falls that ensue from vision's performance. A vision notably demands corporeal substantiation, since its ocular status is fragile.

Henselmann and his architect colleagues initially formulated the Stalinallee's design and that of its surrounding annexes in the same medium in which Speer prefigured Germania: as models and plans intended for the eye. Photographs and filmed newsreels of 1951–2 show visitors' intent ocular scannings of plans in exhibition halls. But that vision also possessed an acute urgency, in contrast to Speer's deferred plans. The GDR leaders' vision of that avenue foregrounded the Stalinallee as a pre-eminent catalyst in creating the GDR state itself; the tenuous entity of the GDR was effectively concentrated into the ruin-risen *Hauptstadt*, East Berlin, itself then focused down once again into the vision of the Stalinallee, with the remainder of the GDR forming a polluted wasteland, void space or collectivized rural hinterland, its occupants expected to make sacrifices in the form of donations to accelerate the Stalinallee's construction, or even physically travel to it to expedite its completion with manual work. The vision of the Stalinallee entailed extremely tight construction dead-lines. Whereas Speer and Hitler infinitely pored over their delirious projections and instigated only prepar-atory demolitions and ground-level tests, Henselmann and his colleagues had to surrender their plans in mid-formulation to construction gangs that were already at work. Filmic documents narrating the Stalinallee's construction, especially *Geschichte einer Strasse* (*Story of a Street*, 1952–4), emphasize the immediate, linear transaction of those gangs' mass corporeal gestures into the urgent realization of architectural 'vision', in contrast to other East Berlin street films of subsequent decades, such as those filmed in the 1970s in the run-down Auguststrasse and Ackerstrasse, their spaces projected via fragmentary, visionless street history. The misfiring of that urgency, manifested in the June 1953 East Berlin riots – precipitated in part by the excess of corporeally exhausting Stalinallee work quotas – is entirely absent from that film's narration, since even a split-second hesitation or corporeal aberration annuls vision.

Berlin's vision, across much of its twentieth-century corporeal history, was principally located in unitary political commitment, above all towards Communism or Nazism, so that the eye served to focus a content that appeared already fully formulated. Such apparitions of vision required no rational communication, only the exclaimed and asserted articulation, with devoted commitment, of a set of tenets. But such commitment and its tenets proved subject to abrupt reversals, resulting in impossible urban eye manoeuvres; the vision-negating denunciation of Stalin by Khrushchev in 1956 at the Soviet Union's Communist Party Congress, for example, impacted directly upon East Berlin's own vision and its urban manifestations, in the eventual stripping of the Stalinallee's name in 1961 and the removal of the statue of Stalin's figure that had been prominent along its course. The annulling of the Stalinallee's originating vision, as devoted and dedicated to Stalin corporeally (in his envisioning as having singlehandedly resuscitated Berlin from its razing, through the negligible intermediation of Berlin's bodies), led to other, successive visions, notably that of the 1960s avenue with its newly added cinemas – the Kino International and Filmtheater Kosmos – and well-stocked shops as embodying, notably for Eastern European eyes, East Berlin's capacity for urban-instilled ocular pleasure. Vision's momentum, together with its architectural and corporeal embeddings in urban space, often heads in awry, unforeseen directions, once its originating tenets are voided; by the 2010s, the Stalinallee's 1950s visionary status had transmuted to that of the Berghain nightclub – occupying the dilapidated heat-generating power plant that had formed one of the avenue's peripheral annexes – in its carrying of that era's distinctive vision of Berlin as a nightclub-city Eden.

The Stalinallee's other vision-originated annex manifested itself directly to the east of the city, close to the Oder river on the border with Poland, as East Berlin's 'Stalinstadt' sub-city, inaugurated by Ulbricht in May 1953, shortly after Stalin's death, beneath a banner proclaiming its name, in the form of multiple avenues constructed in an identical socialist neo-classical architectural style to that of the Stalinallee, and populated by vision-impelled young Communists (transplanted both

from East Berlin and internationally) determined to produce the maximum quantity of urban-enhancing high-grade steel in the shortest possible time in that sub-city's steelworks. Meeting halls and ornate cafés, such as Café Aktivist, were provided for Stalinstadt's young inhabitants, architecturally resonating with those constellating the course of the Stalinallee in East Berlin. In time, across sixty years or more, the Stalinstadt sub-city's name changed to Eisenhütten-stadt, just as Stalinallee's name had shifted to the Karl-Marx-Allee; the GDR lapsed, the downsized steel-works were sold off to multinational conglomerates, its occupants' activist bodies aged and its avenues' surfaces – though largely unchanged – grew corroded; but vision remained cryogenically tangible, in conjunc-tions between those aged bodies and the time-scoured avenues they transited, and in vision's urban and corporeal disintegrations and detrita.[20]

Vision, once separated out from Berlin's urban Edens, also has its material properties. While Berlin's projections undergo malfunctions, its vision is exposed to and holds its unique ocular diseases, provoked to an indeterminable extent by the eye's contact with the city's space and determining, to a greater or lesser degree, the envisioning of Berlin: retinal scrapings, reddenings, inflammations, searings, conjunctivitis-induced blurrings, vein burstings, irradiations, blindings and self-blindings.

EXPOSURES

All ocular and corporeal contacts with Berlin – however glancing or peripheral – constitute exposures, in which the body's skin and the eye's retinal surfaces are transformed into porous screens designed to receive the infiltrations of Berlin's obsessions, striations, scars and projections. The corporeal 'screens' formed by the surfaces of bodies and eyes in their transits across Berlin undergo transmutations once a process of exposure is under way, notably when they come into direct, intimate contact with the city's own screens and media, such as its surveillance cameras; the sensation of being exposed in the city may then lead to corporeal interventions upon urban space, notably in the frequent smashings in Berlin's streets, during the course of May Day demonstrations, of elevated surveillance cameras and other devices of ocular control, alongside confrontations with riot police. Urban exposures are engaged in overpowering or erasing the most vulnerable, sensitized components of the body, notably those of the eye itself. Often, it appears that Berlin as an entity exists to expose eyes to it.

In amateur film footage and photographs of Berlin's pivotal twentieth-century events, archived in the city's local-district museums such as those of Pankow and Kreuzberg, it frequently transpires that the sequences and images have been captured with malfunctioning or misjudged light-readings, so that the films' celluloid and the photographs' emulsion appear bleached or irradiated. As a result of the amateur camera operatives' lack of proficiency, or their distraction, exposure itself irresistibly seizes such images from the twentieth century's early and middle decades: for example, images of attendances at open-air political events around the end of the 1920s, such as Communist or Nazi rallies and the sporting contests that often accompanied them, or at popular leisure mass spectacles of the same era such as six-day non-stop cycling races; images of survival in bombed-out or besieged streets in 1943–5; and images of engagement in clearing urban rubble and repairing or reconstructing buildings in the subsequent years. The bodies in such images often appear already to be in the act of vanishing, drowning in light and barely imprinted on the celluloid or emulsion. Among the many sequences of 16mm footage that the amateur film enthusiast Herbert Kiper shot on his daily transits on foot around the Schöneberg district in 1946, recording its wide-scale destruction and first attempts at reconstruction, the most vitally resonant sequences are those in which his habitually accurate exposures go awry, either via his light meter's malfunctioning or through the maladroit urgency with which he sought to record a particular ongoing act or incident, so that his exposed bodies are simultaneously engrained deeply into Berlin's surfaces in their attempts by sheer corporeal effort (clearing and transporting debris, pickaxing unstable facades) to rectify its destructions, while also melting into those incandescent surfaces, which themselves are poised at the precipice of disappearance.

In the domain of overexposure, the constellations of wounds and striations which Berlin bodies and urban surfaces simultaneously endured in conflictual events, such as the vicious street clashes of the early 1930s between opposed political factions in districts such as Wedding and Prenzlauer Berg, or in aerial attacks, as during 1943's great conflagrations, are rendered null and void, since the excess of light admitted into the lens prevents those scars from being imprinted in depth upon celluloid's skin or photography's emulsion, as memorial residues, with the result that those assaulted bodies and city spaces appear pristine and inviolable in their near-vanishing. Such light-engulfed bodies cling to their last-ditch subsistence as memories in Berlin's urban arena.

Contemporary scannings of Berlin's space – by the eye or via media such as digital devices, now possessing infallible light-gauging technologies – constitute often involuntary interrogations of its fluctuating components of light and darkness. Whenever such probings catch the juxtaposition of Berlin bodies against built forms, as for example on light-attracting plazas such as the Alexanderplatz (reactivated from the ruins of dense streets in the 1960s as a barely obstructed, immense plain designed to be inundated by daylight and also by its surrounding towers' nocturnal neon signage), they also register the respective exposures of corporeality and urban surfaces. In exposed high-lightings of Berlin bodies, the moments of sudden gestural deviation from corporeality's habitual integration within urban space, into the form of

aberrant acts (protests, performances, collapses),
are illuminated and readily registered by surveillance
media. Bodies are at their most exposed in Berlin's
space when they can be violently torn from it and their
more usual invisibility or low profile is cancelled, as
for example in the seizings during the Nazi era of the
bodies of the city's Jewish population for deportation
and of dissident figures for torture and execution, in
the exposure of bodies in Berlin's bombed-out streets
such as those of Pankow and Prenzlauer Berg to
extreme sexual maltreatment at the hands of the
invading Soviet army in April–May 1945, and in the
searchlight-exposed vulnerability to capture or
shooting of figures attempting to traverse the voided
death strip between the Berlin Wall's outer and inner
barriers. Exposure to physical punishment may also
take the form of self-willed acts in which the skin's
surfaces and orifices are unscreened for beating or
penetration, as in the glaringly floodlit environments
of contemporary Berlin's nightclubs (and their ante-
cedents in the city's nightclub culture, notably in
the late 1920s and at the beginning of the 1990s) and
specialist venues devoted to masochistic practices
of corporeal abuse.

Exposures of Berlin's bodies form a principal means
of the city's regulation and reconfiguration, by which
malpractices (notably those relating to the exploitation
or trafficking of migrant, prostituted or in-transit bodies,
or their arduous working conditions in Berlin's space)
are 'exposed' in order to be rectified, by such processes

as sustained ocular observation and infiltrations by covert investigative agents into contested or dangerous locations, often equipped with image-recording devices such as infra-red cameras able to operate in light-denuded conditions such as those of subterranes, sex venues or sweatshops. Dialogues with unsuspecting members of criminal gangs and traffickers can be filmed secretly with obscured lenses. The perpetrators of malpractice may then be exposed for legal prosecution or for vilification in Berlin's media. An intentional act of exposure often intimates an insistent process in which the eye attempts to see something which is occluded, or in which the eye itself, along with exposed corporeality, is rawly scrutinized and subjected to excessive illumination; such processes can extend in destructive intensity to ocular searings, in which entire visions of Berlin are burnt out and lost.

GUIDING BLIND BODIES

The loss or burning out of the Berlin-inhabiting eye's visions and of its capacity for projection, along with the eye's originating incapacity even to conjure vision and projection in the first place, form seminal Berlin malfunctions that result in the annulling of that eye's visual engagement with the city and the compensating need for other sensorial dimensions – such as those operating in sonic and tactile domains – to be explored and accentuated.

Berlin's first institution for the blind was established centrally and with imperial patronage in 1806 in the Mitte district's Gipsstrasse, but the city's principal school for the blind would be constructed much further to the south, in the Steglitz district, in 1874–6, in the era of a vibrant, growing obsession in Berlin with the status of the ocular that, at that same moment, generated Kühne's wayward science of optography, with its fascination with the legible imprintations of images upon the retina at the moment of death. The imposing complex of immense brick buildings located in its own grounds, with workshops and residential blocks, extended around the foot of a hill. As the school's archival documentation indicates, the occupants of that sub-city of the blind had lost their vision in accidents, such as those incurred in searing contact with corrosive chemicals or beams of light in Berlin's industries, or else through injuries inflicted with ill intent (as with the violent infiltration of the retina with broken beer bottles), or unintentionally, in playful fights; others had been born blind and so visualized Berlin as an urban entity largely through its sonic traces and by touching its surfaces. At the Steglitz school for the blind, the occupants' principal work was to manufacture brushes, brooms and other hand-assembled implements, sold at a shop on the site which still operates. The complex was aerially bombed in 1943, inciting acute terror among its residents, with most of the buildings severely damaged; in 1975 the school was named the Johann-August-Zeune-Schule after one of the nineteenth-century Berlin pioneers of the

institutionalization of the blind. Other than repairs of bomb damage, the school remains almost unchanged since its construction, with walks along its corridors generating an intricate echoing soundscape of wood-floor creaks and splinterings intercut with the whispers and gestures of the school's population from their workshops.

The loss or eradication of vision in Berlin can also lead to the concealment from exposed urban sight of its bodies. During the Nazi era, that secreting of the blind formed a means of provisional survival for the Jewish workers in the small brush and broom factory of Otto Weidt, located in the Mitte district in the back courtyard of a building in the Rosenthaler Strasse, not far from the site of Berlin's first institution for the blind. Weidt, who had military contracts for his products, was initially able to protect the Jewish members of his workforce (which also included sighted members) from arrest, but intensi-fied deportations in 1942 led to the need for him actively to conceal them in his factory's space and also to rescue – by bribing their captors – members of his workforce already arrested and taken to the nearby, newly estab-lished Grosse Hamburger Strasse deportation centre (from where Coco Schumann's journeys of concentration-camp deportation would originate in the following year). Eventually, despite Weidt's efforts, almost all of those concealed at his factory would be deported from Berlin. As well as forming an urgent justification for the concealment from exposure of bodies in Berlin, blind-ness may also generate the sensory acuity necessary for the urban locating and revealing of bodies; in Lang's film *M*, a blind balloon-seller identifies the child-murderer Beckert sonically, in the act of whistling, and his vocally exclaimed guidance then leads to sighted criminals' ocular tracking down in Berlin's streets of Beckert's body.

As well as guiding sighted bodies, the blind also guide one another, as in film documents and photographs of chlorine- and mustard-gassed First World War soldiers' transits – configured in chains of bodies with hands placed for guidance on the shoulder of the figure in front – through Berlin's railway-station concourses and streets on their journeys from distant battlefields to institutions on the city's periphery such as Beelitz-Heilstätten, adapted from its habitual role as a tuberculosis sanatorium for the treatment of ocular and other injuries for the duration of that war and thereby forming an annex sub-city of the Berlin blind to the Steglitz school. Hitler, who had spent time at Beelitz-Heilstätten with war wounds in 1916, would have undertaken such a traversal between Berlin railway stations, in October 1918, close to the war's end, on his journey by train from Belgium, where he had been mustard-gassed and part-blinded in combat at Werwicq, to the military clinic in the town of Pasewalk, north of Berlin; alternatively, Hitler's loss of vision may have resulted from a psychosis or hysteria of self-induced, temporary blinding, already very familiar to psychiatrists in the overwrought 'electropolis' of early twentieth-century Berlin as one of the real or fabricated symptoms of its inhabitants' unscreened exposures to the sensorially shattering city.[21] As an urban phenomenon of Berlin's cityscapes, the 'schooling' and homing of the blind, together with the vision-voided guiding of the blind by the blind, recurs as a spectacle in the contemporary city, with the guiding of amassed international groups of unseeing or oblivious schoolchildren and students from site to site of Berlin's recent monuments, along with the construction of immense hotel complexes (their low-grade fabrication primed for future obsolescence, unlike the more resilient forms in Berlin's peripheries of late nineteenth-century hospitals built to house the blind) to accommodate them.

The great swathes of Berlin's monuments to its own historical blindness, constructed primarily as enticements for visitors to the city in the decades following its reunification, or as manoeuvres of conjuration to divert attention from its contemporary dilemmas, encase the city's surfaces as anti-screens that petrify the eye and annul its capacities. Berlin's urban space demands intensive ocular and corporeal excavation in order to reveal its own entrenched obsessions – always deeply inscribed into its surfaces – with the power of vision, the elations of projection and the exposure of the eye. Once opened up, the detrita and traces of those preoccupations form an exposed exhibiting of Berlin's vital fissures and apertures.

BERLIN ART

The act of exhibition in Berlin is one which exposes the body, especially in its urban-induced transformations and disintegrations, in artworks; the French-language art exhibition noun 'exposition', especially in connection with figurative art preoccupied with corporeality's intersections with urban space, carries simultaneously the spatially located event entailed in exhibiting the body and the specific act of exposing, along with all of its eye-searing or violent skin-unpeeling implications and its two-way dynamics of projection. Exhibiting the body in Berlin intimates the need pre-emptively to erase all obstructions or screens that would impede its visibility, in order to secure the maximum capacity for its infiltration and projection; the presence around or within the body of Berlin's abrasive surfaces can serve only to accentuate that corporeal propulsion into the eye of its spectator, who characteristically views it from vantage points in city space. In corporeal exposition, the eye looks out of the body (in performance) or from its image (in photography, art film and other art media), and ocularly transmits its urban experience in fragments. Exhibition in its corporeal projection precludes solitude, even when its enacting is prepared in acute isolation; exposing the body in Berlin necessitates a watching eye's seizing of that act, even momentarily.

In Berlin, bodies may choose to exhibit themselves and enact that self-exposing in particular locations – streets, nightclubs, art spaces – or their exposure may be overseen by a curator who is assigned to conceive the space and time of that corporeal exhibition for its maximal envisioning. In the aberrant visual dynamics endemic to Berlin, such eye-directed curated acts may take place in utter darkness, as in the spaces of night-clubs located in former bunkers and industrial buildings, or in subterranes, and be illuminated for only a split second. Conversely, acts of exhibition can be externally situated in Berlin's most exposed plazas, such as the Alexanderplatz, or in transparent plate-glass-enclosed spaces, the formative model for which is the upper pavilion of Ludwig Mies van der Rohe's Neue National-galerie building, installed in West Berlin in 1968, whose ocularly exposed street-level space interconnects, via a stairway descent that excludes natural illumination, with the subterranean exhibition rooms directly below it.

Throughout its twentieth-century history, Berlin's art was instilled with compulsions of the body to expose and reveal itself, even in its most shattered forms, or in sexual excess; self-portraits by Berlin-based Brücke and Expressionist artists exhibit that obsessional self-exposure and its gestural articulation, also manifested in the same era in such choreographic forms as Anita Berber's performances. Once a body's desire for extreme ocular self-exposure consumes all aspects of individual life in Berlin and becomes the primary mode of urban existence and corporeal projection, in 'exhibitionism', as exemplified in mid-1970s West Berlin by the cultures of style and performance pivoting around the Chez Romy Haag nightclub (and especially in the figure of

Romy Haag herself), it oscillates between the status
of an ephemeral, embodied urban artwork – a Berlin
body that exists to transit the city between nightclubs,
solely to exhibit itself, as in Iggy Pop's West Berlin song
'Nightclubbing' – and a manifestation of Berlin's own
outlandish, excessive urban envisionings, which encompass all bodies that inhabit or transit the city and
possess the capacity to tip them into vertiginous falls
into psychosis, addiction and vanishing. The intersection in the 1970s between Berlin's art and its corporeal
exposures, especially in nightclub spaces of sonic as
well as visual excess, generated music performances
of cacophony and sexual self-exhibition by the city's
ephemerally prominent figurative painters (grouped
in that era as the 'New Wild Ones': Salomé, Luciano
Castelli, Rainer Fetting, among others) in Kreuzberg-
district clubs such as the SO36 as well as at exhibition
openings in their self-run studio space, the Galerie am
Moritzplatz, and in the city's galleries and art museums.
Such infiltrations between art cultures and nightclub
cultures in Berlin prefigure many further acts of exhibition and exposure, notably from the 1990s, that focused
around a culture of relentless self-projection as a counter
both to the dynamics of ocular self-concealment or
self-annulling induced by urban psychosis, and also
to the perceived necessity for fragile, 'exposed' bodies
to be integrated into institutional structures, as in the
segregated institutionalization of the blind.

In 2014, the cavernous main hall of the Friedrichshain district's former power plant – originally

constructed to serve the Stalinallee area, but disused
for many years and subject to engrained dereliction in
its striated interior surfaces – was used for an exhibition
tangentially tracing, in the form of photographs and
installations, the ten-year visual cultural history of the
notorious nightclub, Berghain, that occupied the adjacent generating station hall, that history itself seeping
back in time to the reunified city's 1990s nightclub
culture with its proliferating engagements with sexual
self-exposure and the demanding, durational performance of dancing in conditions of extreme cacophony,
often located in obsolete former-GDR industrial buildings and subterranes. A soaring internal wall divided
the exhibition space, in the building's turbine hall, from
the Berghain nightclub space (itself open and filled
with its usual clientele during the exhibition's nocturnal
opening hours). In the main hall, the scattering of
exhibited artworks as memorial traces and corporeal
residues, such as glass-enclosed sweat and nightclub
toilet doors inscribed with graffiti proposing sexual
assignations, were secreted in partial darkness into
the immense space, glimpsed in transit across gantries
and from balconies over plummeting voids; the rusted
ladders extending far up the hall's blackened walls,
formerly used by workers to inspect the now-vanished
turbines' operation, appeared to have been presciently
installed in order to provide vantage points for
obstructed, fragmentary viewings of those artworks.
In that space, the corporeally exuded or inscribed

artworks took on the status of incidental but deeply

embedded urban entities, memorially monumental in their simultaneous self-exposure and effacing, within the encompassing terrain of Berlin's wider disintegrations of memory.

A distinctive corporeal art of Berlin was last attempted in the final years of the GDR, instilled with its own imminent urban and ocular vanishing, and gleaned from the surfaces of the city, as in York der Knoefel's *Slaughterhouse Berlin* (1986–8) photographic installation, which enabled its spectators to inhabit and transit its image-imprinted panels, as an artwork constituting an exploratory, engulfing Berlin sub-city, along with other interrogative photographic works of that same era by Gundula Schulze Eldowy and Sven Marquardt, that track the journeys of broken-down or desperate bodies through the eroded streets and improvised drinking venues of the Mitte district. Marquardt (then often engaged in photography assignments for the GDR's *Sibylle* fashion magazine, but by the 2010s a glaring and facially tattooed figure posed at the entrance to the Berghain nightclub's interior, ocularly appraising bodies for admission or expulsion) amassed portraits of East Berlin's disdainful and disabused subcultural bodies, who occupied the peripheral urban space left emptied by the GDR secret police's eradication of East Berlin's punk rock culture around 1982–3. Towards that decade's end, those bodies engaged in art-inflected obsessional self-exposings that resonated with those conducted in the previous decade in West Berlin's nightclub culture. Gundula Schulze Eldowy, who collected her photographs of East Berlin's bodies under the title *Berlin on a Dog's Night* (*Berlin in einer Hundenacht*), undertook endless nocturnal walks across the first half of the 1980s in the crumbling, semi-abandoned area of the Mitte district around the Alte Schönhauser Strasse, in what she retrospectively viewed as guileless, eye-exposed urban journeys during which she caught images of elderly and young bodies – stranded and bewildered, dissident and hostile – in those streets, their figures foregrounded against neglected, near-collapsed facades holding bullet-holes and the near century-old inscriptions of dealers in coal and subterranean bars; during the same era, she also documented many of East Berlin's nakedly exposed bodies in their apartments' denuded interiors. Such eye-oriented street anatomizings of Berlin's bodies, often exhibited in the city's memory-saturated spaces and rawly engrained by them, form essential future-oriented art for Berlin's oncoming ocular ruinations.

5

SONIC BERLIN: URBAN EXCORIATIONS

SOUNDS EJECTED INTO THE STREET . SONIC ACTS OF PERFORMANCE . SOLITUDE'S NOISE . EXCESSES

SOUNDS EJECTED INTO THE STREET

When you listen to Berlin, you hear an urban corporeal entity of malfunctions, ecstasies, screams, appeals, incantations, enumerations, mid-exclamation cut-off silencings, mishaps of the vocal tract, murmurings of the city dead, whisperings of the blind, gesturally beaten-out cacophonies, that together – as the sonic projections of Berlin bodies – infiltrate the city's prevalent noisescape: hums, turbine drones, drillings, hammer blows, digitized echoings of voices, engine accelerations, S-bahn trains' shrieks and announce-ments, ringtones, cracklings, sounds of unknown provenance almost out of earshot, and the noise of things falling. Berlin's sonic corporeality – as with its body-instilled contents projected from and into the eye – takes the form of fragments, but sound fragments will not vanish as eye-contents' fragments can. Vital corporeal sonic traces endure as strata in urban space and on Berlin's streets, notably taking the form, among others, of ejected detrita of noise, originally sourced deep in Berlin bodies' vocal tracts and organs, often expelled as variants of cries, and left behind by those bodies, especially on late nights out, in near-deserted nocturnal avenues, as sound serratedly driven from the body in desperate solitudes, or in the course of heated altercations and of attempted persuasions or seductions between two or more bodies, that are then discarded into abrupt obsolescence, as those bodies move on, the immediate focus of the altercation or contestation cast into oblivion, so that those intensive sonic traces are rendered into abandoned ones.

The streets that surround those traces' momentary eruption and the bodies that will come to repopulate those streets may then be transformed almost beyond recognition, as with the future of the striated streets of East Berlin's Mitte district, with their broken and disabused figures, photographed in the 1980s by Gundula Schulze Eldowy, but those sonic detrita still possess their embedded existence there, intangibly archived within Berlin's histories of noise, alongside many other sonic layers. Often, noises heard in Berlin appear so diffuse and in flux, able to transit time and space, that they seem not to belong identifiably to the contemporary moment, but instead to an otherwise vanished decade or era still emanating its presence sonically, in Berlin's streets, generating noises that are as ineradicable as deeply gouged voids in buildings' surfaces, even when the mouths and lips or the turbines and exhausts that emitted those sounds are long gone. Such Berlin-ejected noises, left out in the street, constitute unnamed things; all that is definitively known of them is their spectral survival as sonic excoriations from the city's skins and surfaces.

From the interiors of Berlin's buildings, the surrounding city seeps in as a sonic medium that is able to traverse walls, glass panes and screens; often, the corporeal gestures that generated the sounds heard have already been executed, but their propulsion of sound endures for a split second beyond their lapsing, so that the ear catches Berlin corporealities that have already ceased to exist and now taken on new configurations. Even in the most isolated, soundproofed building interiors of Berlin, a sonic, body-instilled fragment from outside will almost always find a medium of entry, bringing its charged history with it. During Berlin's aerial destruction of 1943–5, that habitual sense of an already lapsed corporeal origin for sound was reversed into that of a prefiguration of imminent engulfing noise-impacts upon bodies whose sense of anticipatory hearing became acute, accentuated to its maximal extent in that of the inhabitants of Berlin's Steglitz-district institution for the blind, whose entire sensorial capacity must have focused upon the sonic indicator – falling bombs' air-displacing rushes of noise – of the next moment's explosive detonation and its resulting conflagrations. In above-ground air-raid bunkers, such as that (later occupied, in the 1990s, by a hardcore techno nightclub) constructed in 1942 in the Reinhardtstrasse, close to the Friedrichstrasse railway station, the multiply reinforced walls' resistance to all exterior sounds formed unique, total annullings, in utter darkness, of external Berlin's sonic infiltration of their interiors, thereby creating inner worlds of transacted corporeal noise for those bunkers' occupants.

While the inhabitants of Berlin's interiors perceive blurred amalgams of corporeal noise and city noise from sources outside their spaces, bodies in transit through Berlin's external space intermittently hear, at unforeseen moments, the sounds emitted into that external arena of noise from buildings' interiors and auditoria, such as those in which bodies have amassed in a concentrated form: music venues, cinemas, sports halls, nightclubs. Internal noise exudes eruptively through Berlin's surfaces to inhabit city space in a mutated form; it becomes irreparably separated from its origins in a collective corporeal existence, such as that of the ecstatic exclamations of an overheated nightclub's frenzy of bodies, and so possesses an anachronistic status in external space, as in deserted nocturnal avenues. That obsolescence of bodies' sonic traces once they have escaped their auditorium manifests itself in its most exposed form in the streets or alleys outside Berlin's cinemas, especially those with only fragile or narrow boundaries between external and internal space, such as the Tilsiter Lichtspiele, or those whose emergency exits' doors are opened out to the street in conditions of summer heat; the resonant voices and cries of film's figures, often amplified to distorted sound levels by malfunctioning or overloaded speakers, along with the live voices of unruly audiences (such as those of uproarious all-night cult film spectators, or those of audiences protesting in dissatisfaction with the projected film), traverse the cinema's carapace and become stranded, still in the act of exclaiming, in Berlin's streets. Such sonic traces of film then have to negotiate their autonomous existence as fragmentary elements among Berlin's intricate urban noisescapes.

Berlin's sonic existence is integrally a corporeal one, with its dense cultural history of instances of seminal eruptions and imprintations of urban sound and noise, encompassing the sounds of city-salvaging appeals directed to immense audiences such as that of Reuter's voice, recorded in external space on the Reichstag steps, and of delirious incitements to risk the very existence of the city, as with Goebbels's 'total war' speech, recorded five years earlier in the internal space of the Sportpalast auditorium, among untold other pivotal sonic gestures traced on cylinders, discs, tracks and tapes and in digital formats, amassed in Berlin's archives or consigned to loss. The status of sound in Berlin could be re-envisioned, along with that of art, as a distinctively urban-originated and urban-shattered entity, always intimately bound to the acts and projections of Berlin's bodies.

SONIC ACTS OF PERFORMANCE

In Berlin, even to make a sound at all is an act with multiply charged resonance; it immediately intersects with all of the city's histories of vocal or physically generated sound, such as histories of city authority pronouncements curtailing or forbidding gestures and transits of Berlin bodies, or contrary histories of sound projecting the body in outlandish and aberrant ways into urban space, in contexts of social tension, contestation or subjugation. Sound itself has often been a target of subjugation in Berlin, as in the GDR's strategic

obliteration in 1982–3 of East Berlin's punk rock culture

with its sonic insurgency, in the violent dispersals of vocally protesting activists on many occasions in the 1960s, '70s and '80s in the Kreuzberg district – when that district formed the most fiercely animated part of West Berlin, sound-striated by its demolition-opposing inhabitants and by the noise of the demolitions themselves – and through to the contemporary moment; the city's officially overseen sensory regime is oriented far more towards expulsions and prohibitions of sonic manifestations than to their open permeation of primarily corporatized urban space.

In Berlin, even the making of sound in a condition of nonchalant oblivion instantly amalgamates that intervention into the city's proliferating cultural histories and archives of sensory obliviousness, with their accompanying, imminent dangers for that oblivion's perpetrators. The intention to undertake a sonic act, as a barely enunciated whisper or maximally expectorated scream (the night in Berlin can be full of screams, from those of narcotic or alcoholic derangement in the streets of the Mitte district, to those of desperation or reactions to assaults in peripheral districts such as Marzahn or Lichtenberg), demands a close awareness of how the city's sound-scrambling dynamics will invariably sieve, dissect and reconfigure that act, potentially transforming it so fundamentally that it becomes implanted into other bodies or into the city's own noise-emitting organs and orifices. The performance of sonic acts in Berlin is undertaken always with an audience, even one situated at a tangent.

As with the city's now near-extinguished twentieth-century sonic culture of back-courtyard musicians performing accordion and barrel-organ music, directed upwards, storey upon tenement storey, towards audiences located in intimate proximity to that music, Berlin-inhabiting listeners are always inescapably exposed to such performances' multiple sonic layerings and infiltrations of urban space.

While sound may be launched with intended obliviousness into Berlin, as a performance of urban insolence that counters the vocal coursing of Berlin with sounds of passionate engagement or the intensively gasped noises of sex acts, the city's listeners may also perform obliviousness to the sounds they receive, as for example with the vocal recitations by the desperate of their calamities during the course of S-bahn carriage transits. In such instances, those passengers not carapaced with iPhone headphones, but unreceptive to the performance's enumeration of endured urban maledictions, must undertake intricate corporeal gestures – conjuring obliviousness or the negation of all sound – that themselves constitute intricate performances: affected turnings away, starings out of the window into the passing cityscape, dismissive hand gestures, ocular fixations on void floor space, or the issuing of their own sounds (exasperated sighs, rhythmic intakes of breath). But the desperate in Berlin will not be silenced, and often insurge into the streets to protest their contestations at maximum vocal volume, as with the frequent apparitions in the gentrified,

overhauled streets of Prenzlauer Berg of maddened
solitary figures who scour those pavements on foot while
expelling vocal-cord-rending streams of salutary curses
directed upwards at the buildings' concealed new
occupants, whose arrival across the two decades
following the city's reunification led to the expelling
or financial driving out of almost the entirety of the
pre-unification population, and thereby became bound
into Berlin's extensive urban-historical lineage of
corporeal expulsions of populations. That high-volume
street cursing, as an act of sonic excoriation and even
when performed in derangement, possesses a specific
activist agenda that belongs to Berlin's histories of
urban intervention; by contrast, other high-volume
night-time cries, expelled in multiple languages,
performed by unknowable recitants, and often
inflected with exilic tearings open of the senses,
possess the mystery and unprecedented status
which Kracauer noted in his Berlin writings of the
early 1930s on the sudden eruptions, erasing the city's
periodic nocturnal silences, of street cries.

Berlin's accumulations of discarded noise, ostensibly
used up and left out as detrita in the streets, are often
collected with obsessional commitment (as a contrary
response to Berlin inhabitants' real or feigned obliviousness to urban sound), notably by sound artists special-
izing in 'found' residues of noise. Such performative
seizings of sound – recorded as fast-moving amalgams
of noise on transits through the city via mobile recording
devices, or else in states of durational stillness that aim

to record the sonic emanation over time of a particular location in Berlin – also hold their own lineage, from the first experiments of the city's sound artists in the 1950s (notably those visiting West Berlin on international artists' invitation programmes) and the work of the Einstürzende Neubauten group in 1980s West Berlin, with their interest in repetitive sonic hammerings, to the contemporary city's innumerable urban-sound archivists. In turn, such performative collectings of Berlin's urban sounds – many with their corporeal origins, and scraped as distorted reboundings, projections and echoes from the city's facades – are then incorporated and transmutated into new usages, combined with synthesized sound or other corporeal sound elements, in the form of urban ambient compositions, urban cacophonies or other urban-noise media, and performed in Berlin's art-oriented nightclubs and gallery spaces.

To momentarily overhear sounds in Berlin's space, over shoulders, between partitions, from the mouths of rapidly path-crossing figures, behind screens or seeping from subterranes and cellars, is always an experience of intercut fragments, in which other manifestations of urban noise will instantly attempt to dislodge and render redundant those fragments that – through their distinctive resonance for memory or corporeality, concentrated into the instant of their overhearing, even when sonically blurred or misheard – remain with you, and become part of your own body's sensorial archiving, as seminal Berlin noise fragments.

SOLITUDE'S NOISE

A receptive exposure to Berlin's noisescapes is most intently at stake whenever transits of the city are durationally undertaken in intentional solitude, across months or years, notably enforcing the maximal intersection between sensorially torn-open corporeality and Berlin's sonic projections. Berlin's solitary passengers, driven by urban compulsions, undergo immersals in noise, receiving sonic inputs at the same time as visual emanations; the sensory organs of such passengers are accentuated by their corporeal separation in such a way that sound and vision may conflictually mesh in their dual propulsion of urban fragments, and thereby upend the fixed status of eyes and ears. Solitude also recasts skin as a sensitized medium or screen for the absorbing and transformation of such projections, and – as with the operation over time of a cinema screen – that skin is imprinted with the same contents again and again, in repeated traversals of such pivotal avenues as the Karl-Marx-Allee, the Oranienstrasse, the Schönhauser Allee and others, along with wastelands, interzones, peripheries and locations of Berlin, each time corporeally appropriated and rendered, through their spatial transit, in an utterly different form, in irreplicable repetitions. Noise forms a reinforcing carapace for the solitude of Berlin's passengers, heightening their sense of separation but also reassuring them, with insistence, that solitude is Berlin's optimum corporeal medium.

In their solitude, Berlin's passengers pass by other solitary figures, with whom contact is foreclosed if solitude as a prized urban entity is to be maintained. Along with those whose eyes are engaged in parallel sensory excoriations and anatomizings of Berlin's urban forms, passengers also cross the paths of the furious vocal cursers of such districts as Prenzlauer Berg, but may be exempt, through the unspoken equivalences of solitude, from exposure to their remonstrations, which are primarily directed towards the isolated occupants of luxurious loft apartments converted from what, until the post-reunification era, had been void attic space of semi-abandoned tenements; cursings rarely form a dialogue, since they are vocally delivered at such high volume and with such unbroken speed that their inter-locutors are habitually enclosed by them into solitude. In Berlin's sonic regime of solitude, there are few coherent conversations or dialogues in which urban knowledge is imparted or exchanged, only variants of obsessional or oblique vocal projections, or fragments of cries; what is vitally known of the city (if anything is known) is predominantly transmitted, directly into the body, as though intravenously, from Berlin's infinite archives. Along with those street-located cursers, Berlin's solitary passengers also intermittently intersect with the zigzagging trajectories of the city's mad or deranged, no longer confined to lunatic-asylum sub-cities such as Buch but now relocated into the city itself, and vocally active, as recitants, monologuers, internal-dialoguers (engaged via solitude's hallucinations in interactions with another body of solitude, conjured for dual deliria), performative emitters of corporeal noise, including the obsessive-compulsive imitation of urban sounds, and paranoid imaginers of maleficent threats from all passers-by, among many other variants of the contemporary urban mad. Delirious solitude is always outwardly directed towards spectators, even when its performers appear solely to be addressing themselves, and the inbuilt lack of response from those oblivious spectators consolidates solitude's armatures. Oblivion can also take the form of a performer's own carefully guarded attribute; in many of Berlin's sites of alcoholics' amassings, with historical lineages as locations of corporeal dissolution, such as Prenzlauer Berg's Helmholtzplatz, figures of solitude gather together to perform monologues and cries of maddened fury in utter oblivion towards those in intimate proximity to them.

Renderings of Berlin's solitude in sound, art and film often envision a body in relentless, lonely transit after a calamity has taken place. After opening with a series of panning shots over Berlin's ruins in which almost no figures are visible, Roberto Rossellini's film *Germany Year Zero* (1948) follows the directionless movements of the young boy Edmund through wastelands. Berlin's razed streets no longer delineate a cogent city for solitude's transits, and when Edmund attempts to approach other figures, solitude's suspension only exposes him to abuse. Newsreels and feature films of the GDR's first years of existence often attempted to emphasize the desirability of corporeal communality, especially in its instigation and inhabitation of new architectures such as that of the Stalinallee; but solitude in that era appears broken instead primarily through the eruption of dissent, as in the filmed documents of the June 1953 East Berlin riots, in which masses of bodies gradually join the protest as it traverses the city.[22] Contrarily, in more recent films and digital sequences of Berlin's riots, such as those of West Berlin's Kreuzberg-district activist protests of the 1970s, and those of contemporary protests demanding the spatial autonomy from police and city-authority surveillance of contested sites, such as Kreuzberg's Görlitzer park, the confrontations and exposures of Berlin's bodies often appear to lead to the intensification of solitudes; in the fierce corporeal interactions, especially in hand-to-hand struggles and beatings between riot police and protesters, those protesters are often adeptly segregated by intricate police manoeuvres to facilitate an isolated body's beating, so that an envisaged corporeal solidarity and communality can be readily disintegrated via such violent manoeuvres into subjugated and bloodied solitude.

Visual art's preoccupation with the seething megalopolis of Berlin across the twentieth century's first decades pivots on the unbreakable solitude of its figures isolated in the heart of the city, such as those of Kirchner's 1914 Potsdamer Platz prostitutes, whose spectacular enticements perversely adhere them irrecuperably into urban space and appear to withdraw their bodies from all potential transactions. Photographs of corporeal traversals by the dissident, mad or askew figures of Berlin's run-down streets – such as those taken by Ludwig Menkhoff in the Kreuzberg district and by Gundula Schulze Eldowy in the Mitte district, during the 1970s and '80s – occasionally transmit a sense of active solitude that aberrantly determines and re-envisions Berlin's urban space. The sensory flux and oscillations of the city's solitudes are also mediated by the work of contemporary Berlin-based, often exilic artists such as Kader Attia and Rabih Mroué, as in Mroué's *The White Sheets of Berlin* (2013). Sound-art excoriations and evocations of Berlin's districts and their occupants' bodies, from those undertaken by Bowie in 1977 with their focus on the melancholy, dilapidated Neukölln district (then an area of bewildered children wandering decrepit streets and of recently displaced, homesick workers, especially from Turkey, brought to West Berlin to undertake its most menial tasks) to contemporary sonic embodiments of Berlin's cityscapes, form multiple projections of the city's infinite solitudes. The singularity of Berlin's engulfing solitude always accumulates into plurals and proliferations.

In the late winter of 1985–6, snow fell so heavily on Berlin that the city was silenced. Streets were impassable to vehicles and S-bahn tracks blocked and frozen; the temperatures dived, schools closed and the city's inhabitants stayed inside, though in East Berlin's fissured tenements, barely heated by their ovens' lignate coal bricks, it was often colder inside than outside, and ochre chimney smoke from that low-grade burnt coal overlayered the brilliant blue sky. Icicles with the dimensions of human bodies hung jaggedly from the gutters of tenements, ready to plummet to the streets below if a thaw ever came. Wrapped up, and with the aim of keeping warm, I walked right across the city, breathing ice, from Kreuzberg via the Zimmerstrasse Wall-crossing to the northern end of Prenzlauer Berg, then south again via the spectral Mitte streets and wastelanded bombsites, and across the frozen Spree, back into West Berlin and further south, along the course of the S-bahn tracks into Schöneberg, before following the embankments of the Landwehr canal, also sealed down by thick ice, eastwards to Kreuzberg, seeing almost nobody (apart from border guards) on the entire journey. All the way, Berlin's extreme, resonant solitude around my body propelled me on.

EXCESSES

Berlin's excesses, such as those which accentuate solitude into a distinctive anatomical capacity to maximally absorb and re-permutate the city's prolifer-ating sonic propulsions as well as its visual projections, constitute the vital demand upon the body which aligns Berlin's corporeality and urban space into unique amalgams, tangible in no other city; even oblivion is demanding in Berlin. Excess intimates sustained cancellations of the limits of what the body's urban inhabitation habitually entails, so that Berlin's occupation or transit is always enacted in liminal zones.

Urban excess can only be determined in relation to the experience and inhabitation of other cities; when excess manifests itself incessantly, as a city's liveable medium, then it separates that city, Berlin, from other cities, and casts it into an urban solitude – as a city resolutely alone, resonating with West Berlin's stranded island status within the GDR's space and Reuter's urgent appeal on the steps of the Reichstag in 1948, at the time of the Berlin Airlift, for city populations worldwide to turn their eyes upon West Berlin, in its ruined solitude and exposure to being territorially swallowed alive – that is demarcated by its excesses as well as by its voids. In its self-presentation as an expansively thriving, all-enveloping *Weltstadt* megalopolis in the 1890s and 1900s, Berlin appeared tumultuously in sensory over-load, transformational in all domains, producing vastly superfluous quantities of luxurious experiences and industrial materials, and propelling its newly teeming, hyper-stimulated population in madly overspilling corporeal frenzies across its immense space. In the subsequent decades, Berlin's excess indicated its surplus capacity voraciously to appropriate and *consume* all other cities; once all other cities were rendered into marginal sub-cities of Berlin, that megalopolis could exist only in solitude, maintained in its velocity by its own sheer excess. By the 1930s, the project of Hitler and Speer for the world capital of Germania as an invasively all-conquering supreme urban power carried far more maleficent *Weltstadt* dynamics, in its conception of a city which gains pre-eminence by violently absorbing its adversarial 'rivals' and simultaneously expelling its alien elements (its Jewish, homosexual and Communist inhabitants, among others) from its own space; such conquests could only take excessive, outlandish forms, embodied in Speer's Germania modellings and urban test zones in Berlin.

Across its existence from the 1890s – as an expansive megalopolis, nerve-ridden electropolis, ruination-intent world capital of madness, isolated and divided history pivot, and contemporary city – Berlin projects an apartness which is integrally corporeal as well as urban, and requires the generation of that solitude via variants of excess. As a solitary, outlandish urban entity, Berlin, across that history, also configured its bodies as specially adapted for its inhabitation: in the capacity for physical consumption, in neural meltdown, in political obsession, in transpiercing sensory exile, and in contemporary digital culture's multitude of urban excesses that serve to exacerbate Berlin's multitude of solitudes.

In Berlin bodies' anatomical adaptation for excess, the opening of receptive sensory organs for sonic contents forms a primary prerequisite in the act of approaching and facing the city. The inhabitation of always-liminal urban zones in which boundaries to sound and noise, and their intersections with corporeality, always appear profoundly uncertain (even when ostensibly delimited by prescriptions from the city authorities), allows excess to mutate seamlessly into obsolescence. Urban noise may only be excessive for a single instant, in the sudden delivery of its overwhelming, ecstatic or nerve-wracking corporeal charge; from that moment on, excess is dissipated and lost. As a result, noise's excess generates detrital fragments of redundant sonic scatterings across Berlin's streets, which are collected for reusage, disposal or archiving along with the discarded concentrations of body-ejected, left-behind nocturnal noise and those streets' unwanted ocular residues.

Excess in Berlin is often closely associated with the cultural history of sensorial and corporeal engulfings successively experienced across time in its nightclub spaces: from performances of multiple sexual promiscuities, gestures and rituals in the city's 1920s nightclub culture, exemplified in their excess by the Eldorado club and the short-lived figure of Anita Berber, who died at the zenith of that culture's excess (and contrarily exemplified by the figure of Hitler, whose election in 1933 immediately shut down and silenced that culture), to the art-inflected, transsexual and punk rock excesses of West Berlin's 1970s nightclub culture, in such venues as Chez Romy Haag, the Dschungel and the SO36, and their many iconic figures such as the artist Salomé in his near-naked, shaven-headed, lipsticked and stockinged role as resident performer of excess at both the Dschungel and SO36, and to the durational industrial techno-culture excess of Berlin's nightclubs of the 2010s (resonant, in their events' temporal endurance and exhaustive excess, to the terminal point of an aberrant austerity, of the six-day non-stop indoor cycling events that formed such a prominent element of Berlin's popular culture in the 1920s), equipped with zones for intensive sexual activity, as at Berghain, with its door-barring figure of Sven

Marquardt as the potential denier of excess. Equally, that nightclub lineage of excess could be traced via far more peripheral nocturnal cultures, often staged covertly in alternating apartment spaces, arranged across disparate Berlin topographies and always subject to imminent suppression, as with those run by activists, musicians and sexually marginalized figures in 1970s and '80s East Berlin. Excess is always vitally magnified, across those cultures, by the projections of noise: the cries, altercations and impactings of bodies, and variants of music from jazz and swing to punk rock and hardcore industrial techno beats, as well as sonic experimentations into fragments of noise-detrita with the aim of interrogating the ways in which excess is perceived and transacted, across Berlin's urban arenas. Excess is finally delineated – after exceeding all criteria, monitorings and corporeal limits, in its generation of Berlin as an excessive urban entity – by its abrupt silencing.

Berlin's excesses emerge from collisions of contraries, as in excess's own constitution from and against corporeal solitude. Sites of junctures and oscillations in Berlin's urban space – as with those between emanations of noise and eye-directed images, between voids and proliferations, and between repetitions and uniquenesses – all endure or precipitate sensitized city fractures which excess compulsively infiltrates, in order to animate the auditory and ocular domains of Berlin bodies. Once the street-facing skin is torn off Berlin, its excesses pour out, and the city's sonic traces signal and locate the seminal apertures in urban space.

6

APOCALYPTIC BERLIN

AN EXTREMOPHILE HISTORY OF BERLIN .
WEST PUNK ROCK BODIES . *EAST* PUNK ROCK
BODIES . NEGATORS . UPROAR . CITY AS
RIOT-BODY ZONE

AN EXTREMOPHILE HISTORY OF BERLIN

An extremophile body loves extreme, last-ditch
environments, actively preferring them, for motives
of survival or for unknowable reasons, to banally
inhabitable terrains. Most extremophile organisms
are microbial in form (as with the human body, itself a
malfunctional assemblage of skin-enclosed microbial
elements and fluids), but they also take the biological
forms of insects such as spiders and beetles. All
extremophile entities attach themselves entrenchedly
to extinction-prone, apocalypse-inviting, resolutely
hostile sites, often located at profound subaqueous
or subterranean depth, notably alongside ocean-floor
vents expelling contents that would annul all life
forms except for extremophile ones. Such bodies often
need to transform their own internal and external
constitution in order to survive, rendering their interiors sites of 'extremozymes' that allow them not to
explode in excessive heat or to petrify in acute cold,
and amassing carapaces around themselves whose
apertures allow in only the most essential light or
sustenance. An extremophile body possesses its own
distinctive rapport to time and space in antithesis
to that experienced by other sentient bodies, and
usually exists in solitude, since it inhabits a zone
which predators are reluctant to enter (they may
instantly be expelled, combust or freeze). Its attitude
towards its fellow extremophiles is usually one of utter
oblivion, except at moments of reproduction; even

extremophiles possess genealogies. But whenever an extremophile body is engaged in contesting or absorbing multiple incursions or threats to its sensory configuration and surroundings, it is known as a 'polyextremophile', and may then be induced to undertake aberrant acts detrimental to its stability in extremity, such as manoeuvring itself into too intimate or complex a contact with its adversaries, or unwisely adjusting its own resistance to over-heating and freezing, with apocalyptic consequences for itself and its world.

Berlin bodies form the city-inhabiting manifestation of extremophile entities, genealogically generated in many ways by past urban-apocalyptic or meltdown conditions, subject to the anatomical overhaulings demanded by existence in extreme city conditions, and aware – often against their intentions – of the always imminent collapse of their loving, exposed attachment to those excessive, extreme sensory conditions. Berlin bodies' active adherence to their site is often as intensively rooted as that of extremophile entities, embedded intractably into the city's surfaces, with their wastelands, peripheral spaces and subterranes that ostensibly defy inhabitation, but simultaneously provide ideal zones of occupation; in its turn, Berlin's ground-level surface is encrusted onto the volatile skin of Europe, in proximity to vents of historical combustion (all the more threatening for their apparent dormancies) and itself a pivotal vent, as though its many brick chimneys still surviving from its nineteenth-century and early twentieth-century industrial era, along with its contemporary vents such as immense image-emitting digital screens in its corporate plazas, formed outlets for Europe's periodic catastrophic outbursts.

To live as extremophiles on that exposed, cracked and initially unpromising surface, Berlin bodies must, across time, transform themselves corporeally in response to the extreme urban mutations that enable their survival, incorporating polysexual, noise-receptive and image-attuned amendments to habitual urban anatomies, together with the capacity to reverse and fundamentally upend their own sensory perceptions and attachments, as in Berlin inhabitants' large-scale accommodations to 1930s Nazi-era political extremism with its urban manifestations of expulsion, deportation and subsequent conflagration (and final apocalyptic ruination), and, with East Berlin's inhabitants, in the cancelling in 1990 of all defining strata of existence in the GDR. Just as an extremophile body is deeply attracted to its site of residence and undaunted by that site's multiply apocalyptic potential, Berlin's bodies – even its most ephemerally in-transit, surface-skimming passengers – absorb the city's apocalyptic emanations and resonances as an integral element of the elations and ecstasies attached to the act of tenuous inhabitation. Berlin's space emits many intimations and fragments of apocalypse, both visually and sonically, and notably via the gestures and faces of its inhabitants in states of desperate crisis. In its entirety, that space forms the immediate projection into the contemporary city of the twentieth-century ordeals it holds, as though that present city comprised the residual apparition of the previous century's historical and corporeal convulsions, now vitally animated – and made inhabitable through the amassed adrenaline generated via that animation – by the urgent need to screen away the twentieth century's horror and live obliviously.

In the church foyer of the thirteenth-century Marienkirche, adjoining the Television Tower on the exposed plain between the Alexanderplatz and the imperial city-centre palace reconstructed in the 2010s, the extended panels of a fifteenth-century *Totentanz* (dance of death) fresco serve to project a corporeally focused, plague-choreographed apocalypse, as a sequence in which the figures of death and their selected victims appear together. That sequence, restored in the early years of the GDR era through a process that involved the meticulous excoriation of all painted-over layers (including traces of a seventeenth-century whitewashing that had made the dance invisible for several centuries) to leave only the severely eroded original figures, incorporates the near-illegible, part washed-away text of dialogues, which emphasize the necessity for speed in the transit into death, conducted between the figures of death and the bodies – workmen, wealthy merchants and bishops – who will now be conjured into the status of the forma-tive Berlin city dead. The figures of death, visually pre-eminent through their repeated appearances in the fresco, seize the eyes of the imminently dead through their stares, while at their feet a monstrous, bagpipe-wielding figure emits a sonic cacophony.

The sonic projections of apocalypse also appear in unforeseen, spectral ways in Berlin, as in the process of exploring the Bethanien building's courtyards at night, and abruptly hearing, immersed in darkness, Marlon Brando's voice whispering his final monologue – 'the horror . . . the horror . . .' – at an open-air projection of Francis Ford Coppola's film, before the screen and its jungle-canopy combustions come into view.

Apocalyptic Berlin may take on multiple forms, and generate numerous contrary sensations. The aura of an urban apocalyptic threat (or the sense that a calamity had already happened) seemed unnervingly palpable in the West Berlin Kreuzberg district's scarred streets and the East Berlin Mitte district's spectral wastelands, during my first walks through them at the end of the 1970s. For Berlin's extremophile existences, the act of inhabitation, over time, can assume the form of an urban continuum of acute vulnerability, marked by a sense of dread and oncoming calamity, often muted but intermittently taking on more intensified and tangible forms, in their diverse idioms (as in Cold War crises of confrontation, West Berlin's 1970s and '80s subcultures' apocalyptic preoccupations, and contemporary urban 'dark ecology' art and theory, at their most prescient and intently focused in Berlin). Through its durational form, that extremophile existence acquires an aberrant ocular and corporeal habituation to extreme situations, and comes to possess its own distinct time, notably marked in anniversaries (such as the 25th anniversary of the Berlin Wall's fall in 2014, or the 70th anniversary of the Soviet army's assault on Berlin in 2015), as though that extremophile existence, poised at the moment before apocalypse, could go on forever. Apocalyptic Berlin may also instil a sense of deep somnolent obliviousness in its extremophile terrains' residents, with an accompanying disregard for urban history and that history's vanishings. But contrarily, the inhabitation of Berlin's extremophile locations can impart such a sharpened degree of immediacy into its bodies' pre-apocalyptic acts that it also infuses a concertinaed historical awareness into them, infiltrated by fragments from Berlin's past-apocalyptic detrita and its dead bodies.

WEST PUNK ROCK BODIES

In the cultural history of twentieth-century Berlin's bodies, and in the exacerbated, self-testing dimensions of extremophile corporeality which are unique or most concentratedly present in that city beyond all others, the status of its punk rock bodies of the late 1970s, in West Berlin, and into the early 1980s, in East Berlin, is critically at stake. Punk rock bodies interrogate and negate the city and its subjugating power structures, while also affronting and anatomizing one another;

they inhabit an outwardly directed corrosive medium of cacophony and of intent visual glarings and sensory blackouts, while often immersed in narcotic and alcohol-induced crises. They spend most of their time on the city's streets, subject to hostile visual or gestural abrasures even from the notoriously blasé, unshockable population of West Berlin, and, in East Berlin, from state security agents who also scan their urban transits with surveillance cameras and envision their imminent eradication. The self-engulfing obliviousness of Berlin's punk rock bodies is intercut in their prominence in urban space with an acute sense of historical provocation (in the incorporation into their clothing of Nazism-resonating elements, for example) and of history's immediacies, so that intervals of relatively banal time between seminal moments of urban apocalypses, such as that extending from Berlin's 1945 destruction to the contemporary moment, are nullified. Their mission as Berlin bodies is to sustain and magnify the city's catastrophic aura, instilled in that punk rock era into its still-ruined, degraded architectural infrastructure as well as infused into the choking lignate-coal air to be breathed in Berlin – and then to vanish from the face of the city.[23]

In West Berlin, punk rock culture rapidly generated its own distinctive obsessions and sonic intensities once it had received its originating input in 1976 from experiments in such cities as New York, Detroit and London. The presence in West Berlin and its punk rock clubs from that same year onwards of Iggy Pop, whose group The Stooges had been among punk rock's prefiguring instigators around that decade's opening, living in the same building as Bowie in Schöneberg's Hauptstrasse, added to punk rock's precarious corporeal strata in Berlin, along with Romy Haag, whose own club, Chez Romy Haag – initiated in 1974 and still extant at that time – attracted a punk rock clientele alongside its transsexual adherents and those absorbed with performance art and 1920s Weimar-era nostalgia, and Nina Hagen, who had departed East Berlin (where she had already generated a provocative teenaged presence with her first televised performances) in 1975 and, after extensive travels, based herself in West Berlin from 1977. West Berlin's punk rock clubs and bars, such as the Mitropa and the earliest incarnation of the Dschungel – together with their accompanying record and clothes shops – were initially concentrated in close proximity to the building of Bowie and Iggy Pop, in the Hauptstrasse and along the street which led northwards from it towards the Winterfeldtplatz, initially as the Akazienstrasse and then as the Goltzstrasse. When punk rock groups visited West Berlin from Western Europe and the USA, rarely flying and more habitually driving in transit vans through the GDR's autobahn corridors, they often performed in the auditorium of a run-down 1910s cinema, the Kant Kino, to the west of the Zoologischer Garten station in the Kantstrasse, from whose foyer lines of outlandish bodies gathered.

From 1978, with the opening of the SO36 punk rock club, a former slaughterhouse adjacent to the

Heinrichplatz in the most acutely disintegrated and restless part of the Kreuzberg district, then newly populated by exiles from Turkey and subject to systematic demolitions of its eroded nineteenth-century housing stock, the West Berlin punk rock scene shifted eastwards, allying itself with Kreuzberg's activist culture of tenement occupations and anarchist provocations, with its focal points in such buildings as the semi-derelict Bethanien hospital, by then an emergent experimental arts centre after activists violently opposed its razing. Nights at the SO36 club, with its densely stained flooring and cacophony-fissured, strip-lit walls, formed gruelling endurance events of ecstasy and obsession for West Berlin punk rock bodies. Also close to the SO36 club, by the Landwehr canal and beyond the immense housing developments then recently built around the Kott-busser Tor U-bahn station, such as the already decrepit Neue Kreuzberger Zentrum constructed in 1974, was the Exil restaurant, opened at the previous decade's end by Viennese performance artists and writers whose work had caused extreme outrage there. Those nightclub and nocturnal locations for West Berlin's punk rock culture formed insurgent corporeal spaces in the otherwise catatonic island half-city.

In the 1970s' final years, West Berlin's punk rock bodies formed spectacular, outrageous but simultaneously spectral and calamity-emanating presences, attuned to the fragmented half-city while casting caustic gazings on its consumer frenzies, corruptions and subjugations to zonal military authorities; in that era, districts such as Schöneberg and Kreuzberg were still engaged in the final stages of demolishing war-era ruins and renovating or erasing fissured buildings with abraded facades whose barely heated interiors froze in winter. To the north and east of Kreuzberg, the densely graffitied course of the Berlin Wall and the razor-wired river Spree gave the district an engulfing world's-ending aura, especially at night; to its south, the Neukölln district of abandoned buildings and bewildered Turkish exiles reinforced West Berlin's overwhelming sense of dispossessed solitude and urban negation. The virulent corporeal culture of West Berlin punk rock flared intensively, and had evanesced, or embedded itself into other cultures, by the 1970s' end.

EAST PUNK ROCK BODIES

Punk rock culture manifested itself on East Berlin's streets and plazas only after its most coruscating negations had diminished or vanished in West Berlin; on my first explorations of East Berlin's plazas and night haunts in 1979, the traces of an emergent punk rock culture appeared only intermittently, on the immense expanse of the Alexanderplatz and in bullethole-indented back courtyards and peripheral bars in Prenzlauer Berg. The inspirations for East Berlin punk rock culture developed in part from covert viewings of West German television transmissions of punk rock concerts in the *Musikladen* and other series (the elderly nemesis of East Berlin's punk rock bodies, the GDR state security agency director Erich Mielke, astutely identified those inspirations as issuing from 'electronic mass-media' sources, before they became adapted into East Berlin's street-located corporeal acts and furies), as well as from the nihilist inflections of experimental music in other Eastern Bloc countries such as Czechoslovakia. Since the elderly had relative freedom to traverse the Berlin Wall's crossing points by the end of the 1970s, retired grandmothers would habitually be dispatched to record shops in the Goltz-strasse and Oranienstrasse to buy vinyl punk rock records and then carry them back into East Berlin, unnoticed by negligent border guards; punk rock bodies attempting that same crossing, from West Berlin to East Berlin, were more rigorously excluded, and had to dress down or conjure anonymity in order to explore East Berlin's extremophile punk rock culture.

While West Berlin possessed many low-rent bars, performance venues and rehearsal rooms explicitly assigned to its punk rock culture, East Berlin had almost none, and punk rock bodies – always crossing the city in small gangs, since they never numbered more than a few hundred in total and so became intimately bound together as well as being exposed (far more so than in West Berlin) to violent assaults – often spent their nights in transit through the deserted streets, refused entry by bar after bar. The vast, interior space of an abandoned gasometer on the eastern perimeter

of Prenzlauer Berg, in the terrain of already semi-razed industrial installations that would later become the Ernst-Thälmann Park, served as a rehearsal space and locus for encounters for East Berlin's punk rock culture, until that gasometer was detonated in an explosion that immersed the entirety of the district in a cloud of toxic dust; the neglected ruins of that gasometer and its adjacent terrain, largely beyond the gaze of security agents' surveillance cameras, then became a detrital cityscape intensively inhabited by that punk rock culture's bodies, photographed and filmed in Super-8 footage by Marquardt, Sabine Bading, Brigitte Bludau Munroe and others. In the summer months, East Berlin's punk rock culture had its preferential locations at the Spreepark funfair and the unsupervised grounds of lunatic asylums; whenever it intersected with central East Berlin areas such as the Alexanderplatz, in alcohol-propelled zigzaggings of vocally cacophonic figures, that culture's bodies were extensively filmed by state security agents from towers' vantage points and the footage archived for future prosecutions and exclusions, by which bodies were often officially prohibited from the central districts of East Berlin and consigned to its peripheries.

By 1982, Mielke had become exasperated with the disruptive urban visibility of East Berlin's punk rock culture, which he equated directly with the prominence on Berlin's streets of the Nazi gangs he had battled as a young Communist activist on those same streets' previous incarnations, exactly fifty years earlier, prior to Hitler's election; Mielke ordered that culture's total eradication, his voice wavering with confusion over subcultural variants, in a recorded speech – as momentous in its way, in its implications for survivals of Berlin's corporeality, as those of Reuter from the late 1940s – which also criminalized what he called 'heavy metallers', among other disorderly urban manifestations. East Berlin's outlawed punk rock figures were then comprehensively arrested, notably after their gangs' infiltrations by informants controlled by the GDR's secret police agency, and were threatened with lengthy imprisonment in detention centres or military conscription unless they immediately renounced their affiliation to punk rock culture and integrated themselves instead into the GDR's own official youth cultures, such as its Freie Deutsche Jugend organizations. Some of those arrested were detained for a year or more, and all were blacklisted from ever occupying positions of social prominence and responsibility in the GDR (though for most of that punk rock culture's adherents such a prohibition met with oblivious disregard). Mielke's corporeal dispersal of East Berlin's punk rock culture was exacted so thoroughly – in a form of apocalyptic scorched-earthing – that the culture entirely vanished from urban space for several years (as West Berlin's punk rock culture itself had, through its own contrary, abrupt self-combustion four years or so earlier), reappearing only in less inflammatory, fashion-oriented forms in the period leading up to East Berlin's own

disappearance.

In most cases, those punk rock bodies of early 1980s East Berlin never met again, or not until the 1990s or 2000s, when documentary film-makers reassembled them, as for a riverboat cruise through Berlin's Mitte district in the 1996 documentary *Störung Ost* (*Disorder East*). That experience of disabused bodies' reluctant reassembly could be marked by extreme anger and rancour, since the participants had been able to identify – through secret police and state security archival disclosures that followed the GDR's dissolution in 1989–90 – which of the once trusted friends that had intimately formed part of their East Berlin-traversing gangs, in wild abandon and elation, had been implanted, fraudulent bodies: those of security agency infiltrators recording or memorizing the emission of every last vocal curse of that punk rock culture, and preparing its unsuspecting bodies for incarcerated disappearances from Berlin.

NEGATORS

As the twentieth century recedes backwards from the current instant, but obstinately demands ever greater and more immediate attention from Berlin's contemporary inhabitants and also from contemporary Europe as those urban bodies and that contested entity approach eras of new transformations and conflagrations, the scars and voids of that catastrophic century become still more exposed and tangible. Their attempted architectural screening away in Berlin, undertaken for example through comprehensive renovations over the decades since the city's reunification, notably in the once-ravaged streets and courtyards of East Berlin, often appears only to exacerbate and render more profound those resilient scars and voids, in their virtual, archived and city-dead dimensions, and also in the sense of an imminent, apocalyptic falling away of that attempted screening. The twentieth-century cultural history of Berlin, in its intimacy with the contemporary city, simultaneously retracts itself from view and abruptly resurges in sequences of insistent, scathing urban black jokes perpetrated on present-day corporeality. Berlin's twentieth-century diabolical black jokes – with their apocalyptic aura, still palpable and breathable in the city's streets across that century's final decades, even with all of their initiating deliria, cruelty or toxicity long extinguished – remain poised in the air of twenty-first century Berlin, as well as archivally documented in such media as film and also vividly marked into outlying urban spaces, wastelands and neglected interzones, notably as multiple recitations and vocal fragments integral to a corporeal history of Berlin bodies.

An urban historical black joke can become even blacker and still more corrosively cutting in its return, while its new manifestation may possess no imme- diately evident sonic or visual traces. If twenty-first- century Berlin, with its regimes of digital surveillance and the systematic corporate appropriation of public space, remains largely intact but subject to a pervasive dispossession of its bodies, as a terrain of corporeal negation and subjugation, then a still blacker joke is accentuated in its danger by its self-instilled capacity never to be *told*, or heard, and for its corporeal voidings to have become so silently habituated that they are unperceived.

Last envisionings of Berlin, recounted in contemporary activist, dark-ecological and extremophile environments or visualized and theorized in artworks under conditions of corporeal meltdown, often encompass fears or desires for the city's eventual negating and vanishing. In 1945, as one of many permutations for Berlin's future discussed (but soon rejected) in the opening sessions of the seventeen-day Potsdam Cecilienhof conference by the Second World War's victors – Stalin, Churchill and Truman – while the city on the far side of the Havel lake and Grunewald forest from the conference's palatial location remained pervasively in ruins, that projected urban disappearance could take two forms.[24] In the first envisioning of Berlin's negation, the manual accumulation over the post-war years by the city's embattled bodies of detonated rubble and its gradual amassing in peripheral sites into small mountains – such as that of the Teufelsberg, on which the USA security agency listening station with its distinctive white domes was subsequently built from 1963 and, following that construction's obsolescence and ruination, it was planned to install the film-maker David Lynch's envisaged university of transcendental meditation there – would not be the prelude to programmes of wide-ranging urban reconstruction, such as that of the Stalinallee filmed in *Story of a Street* or of the Schöneberg district filmed by Herbert Kiper on his daily walks, but would instead accompany the maximal erasure and uprooting of all traces, archives and strata of the city, ostensibly leaving nothing behind. In that proposition of Berlin's negation, the city's site would then be abandoned and left as a grown-over wasteland, eventually evolving into a lake-constellated immense forest. Its survivors would be dispersed as refugees or rehoused at a distance in a new city, to which the name of Berlin would not be given.

In the second Cecilienhof proposition of Berlin's negation, its ruins would not even need to be detonated or deployed for rubble mountains, but instead would be left in their frozen, jagged precarity, as Berlin's monument to itself in ruination, comprising on a larger scale the model adopted in the previous year, 1944, with de Gaulle's order that the part-razed, incendiary-marked French village of Oradour-sur-Glane, site of a German ss unit's massacre through incineration, in a church and barns, of hundreds of its inhabitants, should be left perpetually frozen in the immediacy of its ruined state, or the variant model that resulted from the British government's order, during the post-war period, that villages evacuated in 1943 to create militarized zones along the Dorset coast of England, such as Tyneham, should not be given back to their compulsorily expelled inhabitants and instead left to fall into ruins that were subsequently preserved in indefinite depopulated memorial suspension.

Many sequences in Berlin's ruin-located films from the end of the 1940s and early '50s, such as Gerhard Klein's documentary about the dangers of ruins collapsing in upon their clearers, *Building-site X* (*Baustelle X*, 1950), shot at night or after the day's rubble clearance had ended, attempt to evoke that sense of a self-monumentalizing, self-projecting city of ruins, with its distinctive anti-architectural mystery and beauty. Such freezings of buildings at the instant of their ruination could equally be the result of neglect or oblivion rather than memorial intention. Ruins such as those of the woodland-surrounded women's pavilion at the Beelitz-Heilstätten tubercular sub-city of Berlin, gutted by fire from aerial bombing in 1945 but with its solid brick-built infrastructure and parts of its tree-grown roof left intact, remain abandoned, almost untouched (other than by covert infiltrators and by the inscription on their exterior and interior spaces of graffiti) from the conflagratory instant of their ruination through to the contemporary moment.

Ludwig Meidner's apocalyptic paintings of Berlin, undertaken in several outbursts of concentrated work, notably in the summer of 1912, in a state of

sweat-pouring, overheated delirium at his heat-
absorbing attic studio in the city's Friedenau district,
and titled as 'apocalyptic landscapes' or 'apocalyptic
visions', with precise indications of their Berlin locations such as the area around the Halensee railway
station, all inflict a spectacular negation upon the
city, whose inhabitants are fleeing in wide-eyed terror
from aerial bombardments or internally generated
combustions, generating convulsed urban fragmentations in which ocular and sonic perception itself
has been negated. Meidner's Berlin-focused drawings
from the same era, of solitary figures in transit within
oppressively dense, hostile crowds in Berlin's central
plazas and railway-station subterranes, or of exposed
figures poised beneath buildings on the point of
collapse, intimate moments imminently preceding
urban annulling. Meidner's paintings and drawings
of 1912–13 collect multiple permutations of Berlin's
negation, with that erasure viewed in each work
from a distinct location in the city, topographically
shifting from image to image, so that Berlin's apocalyptic engulfing for its inflicted negation closes in
upon the city from multiple perspectives that are
assigned to the viewer's eye, as though that eye were
being accorded omniscience as it looks down upon
apocalyptic Berlin. Negation transmutes the city
in Meidner's sequences of split-second explodings.

The subterranes of Meidner's painted and drawn
terminal city are split apart and expel deserts or seas
into ground-level urban space, in a parallel way to

that in which, in the artist Werner Heldt's later paintings from the second half of the 1940s – depicting Berlin negated after its wartime ruination – the near-depopulated city has now become a marine one, exposed to inundations. In contemporary anime artworks' imaginary negations of Berlin – undertaken anonymously by young Japanese digital artists and in which Berlin is only one of many global cities assigned for destruction – an unknown adversary or maleficent deity rains fireballs onto the city's prominent sites such as the Dom cathedral or Siegessäule column; that pixelated disintegration forms an aberrant amalgam across time with the many images and sequences of images – across art, photography and film – of previous negations and destructions of Berlin.

Berlin's projected negations of the twentieth century, in their many variants, often took the form of contestations between opposed performers of dual deliria, such as those of the era of the city's post-war division in which one half or other of the city was glacially dismissed as having no right to exist, while its opposing half threatened to encroach upon and negate it, with potentially apocalyptic consequences in the Cold War period. Such dual deliria, as with that conducted adversarially between Ernst Reuter and Stalin (and his Soviet-zone representatives) in 1948–9 during the Airlift era of West Berlin's territorial stranding and attempted annulling, could possess outlandish historical resurgences, as in that particular pairing's resuscitation of Reuter's previous role in subordination to Stalin during his time as a Soviet commissar, presiding over summary executions, in Saratov thirty years earlier. Once the demarcation between East Berlin and West Berlin became rigidly entrenched, from 1961, that sense of a systematic, contemptuous disregard – to the extent of each half-city's voiding into white emptiness on maps by the opposing half-city's cartographers – took on spectacular dimensions, encompassing filmic, press media, architectural and corporeal domains. Such depths of negatory contestation simultaneously demanded intimate, covert complicity and co-operation between the paired adversaries, from the post-war era through to 1989–90, alongside wily tactics of urban-historical disappearance. While Stalin's wipeout tactic of the 1948–9 Berlin Blockade had been to negate the city's western zones of occupation by isolating and starving their inhabitants, Helmut Kohl's tactic in 1990 was finally to conjure East Berlin out of existence in its entirety, thereby generating a spectral urban entity of deep attachments and nostalgic visions, and of scarred zones for open exploration, more resilient in many ways than either the actual annulled half-city itself or the reunified Berlin.

Corporate contemporary Berlin envisions its bodies' spatial negation or constriction in its ocular and corporeal regimes of surveillance and subjugation, but the city holds many other, contrary negators. In the present-day activist preoccupations with the urban space of Berlin of radical dark-ecology groups and movements (located especially in the Kreuzberg district), a definitive terminal event has already occurred through now-irreparable ecological damage, and what remains, across the city's detrital future-time before its final urban breakdown and extinction, several years or at most decades in duration, forms a marginal survival zone of excess, elating as well as dread-instilled (and spatially evoking in some ways the parallel aura of Cold War late 1970s West Berlin's nocturnal 'end-of-the-line' Kreuzberg) in its final-moment pre-apocalyptic status, and provoking last-ditch experimentation around that projected negation, especially in art, theory and philosophy. Evocative paintings undertaken in Berlin in the 1990s by the ecologically engaged artist Stefan Hoenerloh, of an immense city of seared, surface-abraded tenements subject to acute depopulation which could be perceived as climatic in origin, now appear prescient of that terminal interval. In dark-ecological formulations of Berlin's fade-out, nothing at all can be foreseen of the city's voided future once that interval of tenuous survival elapses. In contrast to the certainty among dark-ecology groups of Berlin's eventual utter vanishing, the city's nihilistic and hard-core anarchist cells manifest their opposition to corporate Berlin more combatively, through street riots and anger-driven uproar, and such direct-action negations of Berlin's current forms invariably envision a new entity that must emerge from that eradicating tumult, even if it is one in which the city – entirely razed as a corporate body – is left in the condition of grown-over Edenic autonomy that was originally formulated as one potential Berlin future at the Cecilienhof in 1945.

UPROAR

Whenever Berlin undergoes a crisis or seminal event in which its bodies' already extremophile existence is exposed to being amended or erased, or in which its amassed crowds are wracked by sensory, ocular and auditory transmutations, those bodies emit *roars*, propelled outwards from corporeal organs into space both vertically and horizontally after initially being projected against the city's resonating surfaces. The status of roaring in Berlin's urban space, such as that occurring insurgently during a political or revolutionary demonstration or in response to the sudden transmission to accumulated bodies of life-changing proclamations or data, is that of a pivotal indicator of the misfiring or unleashing of events whose participants then become collectively con-vulsed, leading them to expel an outlandish vocal content eruptively, beyond coherent language. A roar cannot be performed in solitude, since it must take on a distinctive, multiple corporeal density from its amalgamation of allied expurgings of sensations and emotions: anger, dread, ecstasy or a profound sense of apocalyptic unknowing.

A roar can be expelled spontaneously, but in order to be pervasively experienced by Berlin's inhabitants across maximal urban space, its transmission needs to emerge from a closely choreographed mass of bodies, leading to a crescendo; a roar's projection is optimally enacted alongside a concave or vertically positioned screen, such as that of a multi-storey tower's facade or of a steeply raked stadium or outdoor auditorium, in order to magnify and deepen it. At least some part of that roar's sonic charge will then be directed upwards, collecting in the sky above the city, but the remainder of that charge deflects horizontally from its screen. A roar in transit across Berlin holds an unearthly sonic propulsion, as a city-negating entity that courses at speed over the urban terrain. But the actual emitting of that roar is usually undertaken in stasis, either through intentional corporeal amassings in a particular, sensitized location, as with the roars of elation emitted during the immense demonstration of 4 November 1989 on the Alexanderplatz (projected onwards by such sound-deflecting surfaces as that of the 37-storey Interhotel Stadt Berlin's facade), or else unintentionally, as in the desolate, furious roars emitted by demon-strating or rioting crowds exposed to assault at street intersections and abruptly corralled from all sides by riot police 'kettling' manoeuvres, and thereby locked into suffocating body-to-body intimacies with fellow rioters whose constriction can only be articulated in acts of roaring, such as those undertaken in the Kreuzberg district's Oranienplatz during the protests around its refugee sub-city's voiding in 2014, or in the Friedrichshain district at street junctions adjacent to activist-occupied buildings being voided by riot police, notably, in 2011, the prominent banner-facaded building located in the Liebigstrasse. Roarings' recordings across Berlin's twentieth-century cultural history are pre-eminently rendered in films' soundtracks, often with deficient or malfunctioning equipment that imparts to roars their spectral or shattered aura, as with roars erupting from stadia during political rallies of the 1930s and '50s, or during the final stages of the June 1953 East Berlin protests when tank-assaulted rioters were being pinned down against the Columbushaus and other buildings.

A roar without a vertical outlet and with a limited horizontal range violently compacts itself into space and then returns to its emitters' bodies. In 1990, traversing the long, near-dark subterranean tiled passageway beneath the Lichtenberg S-bahn station, I came across a sudden flaring of violence between factions of neo-Nazi and neo-Communist gangs, its onset marked by a roar of concentrated fury which struck the low ceiling of that passageway and rebounded directly into the tightly enclosed constellation of those thirty or forty young bodies, wielding fists, boots, broken bottles, thereby accentuating that confrontation; after two or three minutes, those gangs abruptly dispersed at high speed, pushing ocularly transfixed spectators aside, leaving behind blood on the passageway's floor and

a detritus of uproar's sonic imprintation, still echoing.

On nocturnal walks during that year's sub-zero winter among the soaring GDR-era housing-towers of Marzahn, I often heard roars from gang warfare eruptions sonically rebounding from those towers' glass and plastic facades, but on reaching the site, I found that the warring gangs' bodies had already vanished while their roaring still hung in clouds of heatedly breathed out ice crystals in the freezing air.

The assembling and choreographing via social media of protests' participant bodies, in contemporary Berlin, itself generates a new idiom of digital roaring, also erupting sonically, in urgent but rapidly dispersed signals, from smartphones that simultaneously film and transmit those protesters' riot police affrontments, in the contexts of anarchistic, nihilistic, anti-capitalist and other street-located activist contestations. Such riots' roarings, oscillating between the digital and the corporeal, may actively desire or urgently anticipate variants of the apocalyptic engulfing of the city which formed such a source of dread or protestation in previous eras' fearful roarings by Berlin's populations. Across Berlin's corporeal history, roars of exultation, such as those collectively emitted by sensorially trans-ported dancers in deliria of physical endurance and ricocheting from the interior walls of nightclubs located in derelict industrial buildings, together with the roars of terror in darkness of crammed bodies anticipating their imminent wiping out in air-raid shelters under relentless attack, and roarings of furies of negation in their multiple forms, all amalgamate as urgent voicings of Berlin's survivals and of the threats to those survivals.

Berlin's urban ethnographers preoccupied primarily with the city's peripheral spaces of dispossessed and abandoned bodies, and conducting extended research-focused inhabitations of such spaces, such as the Spanish ethnographer Iban Ayesta in the early 2000s, have investigated the ways in which silence forms a projection of uproar too, when it is instilled insurgently in Berlin bodies – such as those with marginal or refugee non-status – in the form of an unmanifested roar that is unable to traverse corporeal boundaries such as those between the vocal tract or tongue and the hostile exterior atmosphere. Such Berlin bodies are barred in isolation from the amassings with other bodies required to impart to uproar its city-saturating depth and resonance. As a result, such silent uproars are only projected in curtailed forms, in gestural fragments or facial tics, often on nocturnal, isolated traversals of the city's wastelands and emptied-out avenues, by those self-muted bodies who decline to narrate their own calamities in the way that they are repeatedly recited vocally by the S-bahn carriage riding figures of Berlin's desperate population; such silent bodies in uproar instead occupy the city's unseen, unheard perimeters.

CITY AS RIOT-BODY ZONE

Acts of rioting and violent political contestation frequently occupied Berlin's twentieth-century space, from those instilled in the city by the Spartacus League in the winter months of 1918–19, to those of 1967–8 following such events as the beatings by riot police of protesters during the Shah of Iran's West Berlin visit and the attempted assassination of Rudi Dutschke, and those of 1990–91 transmitting the aftershocks of unreconciled extremism following the city's reunification. Such acts occurred right across the city, from its central plazas and squares, to its workers' districts such as Wedding and Prenzlauer Berg, its embassy quarters, its luxurious avenues such as that on which Dutschke was shot, its eastern tower-block peripheries, and its eroded areas of entrenched historical confrontation, such as Lichtenberg. A riot or eruption of uproar in Berlin is integrally an in-transit phenomenon, in which an amassing of protesters crosses the city in order to reach a sensitized locus, gathering more bodies and eyes along the way, as in the 17 June 1953 event's riotous traversal of East Berlin. Even if a riot event remains static, its uproar, as a corporeal entity in its own right, is propelled across urban space, especially if its location is positioned next to a projecting 'sound mirror' construction, allowing outlandish sonic emanations of disquiet to be heard from one end of Berlin to the other.

The spatial malleability and pervasive physical infiltrations of riots' locations in Berlin invoke the

potential for the entire city's terrain, within the topographical outlines of its administrative boundaries, to
be rendered into a riotous entity, seismically seething
with apocalyptic fury or ecstasy, and in which the city's
most tranquil sites may be abruptly overturned into
its most enraged. Berlin's yearly May Day riots, with
their wide-ranging, expansive urban reach, prefigure
the momentum of such a city-engulfing event of
insurgency in which spatial saturation and protests'
temporal simultaneity exactly coincide, and in which
Berlin bodies are provoked beyond endurance by an
amalgam of such all-consuming outrages (such as
urban-ecological despoliation, city authorities' opaque
or corrupt dealings, imminent or ongoing political
and corporate subjugations of its inhabitants, among
many other provocations) that the city as riot-body
zone is engendered. Throughout its cultural history,
Berlin as anatomical city is one realized in insurgency.

The activation of overwhelming proportions
of Berlin's inhabitants and their convergence into
particular sites can take the form of distinctly
future-oriented amassings, as with the immense
expanse of bodies positioned in front of the Reichstag steps for Reuter's Airlift-era 1948 speech or in
the (more constricted) plaza and streets facing the
Schöneberg town hall steps for Kennedy's epochal
1963 speech, during which West Berlin's bodies, at
those moments of accumulating, acute crises, anticipated words reassuring them that Berlin's urban
time would continue to run onwards. In their filmic

documentation, those speeches of Reuter and Kennedy may retrospectively appear to be vocally emitted through the historical Saratov death-sentence judgements and the imminent Dallas exhalation of assassination of the mouths speaking them. The written materials from which they were delivered or improvised, in the forms of Reuter's few handwritten notes and Kennedy's pronunciation guide, together with both speeches' hesitating, maladroit delivery, intimate the extent to which pivotal urban events, determining the future of Berlin, can be propelled from sparse, fragmentary materials and amassed corporeal expectations.

Other mass occupations of urban space, as with those of autumn 1989 across East Berlin's plazas and streets, such as the Alexanderplatz, Zionskirchplatz and Stargarder Strasse, took the contrary form, of past-oriented acts of participants witnessing with anger and derision the obsolescent GDR's demise, with the absence of any determined, collective future-focused direction in that crowd, almost all of whom had no intention or expectation that East Berlin and its urban cultures would be so rapidly and totally subject to their erasure across the following months. Such public events' particular orientations towards future or past variants of Berlin – in the forms of desired propulsions into the future of West Berlin, in 1948 and 1963, and elated consignings of East Berlin's regime to oblivion, in 1953 and 1989 – inflect the parameters of Berlin bodies' amassings, in unease or protest. But in order for every last periphery of Berlin to be occupied by a potentially all-enveloping manifestation that turns the entire city into a riot-body or protest-body zone, such fixed temporal orientations would need to be annulled, so that body-propelled urban time can oscillate with infinite flexibility, between future, past and contemporary moments.

Berlin's unique capacity to instil deep into its own terrain the aberrant, riotous, zonal, uproar-striated, electrified and contrary contents of compacted urban strata – which then extrude into its exterior space as the city's projections – emerges directly from the insurgent dimensions of its corporealities. That vital intersection between Berlin bodies and the multiply scarred terrain they occupy imparts to the city its distinctive aura as one profoundly marked by corporeal acts, interventions and vanishings. Berlin's many emergency eras – such as those around 1918, 1945, 1961 and 1989, among others, and always including the contemporary instant – have often taken the form of bodies pouring restively onto the streets, to protest, riot, negate or simply to amass, or else of bodies pivotally retracting and disappearing from death-exposed streets, into subterranes, cellars and air-raid bunkers. Whenever bodies are located on the streets of Berlin, or whenever their traces are tangible there even after their vanishings (as with the deliquescing ice-crystal breath of uproar of its Marzahn gangs' bodies after their dispersal, archived into thin air), they are instantly caught up as seminal corporeal entities into urban history's transformational velocities, always at their most intensive and awry in Berlin.

7
BERLIN'S RUINS

BERLIN RUINATION . THE BATTLE FOR BERLIN

BERLIN RUINATION

Among Berlin's infinite ruinations across the twentieth century, that of its bodies constitutes the most spectacular. Bodies were subjected to ruination and disintegration during conflicts, such as those which sheared off body parts and led to the prominent visibility on Berlin's streets, for decades after each of its two world wars, of limbless, eyeless or organless figures. Berlin's bodies also generated and exhibited their own self-inflicted ruination, as in the instances of bodies ruined via multiple abuses intimately interlinked with the inhabitation and experience of Berlin, exemplified in the ruined figure of Anita Berber, still dancing wildly at late 1920s nightclubs such as the Eldorado even in terminal physical dissolution, and in the contemporary city in figures undertaking unfinishable but urgently propelled exterior traversals of urban space as narcotic or alcoholic passengers. Since Berlin's inhabitation is often performed via its bodies' projection into vulnerable contacts with the city's pre-eminently serrated surfaces – as everyday habitual events or during insurgent acts such as riots – those exposed Berlin bodies incur, over years or decades, a gradual process of ruinous attrition, in which corporeal extremities are grazed, indented or scarred. Ruination also takes the form of an obsessively desired act, accomplished rapidly through concentrated abuse or debilitating exhaustion during intensive occupations of corrosive environments such as nightclubs. Markings of Berlin's self-directed corporeal ruination – in facial striations, ocular flaws, collapsings into unconsciousness, gaping orifices, discolorations, uncontrolled emissions of detrita, sensory negation – distinctively resonate with those imprinted upon and constituting the city's ruined surfaces.

Berlin's ruins also embody petrifaction, and the freezing or loss of time. In 2013 I attended an event in the former GDR Mint building, in the Mitte district alongside the Spree – the soaring windows of its reception rooms looking across that sunlit river's weirs to the multi-storey apartment towers of the Fischerinsel – at which the 83-year-old lawyer Ulrich Ditzen, the son of the novelist Hans Fallada, evoked (probably for the last time, since he died soon afterwards) his teen-aged memories of nocturnal walks in the years 1946–7 through the ruins of northern and eastern Berlin, especially the district of Pankow, through streets still devastated by wartime aerial bombing, artillery fire and hand-to-hand fighting, alongside the figure of his morphine-destroyed father – dying of addiction in that era while simultaneously writing at furious, extraordinary speed his final novel, *Alone in Berlin* (*Jeder stirbt für sich allein*, 1947) – whose advanced corporeal ruination bled into the city's ruins and itself was exacerbated by that pervasive urban ruination which, at that moment, appeared irresoluble and irreparable to many of those engaged in traversing it, including Fallada himself. In February 1947, shortly before the publication of *Alone in Berlin*, Fallada died of his physical disintegration engendered by morphine addiction in his room in Pankow at a semi-ruined temporary hospital improvised from an old school.

The Mint building's second-floor reception rooms had been converted into a design studio, but outside them and at the end of a passageway, an uncarpeted stairway led unobtrusively out of sight up two further flights of stairs, and once the event was over, I walked up those stairs and prised open the door, entering the Mint's petrified, dust-encrusted administrative offices, arranged in a sequence of seven river-facing rooms along a corridor, and frozen in time since their abandonment and negligent sealing in the spring or summer of 1990, manual typewriters and fading, cream-coloured letter-headed stationery on their desks, along with unopened packets of VEB Zigarettenfabrik Berlin-Pankow 'Saba' cigarettes and detailed, annulled plans for mintings of new categories of medals for those East Berlin citizens who had devoted thirty or even forty years of *Treue Dienst* (loyal service) to the GDR's Fighting Groups of the Working Class. The windows overlooking the Fischerinsel – their view angled at a higher elevation from those in front of which Ditzen had stood to vocally conjure Berlin's 1946–7 ruins just a few moments earlier – had been closed for almost a quarter of a century, so that filaments and fragments of the final bodies that had occupied those rooms hung in dust or lung-expelled ash in the dusk air and spectrally coated the windows' interior surfaces, rendered into suspended corporeal ruination. In the final office at the corridor's far end,

I opened a reluctant window by a sliver and those corporeal ruin-traces instantly dispersed into Berlin's outside space.

The delicate zones of intersection between corporeal ruins and urban ruins can be explored with acuity only momentarily, in Berlin's spaces, before such dispersals and evanescences. Once those dual ruinations have taken on an acute or extreme form, their interfacing is subject to the imminent collapse of one or other (or both) of its components, so that the ruined faces of Berlin's bodies fade from view and the last tenable surface-layer of ruined architecture undergoes a fissuration so complete that it crumbles away into fine rubble and slips between the fingertips, as with the hand-lettered signage and vividly glazed wall tiles of just-destroyed late nineteenth-century ballrooms which I picked up from former East Berlin's demolition sites in 1990. The eye cannot probe too interrogatively into ruination, or else it vanishes, as with so many of Berlin's resonant spaces of abandonment over the decades since the city's reunification.

Film may often form a more incisive medium than the destabilizing eye for probing the interzones between corporeal and urban ruination, as with the sequences in Klein's film *Building-site X* in which emaciated, burnt-out bodies of ruination struggle, in Berlin's bombed-out areas such as those of Pankow and Friedrichshain, to detonate, demolish or disassemble the precarious columns and precipices left over from otherwise razed buildings, and – their ruined bodies' hunger or hallucinatory exhaustion making them inattentive to danger – risk being engulfed by those ruins' abrupt collapses before the work of urban reconstruction has even begun. Other sequences from films of later decades, focused upon narcotic, psychotic or alcohol-induced corporeal self-ruination in intimacy with West Berlin's enduringly semi-ruined terrains and in-transit wastelands – such as those sequences scrutinizing young, heroin-addicted bodies, including that of the character 'Christiane F.', against the Zoologischer Garten station's far-side exits used for transactions in prostitution and drugs, in *Wir Kinder vom Bahnhof Zoo* (*We Children from Zoo Station*, 1981) – reinforce an exposed precariousness that ensues from encounters between ruined bodies and ruined urban fragments, which serve further to disintegrate one another. Film constitutes the final medium of Berlin's ruination, projected as an ongoing urban catastrophe always infiltrated and enhanced in its apocalyptic aura by the bodies inhabiting it.

In order to assess with clarity the vital, future-oriented form of Berlin's surviving ruins – such as those of abandoned cigarette factories, funfairs and generating plants from the GDR era, or of the rare buildings bombed out in 1943–5 and still left intact in neglect, as voided, tree-grown shells (as with the women's pavilion at the Beelitz-Heilstätten sanatorium), or of wastelanded zones of compacted debris – as a living, body-imprinted entity of the contemporary city, it would be necessary to map, demolish and raze without exception all of the construction work (in such forms as office buildings, hotels, condos, gated communities and governmental or corporate head-quarters, along with their digital image screens) undertaken since Berlin's reunification in 1990, and signalled against the city's skies across a quarter-century by constellations of cranes and at ground level by cacophonies and the dispersal of toxic residues, to thereby create a monumental network of new voids in Berlin's space to function as viewing sites for the study of its seminal ruination.[25] Urban anatomy in Berlin is revealed in the configurations of ruins and their endurance into the city's futures.

THE BATTLE FOR BERLIN

Berlin's bodies may be street-anatomized via explorations and projections of urban cultural histories, of ostensibly detrital, ruined and obsolete locations that, in their apparent voiding, contrarily hold unforeseen revelations, of inscriptions on corporeal and urban surfaces, and of opened-up or burst-open archives. In such anatomizings of the city's ruins and voids, you are always propelled through Berlin's past and contemporary contestations and seizings: the battle for Berlin is a multiple entity.

The most omnipresent Berlin ruin, permeating half of the city, remains that of East Berlin (itself largely constructed on the semi-razed terrain of the 1945 urban battlefield), many of its architectural constructions still there, more than a quarter-century after that half-city ceased to exist, re-facaded, obscured or reconfigured, and often constituting some of the contemporary city's most prominent, densely inhabited elements – as with the former Interhotel Stadt Berlin and the Television Tower, or the peripheral towers of Marzahn – in the form of rigid strata of ruins, but negated so utterly and suddenly as an urban entity in 1990 that it possesses a traumatized, overturned aura that spectrally infiltrates every corporeal and ocular transit through the eastern city. Especially in the cataleptic streets of the north-eastern Weissensee and Pankow districts that are only marginally altered since the 1980s, with their GDR-era street signage and buildings' facades still displayed, East Berlin appears a comprehensively erased, obsolete memory whose content is contrarily still tangible.

East Berlin's ruination, in that half-city's sidelining into oblivion, was only intermittently and ambivalently contested in its former inhabitants' battles for Berlin's memory, but other, more fiercely fought battles for Berlin, in their many variants and conjurations, have been conducted with intensive corporeal engagement and exposure, in the forms of headlong confrontations with riot police, such as those by 1970s Kreuzberg activists protesting against the sleight-of-hand seizing – through covert alliances between the city authorities and redevelopment corporations – from its inhabitants' grip of that district's precious (even at their most disin-tegrated) buildings, spaces and resources. The corporeal commitment devoted to a battle for Berlin intimates that some element of the city is conceived of as being prized, often in inverse proportion to its monetary valuation, and is thereby worth defending or contesting physically, via human barriers or eruptions of bodies which are self-primed to receive woundings as urban 'sacrifices'. Such corporeal battlings for the city also presuppose the belief or enduring paranoid delusion that Berlin – uniquely or to a degree far exceeding all other cities – is always the focus of relentless attempted appropriations and transmutations, in many forms (from 'grabbing' speculators, corrupt political powers, agents of subjugation, digital data corporations, alien bodies or adversaries, among other potential 'thieves' of Berlin), that dispossess it of its distinctive status and thereby render it into irreconcilable non-Berlins or anti-Berlins.

In subjecting Berlin's buildings to pervasive disintegration through rocket fire and shrapnel and in simultaneously wiping out and abusing many of its bodies, the Soviet army's overpowering of the city with over a million belligerent figures propelled *against* Berlin in the final week of April 1945 amalgamates urban and corporeal inflicted ruinations, with that concentrated span of time evident in the form of large plots in Berlin-wide cemeteries devoted to the identical graves of its inhabitants all killed on the same day during that week, as the Soviet army infiltrated the city, at varying speeds and deploying a range of urban-combat strategies, from the south, north and east, aiming to converge on the Reichstag building and (to the extent that it could be established that he was still present in the city) upon Hitler's body. Every Soviet soldier subsequently received a mass-produced brass medal embossed with the definitively assigned date of Berlin's 'capture', as though it were an animal: 2 May 1945.

As the pre-eminent 'battle for Berlin', the Soviet army's overpowering and ruination of the city also generates a retrospective ambivalence paralleling that with which East Berlin's vanishing is contested. In order for Hitler's lethal Berlin (with its proposed overhauling into the Germania megalopolis) to be negated, it had to endure a demonstrative obliteration and large-scale disappearance which still striates the infrastructure of the contemporary city, and whose extensive battle casualties, on the Soviet side, led to a topographic culture of memorial space installed in the second half of the 1940s, still resonant in the contemporary city, especially in the prominent forms of the Treptower Park and Schönholzer Heide monuments commemorating and holding those Soviet soldiers' bodies. The forces who battled to resist Berlin's fall – many of them mid-teenaged conscripts – were contrarily obscured in death. But alongside that erasure of Berlin's urban form, the city's subjection to corporeal abuse – exemplified above all in the wide-scale rapes, in the days immediately preceding and following the city's fall, for which Marlene Dietrich rebuked the Soviet army's commander Georgy Zhukov at their meeting in September 1945 at his villa headquarters in the Karlshorst district, where

the capitulation of Hitler's army had been signed four months earlier – infuses into Berlin's battles, in their many contemporary forms, an enduring resistance to corporeal subjugation.

The 1945 battle that struck Berlin remains so profoundly determining for the urban and corporeal history of the contemporary city that it wields the enduring power to assert itself over and even upend the oblivion-oriented present moment. In May 2015, on the seventieth anniversary of the fall of Berlin to the Soviet army, I visited Zhukov's headquarters in Karlshorst with my friend Maria S., who had been born in 1945 within the tumultuous dead-centre axis of Europe's massacres, refugee displacements and urban razings. We stood under the chandeliers of the austere high-ceilinged salon (originally the dining room of a military school) in which the embittered Nazi commanders had signed the capitulation document under Zhukov's abrasive eye, while on a stage outside in the villa's garden, singers from the Alexandrov Ensemble performed the same song – 'Kalinka' – which their predecessors had performed for an ecstatic audience clinging to the precipices of Berlin's Gendarmenmarkt ruins in 1948. On my visits to the Karlshorst site on previous anniversaries, aged medal-wearing uniformed veterans of the invading Soviet forces had been conspicuous presences, but for the first time, their figures were now entirely absent. The anniversary was marked on the following day, 9 May, by celebrations at Treptower Park, and Maria and I climbed the steps at the base of the memorial's immense bronze statue of a swastika-crushing Soviet soldier, to look out over the vast terrain of wreathed mass-tombs and gilt-lettered friezes, in one corner of which Ko Murobushi had danced his city dead Berlin dance, a year earlier. Many thousands of bodies saturated that terrain, and Maria ascertained from their voices that almost everyone in that celebrating crowd was Russian. Remembering Murobushi's delirious vocal incantations accompanying the final gestures of his abandoned dance, I imagined a seismic momentary inversion of Berlin's infinitely fissured ground-level surface that would supplant the bodies of the living with the dead, propelling the young Soviet soldiers of 1945 from their encased vaults to rise up and spectrally gulp for an instant the exhilarating air of the streets they fought for and scarred, while consigning Treptower Park's current living bodies in their Putin T-shirts downwards to Berlin's city dead subterranes.

The temporal and spatial parameters of Berlin's battles, in their originating moments and final extinguishments or abandonments, leave conflicting traces on the city's surfaces and bodies, as battles for memory. The origin of the Soviet army's battle for Berlin is commemorated, at the Seelower Höhen monument on a strategic spine of hills alongside the Oder river plain fifty miles or so east of Berlin, at the site at which those forces' assault on the city intensified and entered its final phase – marked sonically by a coordinated burst of artillery fire clearly audible on Berlin's streets – but could equally well take its commemorated origin

at other points on that trajectory, with numerous strands and across four years of warfare, from an origin in Stalin's order-issuing body, in Moscow. The terminal location of that battle was marked by the mass of graffiti inscriptions around the Reichstag's steps and in corporeal frenzies of celebratory dancing, as well as in the incineration of Hitler's body by his subordinates and in its autopsying, once discovered and unearthed, by Soviet army pathologists at a clinic of the Buch sub-city of Berlin's mad, and also in the proliferation of Berlin's city dead and of gougings and fissurations of urban surfaces, still tangible in remote tenement back courtyards in which intensive hand-to-hand, body-to-body fighting took place.

In the temporal domain of contemporary Berlin's battles, attempts by activists to avert a particular building's demolition, or a refugee body's threatened deportation, may extend over years, only occasionally flaring into pitched battles with riot police; conversely, an urgently incendiary battle – such as those conducted between gang warfare territorial factions – may be won or lost almost instantaneously. Berlin is often presented as a perpetually 'embattled' contemporary city, always drowning in irresoluble debt, through the media pronouncements of its city authority figures, whose predecessors in West Berlin grew habituated to the regime of covert financial dealings that became engrained during that cut-off half-city's decades of massive governmental subsidies, and whose predecessors in East Berlin experienced a parallel regime in the opaque stultification of that half-city's own operations; such city authority figures' interest is served by the appearance of sustaining a beleaguered urban entity in the face of overwhelming negative odds. For the city's dark-ecological, nihilistic and subcultural activist combatants, a Berlin battle's origins in acute outrage, at perceived city authority hypocrisies or malpractices, will often post-date their conviction that an inflicted or self-generated urban apocalypse has already definitively cancelled out the results of all potential future contestations, even before new battles for Berlin begin. But, even annulled from their origins, those future battles will still be undertaken by their combatants with intense, unrelenting commitment.

Battles for Berlin, exemplified in the contemporary city by the engulfing – via digital media and spatial appropriations, surveillances and constraints – of the bodies occupying it, together with the multiple combative responses of those bodies, can finally only be defused by minuscule, aberrant gestures and acts of urban dissent that instil apocalyptic malfunction and calamitous ruination into all media of corporeal subjugation. The cultural history of the human body in Berlin, across its intersecting forms, always interrogates the capacities and impossibilities of future urban survival.

REFERENCES

1 Avraamov's sonic experiments with the urban space of Baku and Moscow are discussed in the catalogue *Generation Z: Renoise: Russian Pioneers and Musical Technology in the Early 20th Century* (Berlin, 2014, especially pp. 18–20) that accompanied an exhibition of documents, artefacts, films and photographs at the Kunstraum Kreuzberg/Bethanien, Berlin, 2014.

2 I visited the Exil restaurant (now vanished) many times in the early 1990s; it formed the antithesis of the health-oriented vegetarian restaurants Kafka sought out in Berlin in the winter of 1923–4. Brus produced a vivid, caustic analysis of the inhabitation of 1960s and '70s West Berlin in his book *Das gute alte West-Berlin* (Berlin, 2010), and in spoken memories of 'exile' in the half-city at an event at the Berlin Literaturhaus in December 2010 for his book's publication. A distinctive cultural history of the Exil restaurant appears in *Nachtleben Berlin: 1974 bis heute*, ed. Wolfgang Farkas, Stefanie Seidl and Heiko Zwirner (Berlin, 2013), pp. 76–7.

3 The archival film document of the 1950 razing of the Berlin city-centre palace, almost unknown, was projected at the German Historical Museum's Zeughaus cinema, in close proximity to the palace's site and at an inverse, contested moment – April 2014 – in the palace's history: that of the opening phase of its 'reconstruction', envisaged since 1990 and finally undertaken across the second half of the 2010s.

4 Romy Haag's unique, ephemeral map of contemporary sexual persecution and erasure presented an antithetical form of mapping to that multiply replicated across Berlin in more permanent, officially sanctioned displays at sites of war-era extermination and persecution, often in conjunction with the construction of new monuments. In her book *The New Berlin: Memory, Politics, Place* (Minneapolis, MN, 2005), Karen Till analyses the dilemmas surrounding the rise of that pervasive new public-space mapping of Berlin

across the first half of the 2000s, notably focused on the
demolished site of the former Gestapo headquarters,
directly adjacent to the Martin-Gropius-Bau museum
in which the Bowie exhibition took place.

5 Matthew Gandy explores the expansive corporeal and
architectural ideals at stake in Berlin's bathing complexes,
focusing on the era 1919–33, in the chapter 'Borrowed
Light: Journeys through Weimar Berlin' in his book *The
Fabric of Space: Water, Modernity and the Urban Imagination*
(Cambridge, MA, 2014), pp. 35–79.

6 Andreas Killen marks formative events in Berlin's expansion
as a world city 'electropolis' inbuilt with corporeal and
neural malfunction, such as the vast Trade Exhibition held
in Treptower Park in 1896 (in the same era that Berlin's cityscapes were filmed for the first time), and argues: 'Berlin's
transformation into a city of hypermodern urbanity was
tinged with fever, a hothouse air of unreality. The expansion
of the public sector resulting from the state's assumption
of vast new responsibilities for its citizens' welfare fuelled
the growth of the salaried masses but also awakened wide-
spread antipathy towards the increasing bureaucratization
of the everyday.' *Berlin Electropolis: Shock, Nerves, and
German Modernity* (Berkeley, CA, 2006), p. 185.

7 East Berlin's secret police archives are often visualized
primarily as proliferating quantities of paper-based documents, such as those unearthed by protesters in 1989 after
the secret police agency's fall. However, those archives are
also significantly filmic archives, of surveillance sequences
(with extraordinary prescience for the contemporary
moment) of bodies unknowingly filmed as they traverse
Berlin; extracts from such footage were incorporated into
the film *Ostpunk!* (dir. Carsten Fiebeler/Michael Boehlke,
2008).

8 The disposal for demolition by city authorities of large
elements of Berlin's distinctive housing stock to property
speculators and large corporations – notably in the 1970s
and most intensively in the early 1990s, following the
city's reunification – forms a particular focus of attention

of contemporary Berlin's interrogative urban historians and urban activists, such as Andrej Holm and Britta Greil, along with such issues as the exploitation of wasteland spaces previously assigned for ecological urban nature experiments; the construction of Berlin's new airport; the reconstruction of the city-centre palace; gentrification and displacements of long-term residents; and the financial imperatives and opacity or lack of transparent financial regulation surrounding all such urban initiatives in Berlin. Translations into English of pivotal essays on those issues, dating from 1991 to 2013, were collected as *The Berlin Reader: A Compendium on Urban Change and Activism*, ed. Matthias Bernt, Britta Greil and Andrej Holm (Bielefeld, 2013).

9 Artaud's journeys to Berlin at the beginning of the 1930s were made in the context of the then thriving culture of film studio co-productions between German and French companies, in which films were shot at Berlin's immense Babelsberg studio complex simultaneously with entirely different German-language and French-language casts, but with the same director; as a result, Artaud appeared (in the role of a beggar entering the profession) in the French-language production of G. W. Pabst's film drawn from Brecht's musical play, *The Threepenny Opera*, but not in the German-language production. During his stays in Berlin, Artaud wrote letters to friends in Paris evoking his fascination at the proliferation of well-dressed beggars in the city's streets and at what he perceived as an aura of ongoing urban disintegration and collapse. Although Artaud did not work with Fritz Lang in Berlin, he later appeared in Lang's sole French film, *Liliom*, shot in Paris in 1934 during Lang's stay there in transit to California after leaving Berlin on the Nazi regime's election in 1933.

10 In June 2014 the German Historical Museum's Zeughaus cinema presented a unique programme, assembled by the film historian Jeanpaul Goergen, of all the extant archival newsreel film footage of the 17 June 1953 uprising, incorporating materials filmed by cinematographers,

security agents and bystanders in East Berlin as well as in West Berlin.

11 The celluloid copy of Kiper's extraordinary 26-minute silent film (in its German title *Schöneberg baut auf: ein Querschnitt unseres Lebens 1946*) belongs to the historical archives of Berlin's Tempelhof and Schöneberg districts.

12 While writing this book, and without warning during the course of a nocturnal walk in the Prenzlauer Berg district of former East Berlin, I came across the figure of Einstürzende Neubauten's vocalist, Blixa Bargeld, skeletal in the 1980s but obese in the 2010s, battering on the exterior door of an apartment building having lost his keys, cursing and screaming as though irresistibly undertaking a body-focused sonic street-performance, and appealing to passers-by to help him in his predicament.

13 In its survey of Berlin's nightclub culture from 1974 on, the catalogue cited above, *Nachtleben Berlin*, enumerates an expansive genealogy of nightclub silencings, as exacted by the forcible closings of clubs, their expirations of their own accord, the vanishings of their clientele or operators, their incinerations and demolitions, and their unexpected resurgences; the catalogue's tracings of clubs' interrupted histories and spatially in-flux locations, as with those of the Dschungel (pp. 62–71) and Sniper (pp. 170–73) clubs, among many others, serve to map the dynamics of Berlin's silences. Clubs' names may change, so the previous name is silenced on the tongue. In most instances (even when a nightclub's interior is rendered into blackened ash or turned into an eco-supermarket), the urban space infrastructures which held those lapsings of noise endure and are marked with resonant acts of silencing.

14 The voided abandonment and exploratory potential of the Mitte district's urban space in 1990 are palpable in photographs included in the volume *Berlin Wonderland: Wild Years Revisited, 1990–1996*, ed. Anke Fesel and Chris Keller (Berlin, 2014).

15 York der Knoefel's installation *Schlachthaus Berlin* was originally exhibited in Dresden in 1988, before the end of the

GDR state. At the time I knew der Knoefel, in 1993 in reunified Berlin, his experiences and work had been separated by the intervening urban-historical and corporeal events from the extended process of obsessive, gruelling work which had generated that slaughterhouse installation a few years earlier, and he was then involved in and elated by new video works and paintings. Visitors to the 2012 Berlin exhibition on the 'shuttered society' revealed in GDR-era art photography immersed themselves physically in journeys through the reconstructed installation's near-impermeable panels, as documented in the catalogue: *Geschlossene Gesellschaft: Künstlerische Fotografie in der DDR, 1949–1989* (Berlin, 2012).

16 Boris Charmatz's 'dance museum' choreographic project *20 Dancers for the XX Century* at the Treptower Park memorial took place on 28 July 2014, as part of that year's Berliner Festspiele events.

17 Chojna's locomotive roundhouse, a remnant of the immense nineteenth-century railway system pivoting upon Berlin at the time Lars von Trier used it as a *Europa* shooting location, was razed shortly afterwards, but the ruined Marienkirche cathedral (set alight by Soviet soldiers on its capture in 1945) was partly renovated from 1994, its interior space now buttressed with intricate strata of wooden scaffolding and its tower's summit accessible by a vertiginous stairway.

18 The Smithsons titled their Berlin film with the German rather than English word for 'capital city' but with an English-language subtitle: *New Principles of Town Building*. A copy of *Hauptstadt Berlin* is archived at the British Film Institute in London.

19 All of Berlin's local-district urban history museums form invaluable repositories of visual traces invoking the city's sensory and temporal layers that have accumulated since the final decades of the nineteenth century, through such media as photographic plates, glass slides, negatives and prints; materials relating notably to the shifting urban and corporeal forms of the Helmholtzplatz, together with the surrounding Prenzlauer Berg district, are conserved

in the photographic archival collections of the Pankow Museum.

20 Café Aktivist remains extant in Eisenhüttenstadt, its salon occupied by the now-aged, memory-preoccupied bodies of the young 'model' Communists who arrived in the 1950s. The Berlin-based poet Donna Stonecipher explores the architectural and corporeal intersections of Eisenhüttenstadt, among other cities, in her book *Model City* (Bristol, 2015).

21 In *Berlin Electropolis*, Killen emphasizes how crucial and contentious malfunctions of urban vision became in assessing symptoms of neural meltdown as the city's parameters and spectacles rapidly expanded: 'In the early 1890s, the possibility of identifying the true nature of nervous illness came to be focused on the eye, and the visual field syndrome was endowed with a privileged status within the neurasthenic disease picture' (p. 109). In that same era, Berlin's psychiatrists and city authorities began to develop their own acute paranoiac symptoms as they confronted mass incidences among Berlin's inhabitants of devious simulations and undetectable fabrications of ocular malfunctions and temporary blindnesses: 'One expert examiner noted in 1904 that patients who simulated visual disturbances could often be unmasked only by the most practiced eye doctors' (p. 110).

22 East Berlin's immediate post-war period, with its dilemmas of reconciling wounded, traumatized solitude and aspirations for new communalities, also generated Fallada's 1947 novel, *Jeder stirbt für sich allein* (its title adeptly mistranslated by Michael Hofmann into English in 2009 as *Alone in Berlin*), written even before the GDR state's establishment in 1949, and looking back several years to Berlin citizens' isolated acts of resistance conducted in acute solitude and silence against the Nazi regime, specifically that of a factory fore-man and his wife inhabiting a Prenzlauer Berg tenement apartment, whose dissent takes the form of inscribed post-cards denouncing Hitler and left anonymously for passers-by in urban space.

23 For this section and the following one, I am drawing
primarily on my own experiences and memories of the
West Berlin and East Berlin punk rock eras, as well as on
others' experiences and memories, on the fragments of
filmic and photographic documents already at hand in that
era, and on more recent archival assemblings of filmic and
photographic documents, as with (in the East Berlin context) the films *Ostpunk!* (2008), and *Störung Ost* (*Disorder
East*, 1996), and photographic exhibitions such as *East End:
Punks in der DDR*, shown at the Staatsgalerie in Berlin's
Prenzlauer Berg district in 2012.

24 Among the extensive visual and textual documentation
of the Cecilienhof conference, preserved across Berlin's
archives, an especially striking aspect is the apparent
lightheartedness, air of improvisation and atmosphere of
near-delirious joking pleasure with which Stalin, Churchill
and Truman approached the proceedings' initial stages
– notably evident in USSR newsreel film footage of the
celebration genially hosted by Stalin at his delegation's
lakeside villa by the Griebnitzsee to mark the conference's
opening – as though, intentionally or not, impelled by
Berlin's present past to envision Europe's black-joke futures.

25 In 1997, Andreas Huyssen investigated the resilience of
multiple voids in the ruined wastelands, new architecture
and memory of the still-recently reunified Berlin, and noted:
'The history of Berlin as void is not yet over', in 'The Voids of
Berlin', *Critical Inquiry*, XXIV/1 (Autumn 1997), p. 81.

READINGS AND VIEWINGS

Berlin Bodies draws on many archived, published, projected and vocal sources. In particular, this book was researched in the collections and archives of Berlin's city district museums (particularly those of the Pankow and Kreuzberg districts), the Deutsches Historisches Museum, the Kunstbibliothek (Staatliche Museen zu Berlin), the Deutsche Kinemathek, the Filmmuseum Potsdam, the Deutsches Technikmuseum, the Berlinische Galerie, in the library collections of the Freie Universität Berlin, and in private archives and collections. The 'Berlin.Dokument' programmes of rare films, projected at the Deutsches Historisches Museum's Zeughaus cinema, together with film-historical research shared by the programmes' curator, Jeanpaul Goergen, were especially valuable.

Notably, this is a book also researched at street level in Berlin, especially through an exploratory methodology of walking and observation, with the aim of examining, by day and by night, particular sites which I considered relevant for the project of a tentative corporeal (and ocular) cultural history of Berlin, over weeks, months, years, and finally over a quarter-century's duration. Entry to a range of Berlin's auditoria, ballrooms, nightclubs, sites, rooftops, wastelands and subterranes (many of them abandoned or habitually off-limits) formed an essential element of the research undertaken for this book.

Alongside readings and viewings of archival documents, these sources were particularly valuable for this book:

READINGS

Ayesta, Iban, 'Berlin, Fin de Millennium: An Experiment in Corporeal Ethnography', PhD thesis, University College London (2003)

Bernt, Matthias, Britta Greil and Andrej Holm, eds, *The Berlin Reader: A Compendium on Urban Change and Activism* (Bielefeld, 2013)

Braun, Stuart, *City of Exiles: Berlin From the Outside In*
(Berlin, 2015)

Brus, Günter, *Das gute alte West-Berlin* (Berlin, 2010)

Fallada, Hans, *Jeder stirbt für sich allein* (Berlin, 1947)

Farkas, Wolfgang, Stefanie Seidl and Heiko Zwirner, eds,
Nachtleben Berlin: 1974 bis heute (Berlin, 2013)

Fesel, Anke, and Chris Keller, eds, *Berlin Wonderland: Wild
Years Revisited, 1990-1996* (Berlin, 2014)

Gandy, Matthew, *The Fabric of Space: Water, Modernity and
the Urban Imagination* (Cambridge, 2014)

*Geschlossene Gesellschaft: Künstlerische Fotografie in
der DDR, 1949-1989*, exh. cat., Berlinische Galerie,
Berlin (Berlin, 2012)

Gordon, Mel, *Voluptuous Panic: The Erotic World of Weimar
Berlin* (Port Townsend, WA, 2006)

Hessel, Franz, *Spazieren in Berlin* (Berlin, 2012)

Huyssen, Andreas, 'The Voids of Berlin', *Critical Inquiry*,
XXIV/1 (Autumn 1997), pp. 57–81

Jasper, Sandra, 'Cyborg Imaginations: Nature, Technology
and Urban Space in West Berlin', PhD thesis, University
College London (2015)

Killen, Andreas, *Berlin Electropolis: Shock, Nerves, and German
Modernity* (Berkeley, CA, 2006)

Kracauer, Siegfried, *Strassen in Berlin und anderswo* [1964]
(Berlin, 2009)

Ladd, Brian, *The Ghosts of Berlin: Confronting German History
in the Urban Landscape* (Chicago, IL, 1997)

Lupton, Catherine, *The Phantom Sanatorium: Beelitz-Heilstätten*
(Chicago, IL, 2012)

Richie, Alexandra, *Faust's Metropolis: A History of Berlin*
(New York, 1998)

Sennett, Richard, *Flesh and Stone: The Body and the City in
Western Civilization* (London, 1994)

Schlör, Joachim, *Nights in the Big City: Paris, Berlin, London,
1840–1930* (London, 1998)

Schulze Eldowy, Gundula, *Berlin in einer Hundenacht*
(Leipzig, 2011)

Stonecipher, Donna, *Model City* (Bristol, 2015)

Till, Karen E., *The New Berlin: Memory, Politics, Place*
(Minneapolis, MN, 2005)
Zischler, Hanns, *Berlin ist zu gross für Berlin* (Berlin, 2013)

VIEWINGS

Am Bollwerk in Stettin, Max and Emil Skladanowsky, 1897
Baustelle X, Gerhard Klein, 1950
Befreite Musik, Peter Pewas, 1945
Berlin Auguststrasse, Günter Jordan, 1979
Berlin: Gigant der Arbeit, Stadt der Schönheit, Leo de Laforgue,
1942
Berlin Milieu – Ackerstrasse, Veronika Otten, 1973
Berlin Alexanderplatz, Max and Emil Skladanowsky, 1896
Berlin Alexanderplatz, Phil Jutzi, 1931
Berlin Alexanderplatz, Rainer Werner Fassbinder, 1980
Berlin im Aufbau, Kurt Maetzig, 1946
Berlin nach einem Bombenangriff, 1944, anonymous
cinematographers, 1944
Berliner Stilleben, László Moholy-Nagy, 1931
Berliner Stimmen: Ernst Reuter, Paul Karalus, 1969
Botschafter des Friedens, Richard Groschopp/Max Jaap, 1948
Der Frühling erobert Berlin, Will Fischer, 1940
Deutschlandtreffen der Jugend, DEFA newsreel: *Der Augenzeuge*
22/1950, 1950
Die Gebrüder Skladanowsky, Wim Wenders, 1995
Die Kuckucks, Hans Deppe, 1949
Die Mörder sind unter uns, Wolfgang Staudte, 1946
Die Stadt, Herbert Vesely, 1960
Ein Tag in Juli: Berlin 1945, Jost von Morr/John Bandmann, 1974
Escape from East Berlin, Robert Siodmak, 1962
Europa, Lars von Trier, 1991
Germany Year Zero, Roberto Rossellini, 1948
Geschichte einer Strasse, Bruno Kleberg/Walter Marten, 1952–4
Hauptstadt Berlin: New Principles of Town Building, John McHale/
Alison and Peter Smithson, 1957–9

Immer Bereit, Kurt Maetzig/Feodor Pappe, 1950

Jahrgang 45, Jurgen Böttcher, 1966

M, Fritz Lang, 1931

Menschen am Sonntag, Robert Siodmak/Edgar G. Ulmer, 1930

Ostfotografinnen, Pamela Meyer-Arndt, 2006

Ostpunk!, Carsten Fiebeler/Michael Boehlke, 2008

Schöneberg baut auf: ein Querschnitt unseres Lebens 1946,
        Herbert Kiper, 1946

Sommersonntag in Berlin, Albert Baumeister, 1942

Sprengung des Berliner Schlosses, anonymous cinematographers,
        1950–51

Störung Ost, Mechthild Katzorke/Cornelia Schneider, 1996

Symphonie einer Weltstadt: Berlin wie es war, Leo de Laforgue,
        1950

Wir Bauen Wohnungen, Heinz Fischer, 1952

Wir Kinder vom Bahnhof Zoo, Uli Edel, 1981

ACKNOWLEDGEMENTS

I am very grateful to the Gerda Henkel Stiftung for the fellowship which they awarded me for the researching of this book in Berlin, and for their publication grant; I warmly thank them for their invaluable support.

I am also very grateful to the directors and staff of the International Research Center: Interweaving Performance Cultures at the Freie Universität Berlin, and especially to Erika Fischer-Lichte and Holger Hartung, for giving me an ideal base for my research.

I would like to thank all of the many researchers, archivists, writers, film-makers, scholars, performers, urban explorers and artists who gave me insights and source materials for this book in Berlin, with special thanks to Günter Jordan, Sara Piazza and Matthew Gandy, and special memories of Ko Murobushi. And finally, I would like to thank Michael Leaman.

LIST OF ILLUSTRATIONS